To Jan and
Best wishes.
Joanne achieve your dream!
Cheryl.

USELESS
WORTHLESS
PRICELESS

CHERYL CLARY

Trafford
PUBLISHING

Order this book online at www.trafford.com/07-1050
or email orders@trafford.com

Most Trafford titles are also available at major online book retailers.

© Copyright 2007 Cheryl Clary

Cover Design by Dean Horton

Note for Librarians: A cataloguing record for this book is available from Library
and Archives Canada at www.collectionscanada.ca/amicus/index-e.html

Printed in Victoria, BC, Canada.

ISBN: 978-1-4251-2952-1

*We at Trafford believe that it is the responsibility of us all, as both individuals
and corporations, to make choices that are environmentally and socially sound.
You, in turn, are supporting this responsible conduct each time you purchase a
Trafford book, or make use of our publishing services. To find out how you are
helping, please visit www.trafford.com/responsiblepublishing.html*

*Our mission is to efficiently provide the world's finest, most comprehensive
book publishing service, enabling every author to experience success.
To find out how to publish your book, your way, and have it available
worldwide, visit us online at www.trafford.com/10510*

 www.trafford.com

North America & international
toll-free: 1 888 232 4444 (USA & Canada)
phone: 250 383 6864 ♦ fax: 250 383 6804 ♦ email: info@trafford.com

The United Kingdom & Europe
phone: +44 (0)1865 722 113 ♦ local rate: 0845 230 9601
facsimile: +44 (0)1865 722 868 ♦ email: info.uk@trafford.com

10 9 8 7 6 5 4 3 2

This book is dedicated to "DB" and Rob

DB, the child you were, the young man you have become, my son, my friend, I am blessed.

Rob, you complete me.

ACKNOWLEDGEMENTS

This has been the biggest challenge of my life so far, and it would have been impossible without the endless support and love of my husband Rob. You said all the things I needed to hear during the many times I felt I was reaching for stars too high. You have shown me what it is to feel truly loved, thank you forever.

To my children who have encouraged me to tell my story, thank you for your courage and support. I love you.

Sandy, my friend for many years, who shared such a big part of my life in South Africa, your courage during your recent illness humbles me. Thank you for reading my book, and giving me your honest opinion. I could always trust you to say it how it is, and thank you for being my proof-reader.

Last but not least, I'd like to thank Stephen Richards. You have given me so much of your time, and your support and encouragement has helped me achieve my dream of becoming a published author.

1

I was born in August of 1960, in a small town in Africa that most of you will probably never have heard of. At the time of my birth it was called Umtali, and it was in, what was then called, Rhodesia. Apparently I was in a rush to enter the world, and came quickly, and relatively painlessly, for my mother that is, this was possibly the one thing I suppose, that worked in my favour. Apparently, when my Grandfather first saw me, he was shocked that his daughter could have birthed quite such an ugly baby, and he nicknamed me 'nagaapie' which translated means 'night-ape' I believe this was due to a tiny face, huge dark eyes, and a mass of dark hair. I began as an object of ridicule and disappointment, hence, my struggle seems to have begun very soon after birth, because not only was I ugly, but from the time I was born, I screamed. I suppose this is perfectly understandable really, what with the name I was labelled with, and a mother who obviously from the start, felt she had disappointed her beloved father. I was frequently reminded when I was old enough to understand of course, of what a 'problem child' I was, I'm not sure whether that was because it was the audacity of being born ugly, into an otherwise perfect family, or that I didn't comply with their ideal of a happy contented baby. The order for a girl had been put in, to complete the pigeon pair, unfortunately my sex was the only part of that order that was adequately fulfilled.

I had an older brother, by three years, obviously much adored by all, not only did he look like a miniature Greek god, he was the perfect child, quiet, unobtrusive, tidy, bright, cheerful and so on, in short a dream child. Not easy to live up to at all, even if I had tried, which obviously I couldn't, I had barely learnt to breathe on my own, let alone compete with this paragon of virtue.

The backdrop in this first scene of my life, and which set the ones to come, was as follows. My Grandfather's family came from the island of Lemnos, and for reasons I don't know of, they came to Africa. Why they chose this tiny little town in deepest darkest Africa I still don't know. They were, as most immigrants are, very resourceful, and my grandfather eventually owned a bakery, his own company manufacturing factory clothing, and went on to become the Mayor, and an Alderman. During this time, he met and married a young Irish woman, and they had three girls. I'm not sure that their union was love related, as I was told that for whatever her reasons, my grandmother would only marry a man who didn't drink alcohol. My grandfather was fiercely teetotal all his life, for reasons unknown, and this appears to be the basis of their relationship. This rather unusual liaison however, wasn't without its problems. My grandfather was Greek Orthodox, and my grandmother Roman Catholic. When their children were born, both parents wanted them baptised in their respective religions, and fierce battles ensued. Neither won the day. They did however compromise, and all three were baptised in the Anglican Church. There were now three religious followings in one house! Sunday worship was fraught with tensions, and discussion around religion was a subject that was avoided during my childhood.

The eldest child was my mother, and of course this must have been quite a disappointment to him having three daughters, but from what I have been told by my mother, she adored him, and tried to be a replacement son of sorts, joining him in all the male activities, and sharing his enthusiasm for sport, cars, all the things most men enjoy. I think regardless of whether she truly enjoyed these pastimes or not, was irrelevant to her; she did anything to please him. These feelings were reciprocated, and in her, he found his perfect child, and probably his best friend. My mother, due, I suppose to a terrible fear of disappointing her father, attended the local Catholic school, became a prefect, excelled at sport, excelled academically, and socially, in short, an all round belle of the ball. She mixed with the right people, got the perfect job, as a secretary, which at that time was considered the respectable job to have, especially as it was relatively innovative for women to work, and then of course she met and married the right man, in the right way. My grandparents had a large colonial style house on a prestigious road in the town, and they found themselves with new neighbours. My mother and her two sisters befriended the girl next door, as she was close to their age, and subsequently were one day invited around for tea. Whilst there, my mother spotted a photograph of a very handsome young naval officer, and discovered it was their neighbours brother. Later she confided to her two sisters that he was the man she was going to marry.

That was how it was with her, she led a charmed life, this was part chance, and mainly determination, as her social standing was an absolute priority. The handsome young naval officer returned. He had served in the Second World War, and after a fall aboard ship, in which he hurt his back, he decided to become a Chiropractor. In those days this was a relatively new concept, and certainly not one well known in Umtali. He was however confident that he could settle there, and establish his career. Of course when he met my mother, it was mutual love at first sight, and they courted in the right ways, got engaged for the proper amount of time, and then were married. Everything followed a rigid protocol.

I don't know too much about my father's side of the family, but can share what I do, with you. My father was born in South Africa. His mother was of Dutch descent, and was a Jewess. I only discovered this many years later, and I was in my teens when my father told us. Having experienced very closely, the atrocities against the Jews during the 2nd World War, he had a terrible fear that in the future there could be another 'Hitler', and he therefore never claimed his Jewish heritage in any way at all. He waited until he thought we were of an age when we would understand that his reluctance to disclose much about his heritage was to protect us. His father was South African, and he died suddenly, long before I was born. His mother had been married previously and he had step siblings, his step sister, was the neighbour my mother had befriended.

He had a large extended family of nephews, who were just slightly younger than himself, as his step sister was his senior by some years.

3

His nephews were farmers in Rhodesia, primarily tobacco, and my father grew up amongst them, and was keen to become a tobacco farmer himself. It was at this time too, that he developed a rapport with the black labourers on the farm, learning their language, and establishing relationships, that would last during his time in Rhodesia. At some point however, the lure of the goldmines around Johannesburg was strong, and my father left Rhodesia. He worked on the mines, and had all but decided this was where his future lay, until the onset of the war. Again, details are sketchy, but apparently my father volunteered as soon as he could, and spent the next years of his life aboard a naval ship. He never spoke much about his life during the war, but then so many who came back, chose to forget or bury this time, rather than share it.

I believe that their combined paths, patterns and ideals is relevant to the foundations that were laid for me, prior to my birth, the path had been prepared, and all I had to do to fit in, was follow it. Things probably could have worked out very differently if I had just acquiesced and been what I was expected to be. Fate and my own journey however, had very different plans, which would challenge me in every way possible, for many years.

My father was in his early thirties when he returned to Umtali, and his mother, an extremely possessive woman felt confident that he would never marry, and that she would have him to herself for the rest of her days. This went completely awry however, when he met my mother, and although I understand my grandmother didn't make things easy for them, they, ultimately my mother, I believe, won the day, and got married. Of course my mother's wedding had to be the biggest and the best that Umtali had ever seen. There was a large Greek community, and all and sundry were invited. My grandfather was the Mayor, and there were standards to be maintained. My grandfather and grandmother had met King George and the Queen mother, on a state visit to Rhodesia, and they and my parents had been invited to the Princess's Ball, the princesses at the time being, our now Queen Elizabeth, and Margaret, so as I say, it really had to have celebrity status, and within the boundaries of our little town it did.

My parents honeymooned in Mozambique, and after their return, my father continued to establish his practice, my mother continued to work as a secretary, they built their own home, to their specification, planned exactly when to have children, planned a boy first, and then a girl, the perfect pigeon pair, the perfect family, the perfect life. It all went perfectly to plan of course, but they hadn't counted on imperfection, and that was me.

My arrival heralded change and disruption in this ideal world, and I am certain I knew from the start, that I was not really loved, not that deep down gut feeling of being loved, I was tolerated. I know it must have been difficult in a sense for my parents. Everything had so far gone according to plan, even my sex was right, my character however was not what had been planned. As I said earlier, I screamed. They didn't really know what was wrong. My father initiated the help of all the medical people in the town, doctors, pharmacists, possibly even the local witch doctors, as my constant screaming was becoming an enormous embarrassment for them. Neighbours walking their dogs, or taking an evening stroll would often pop in, to confirm all was well, as my crying could be heard from the road past our house. This obviously could not be tolerated, as news travelled fast in our little town, and the implications attached to this were intolerable. There was nothing physically wrong, and they put it down to colic. They tried every known medicine of the time on me, all to no avail. I understand they even tried something called Phenobarbital at some point, quite a dangerous drug, they must have been desperate.

I was told, when I was old enough to understand, that as my father had to work, and his job required focus, he was a doctor after all, and my mother was eager to return to work, they needed their uninterrupted rest. To ensure they achieved this at night, I was put in the farthest room of a large bungalow style house. This was the kitchen, and with all the inter-leading doors closed, they slept, whilst as a tiny baby I was left alone to scream in the dark.

I find this very sad, it must have been very lonely and frightening for such a small baby-me, this is perhaps where my aloneness began, the knowledge that I would face life surrounded by people, but always alone, perhaps this is when in my deep subconscious, I began to build my personal fortress to keep me safe from emotional pain, and perhaps this is when I first understood that I would have to be a survivor, but until I learnt the skills to survive, sadly, for many years, I would be a victim.

It must have been from this point on that I also developed the concept that you had to be good to be loved, and you had to earn love, I didn't know that it should come freely, no price tag attached. I grew up believing that there were conditions attached to being loved, and when you were shown affection, it was something to be grateful for, cherish the moment, like a dog being fed scraps. When love wasn't forthcoming, you had done something wrong or hadn't done something you should have, and even when you couldn't dredge up anything you might or might not have done, you were still to blame for the coldness, the aloofness, the sternness, and the reprimands. And of course I lived in my brother's shadow; he was perfect in every way. I tried to be like him, but that didn't seem to work, so I went back to being me, that was more familiar, and even though we might not like the way we are treated, when we really can't change things, sometimes even the bad stuff can feel good, because at least it's something. I hated it when there was no feeling, no anger, no contempt, no reaction, the feeling of not even being worthy of any feelings at all, was devastating, the nothingness was worse than the coldness.

There were two people in my very young life that I adored, and they loved me back. One was my 'nanny' Margaret, she was a lovely big black woman, and to this day I can remember how she felt, her smell, her touch, her lovely soft melodic voice. She looked after me during the day, and she used to strap me to her back, and carry me this way whilst she did her chores. Most African women strap their children to their back, and it is seldom that you see a disgruntled or fractious African baby. It still surprises me that I can in some very deep recess of my mind remember this feeling, the warmth, the rocking, the lulling, and the contact. Whenever this memory surfaces it still gives me what I call my 'warm fuzzies', a feeling of deep down contentment, that feeling you get knowing you are loved, and all is well with your world.

I loved Margaret, she was all I knew of love, she was my contentment, and she was the only one apparently, that could soothe me, and stop me crying. As I grew from small baby to a very young child, she gave me hope, she showed me how it could be, and then she was gone! I still don't know why, but I suspect it had something to do with how I responded to her, and not my mother, that didn't quite fit into this 'perfect family' picture. I missed Margaret as only a very young child can miss its mother. Fortunately for me I had a replacement, my granny.

I don't' remember my grandfather at all, (the mayor). I only remember when he died. I was about six at the time, and I was collected from school by my mother. I remember it because it was during class, and I was pleased that I could leave early and spend time with my mum. I was always so desperate for her to love me, I thought that any time I had alone with her, might be time I could make use of, to show her I was worthy of her love. Sadly, it didn't work. Nothing changed.

I didn't go to the funeral, children didn't really attend funerals in those days, and I don't really remember anything about it at all, except, that my granny came to live with us! A room was built onto the back of the house, and for years it became my favourite place.

Both my grandmothers were alive at that time. My 'granny' was a large soft cuddly woman, and I adored her. She came from a very large, very poor Irish family who immigrated to Africa when life became too hard in Ireland, during a potato famine I believe. She had seven older brothers, all of whom served in the First World War, two came back. After their return, they literally drank themselves to death; they couldn't live with the memories of the nightmare they had survived so they chose the oblivion of alcohol, and slowly committed suicide. There was little tolerance in those days for people who drank too much, and my grandfather was particularly intolerant of their 'weaknesses'. He forbade his wife, their sister, and his daughters, their nieces to have any contact with them whatsoever. This broke my granny's heart, and my mother has told me how she and her mother would sneak alcohol and food to them. There wasn't any support for them, no alcoholics anonymous, no sympathy, just contempt for the two 'drunks'. I don't think much was known about post traumatic stress, or even shell shock, so they were ignored and isolated, and they chose the only way they knew to block their memories, and their painkiller became their poison. This must have impacted on their relative feelings about alcohol, and I understand it caused an irreparable rift.

Although my grandparent's marriage was more out of convenience than passion, they had been together for many years, and I think they had developed a mutual respect and love of sorts for each other, and she mourned his passing. She was however, very happy living with us, and while she was with us my life became easier in some ways, harder in others. Either way I remember it as one of the happier times of my life. I know she was aware of how much of an outsider I was in the family, and she always tried to draw me in.

As our relationship became ever closer, my mother reacted accordingly. The guilt trip began. She would often tell me how hurt she was that I appeared to love my granny more than her. What had she ever done to deserve this betrayal, and I, true to form, desperately tried to appease her, showered her with affection, withdrew from my granny, anything to make her happy. She also made a big issue about the amount of time my granny spent with me, and the fact that she spent less time with my brother. The fact that he wasn't really interested didn't seem to enter the equation. After all, I don't think he could have coped with much more love and affectionate pride. This sadly put my granny in a difficult position, but I was fortunate that she observed my internal tug of war, and she remained constant in her attention and affection for me. This was wonderful for me, because even though I tried so hard to juggle my time and attention between them fairly, I was so scared I would lose her love. I realised even then that this was more about my mothers pride than anything else, because she needed her daughter to adore her, and her alone. That would present her as the perfect mother you see, and image was everything. I was too young to discuss this with anyone, but granny was aware, after all she knew her daughter.

2

I need to explain that I wanted for nothing materially. I was the luckiest little girl. I had the best party dresses, the best Barbie dolls, I had a Barbie wardrobe which my dad had made, and it was full of clothes. I got the latest toys and clothes, and we were the first to get a TV when we could. We had the best house on the block, the nicest garden, and drove the newest car. We went on regular holidays to the sea, we had a cook and a worker for the garden, and our birthday parties were always the best. We even had the best behaved dogs! My mother gave the best tea parties, and made the best birthday cakes. All the other kids wanted to be on our invitation list, except for one very sad year that I will tell you about later. My mum had regular tea parties with her friends and their children, and they would all compete to make the best most difficult goodies for these parties. My mum always won.

There was no material deprivation, but I paid for what I was given. I know most parents remind their children of what they do for them, for me it was constant. No matter what I did I was ungrateful, didn't know how lucky I was, didn't appreciate anything, how hard my parents worked for it all, I didn't deserve what I had (well why give it to me then), and would I like to go and live with the poor children. I never did know where or who these 'poor children' were, but it scared me nonetheless. So I would go and sit in my bedroom cupboard after one of these very frequent dressing-downs and ponder my very bad ways. What challenged me however is time and again I would try and think about what I had actually done to warrant the ticking off? I soon came to realise that it was probably just because I lived and breathed, and I must be a very bad little girl if I didn't even know what I had done wrong.

In all this my granny was my sanctuary. I would go and tell her about the latest reprimand, if she hadn't heard it going on anyway, and bless her, there was always a hug, and a kiss to make it better, and then she would tell me I wasn't bad, it was just mummy and daddy's way. Funny, they didn't have the same way with my brother, but then I had her, so it balanced out! I remember she went to South America with a friend, they were away for four weeks, and I felt as though the bottom had fallen out of my world. During this time my mum's behaviour was quite different towards me. I felt excluded, lonely and confused, and also quite afraid. She seemed to use this time to give vent to her feelings about me, which were the same as always. Disappointment, anger and frustration, were intensified during granny's absence, as though she had some catching up to do. Once again, I wondered why it was so hard for her to love me, what had I done wrong, what was wrong with me. If only I knew, I could make it better. I also realised how much I now relied on my granny for a sense of belonging and acceptance and without her there was an enormous scary void. After what felt like a lifetime granny came home with loads of stories about her trip and a doll for me. Best of all though, was that she was back, and my fears and isolation lessened.

We also travelled at that time, and once again I was the luckiest little girl in the world, as we went overseas and travelled to so many countries it made my head spin. There was a very profound phase during this trip which would be life changing for me in the future. It was as we came in to land at Heathrow. I was looking out of the window of the plane, and had the overwhelming feeling I was coming home. It lasted the duration of our stay in England. I felt so at home there, I didn't want to leave. This was quite bizarre because I lived in a third world country with a completely different climate. I was ten years old, and the world I knew was so totally different to the one I was visiting, I should really have been like a fish out of water, I wasn't, I felt so at home, I never forgot that feeling, and for the rest of my life in Africa

I longed to live in England. I didn't know it then of course, but there was another very special reason for this yearning.

It's strange how sometimes the smallest things have the greatest impact on us, and affect us profoundly. During the holiday, I had made sure I wrote to granny regularly, and kept a diary so that I could share as much of our time away with her, as possible. I had missed her so much, and now that it was only a matter of hours to seeing her again, and feeling loved and secure in her hugs. We had to travel by train for the last part of the journey, and I knew my granny would be at the station to meet us. It was a sleepover train, and I was so excited about seeing her again I couldn't sleep a wink that night. I was up earlier than the others, dressed in my prettiest dress, and waited at the door, head out the window, soot in my face (it was a steam train) for hours it seemed. We eventually drew up to the station, the tears had welled up with sheer emotion and I was shaking with excitement at seeing her. As the train stopped, the rest of the family was behind me, and then it happened. Someone caught at the neck of my dress, and held me back, whilst my brother was nudged forward. I could see him run down the platform to greet granny, get that first special hug, and then I was let go.

It had been spoilt, my big moment, the moment I had dreamt of, and waited for had gone. Such a small thing one may think, but for me at that time it was such a painful experience, it felt as if the special love we had, had been invaded, and I hated the hand that had held me. I never knew who it belonged to, my mother or my father.

3

Many years later, I was asked to recall the happiest moments of my childhood, and there were some. One of them was the storytelling. My dad would come to say goodnight last, and frequently he would tell me a bedtime story. These were not the standard variety, he made them up, and in my little girls imagination they were the best. I was always the fairy princess, and on many nights, I travelled far and wide, met all sorts of wonderful characters, and of course I was magic! They were very special stories because they were for me alone, and I treasured that time with my dad. I sometimes wonder if this was some form of compensation from him. It was at this time however that I discovered the power of the imagination, and how to escape into my own world. I remember a 'dream' I used to make up when I couldn't sleep, it was always the same, and it always comforted me. My mom and I were shopping, just the two of us, and we had to cross the main road. As we were crossing, I tripped and fell, and a car hit me. Of course my injuries were such that I was going to die, but I was conscious, and as my mother knelt at my side, she was suddenly aware of how much she loved me. There she was, crying, apologising that she hadn't realised earlier how much she really did love me, and would I ever forgive her. Even as I write this I am experiencing the same sense of elation and 'well it's too late now' feelings as I did then. A knowing that once I died she would live with the guilt and pain of knowing she could have loved me better in life, now she wouldn't be able to, and she would understand how much I had loved her. I feel terribly sad, that this daydream comforted me so much, I do however understand why. It was only during this self fabricated fantasy that I felt so loved, so 'needed', so welcome.

Many of the happiest times in my childhood were spent in the bush of Zimbabwe. I went everywhere with the boys (my brother, and cousins), much to their annoyance, and I could shoot with a bow and arrow, and air rifle as well as any of them. I also had my own little 'fort' in the massive hedge surrounding our garden, and I could also climb the twenty foot firs nearly to the top. I was a dab hand at marbles in the sand, and had won a good collection of goons. I rode my bike at top speed, and ran everywhere, barefoot of course; I loved water and swam for hours on end. Some days we would go hiking or climbing for the whole day, a pack of sandwiches, orange cool drink and water, and we were out until dark, we walked for miles, and strangely never got lost.

Like so many children of that time, we adjusted to the environment we grew up in. Snakes were dangerous and to be avoided, but nothing unusual, spiders were big, hairy and very ugly, and I did run from them, especially finding two crawling up my back one day. (They had found a home in one of dresses, and I put it on. This obviously disturbed their comfortable little life, and they soon let me know they were unhappy), all the other bugs and insects however, were just an everyday part of my life. We would compete with each other to see who could find the biggest chameleon, and then put them on our arms and giggle as they tickled their way up our arms.

Our highlight for the week was going to the cinema on a Saturday afternoon. We always went to see a cowboy movie or Tarzan, then we would go home and re-enact it all. Inevitably I was the squaw tied to the totem pole, and it was a good excuse for the boys to leave me and go and play on their own. I would scream until I got my parents attention, wail and howl, and the boys were always reprimanded, whilst I looked on, feeling smug. They would then ignore me, I would sulk, swear never to be the squaw again, and we would repeat the whole cycle the next week.

There were terrible polio scares, as there was an epidemic at the time, some vaccines were still in the pioneer stages, and as my father didn't believe in them at all, he believed we should endure whatever

13

childhood diseases came our way, and recover from them naturally, my brother and I had the lot. I had Chicken pox, measles which I was very ill with, and remember lying for days in a darkened room, mumps. You name it, we got it, and we did recover.

During the summer, which was nine months of the year, we would spend most of our time in the swimming pool at home. This was a great draw card for all the kids on the block, and mostly there were at least about six of us in the pool. We did all the things kids of our age did, played all the pool games, ducked each other until bubbles came up, see who could swim under the water the furthest and longest, even it meant turning blue from lack of oxygen. We chased each other around the pool, feet slipping, bruising elbows, knees, heads, most parts of the body anyway, bombed each other, somersaulted into the water, and we all survived. My poor granny, who looked after us during the day, must have aged ten years every summer. I do have some wonderful memories, in all of it though, I never stopped feeling alone, and I never felt that warm safe feeling I know now, the feeling you have, when you know you are cherished.

I only had one real beating during my childhood, and strangely it came from my father. This was unusual, because it was normally my mother that did the physical disciplining, in the form of smacking, and my father, slow to anger and a quiet introspective man, only seemed to verbally discipline us on her prompts. He would come home from work, and disappear into his workshop for hours until dinner, and not being a tactile person, there was never any romping on the carpet or footie outside. He seemed to live in my mothers' shadow, and he was apparently comfortable with it, as he never took a more active role in our upbringing. Anyway, my mum and granny had gone to bingo for the evening, and my dad was babysitting.

He was working at the dining room table, and had asked us to keep quiet as he needed to concentrate. Well, this was a red rag to a bull for us, and we set about making as much noise, playing cowboys and Indians around the table. Whooping, and screaming, pretend shooting, dying loudly and everything else that goes with a good battle. He did shout at us a bit, but we took advantage of his quiet nature, and of course ignored his warnings. Well then all hell did break loose, and the next thing we knew was that the hidden evil piece of hosepipe, often used as a threat in desperation, had appeared in his hand. I flew

14

into my room, and thought the more blankets I could cover myself with, the less it would hurt. Not a chance, my dad came in, and I had never seen him in such a rage, it frightened me how different he looked; I had never seen my dad so angry. He pulled the blankets off, and hit me repeatedly with the length of hose. All I need say is that he drew blood, and it was one of the most terrifying memories I have. Not just the pain of the beating, but I couldn't believe this mild mannered, quiet man, had turned into such a monster.

Needless to say I was screaming the house down at this point, sore and very frightened, and I was terrified he wasn't going to stop. He did, thank God, and then went into my brother's room, and beat him. I know to this day, my brother and I have different impressions of who got the worst beating, but I do think my father's rage had diffused somewhat by the time he got to my brother. I lay in that bed, not moving, barely breathing, until I heard my mother's car, and it wasn't her I wanted to run to, but granny. I didn't know quite honestly how my mum would react; she could well follow up that hiding with another of her own. We were told from day one, that her and my dad was together in everything, in every way.

I shot into granny's room as soon as I could, and showed her my wounds, and of course had a good cry. At this point, my dad was obviously telling my mum what had happened, and they were talking on the porch. Granny was out there in a flash, and it was the first and last time I ever heard her voice raised in anger, and was she angry. Sadly, my dad told her to know her place, and sent her back to her room, and for days after that there was a frosty atmosphere. That night my mum came into my room, just to say that I had obviously deserved to be disciplined, that I was not to tell anyone about what had happened, and the following morning, my dad told both my brother and I that he would never hit us again. He never did, although his verbal discipline was sometimes more painful than any beating.

This was another of those 'small things' that affected me deeply, when I was very young, perhaps five or six. There was a doll I desperately wanted for my birthday, and I'd shown it to my mum at the shops. One afternoon whilst my parents were at work, my friend Marlene and I were talking about the doll, and she suggested we see if we could find it. She had found her present one year in her mum's cupboard. This was too hard to resist, and we decided to see if perhaps it had been bought and I would be getting it. I remember feeling very anxious as we searched through cupboards, and eventually got a chair to look right at the top of my mum's cupboard. Lo and behold, it was there, in a lovely box. I took it down, and we looked at it, not removing it from the box, and I was so excited. She was so beautiful, and something I could cuddle and love, and look after. After a short while, I put it back where I'd found it, and I was ever so careful to make sure everything was as it had been.

That evening there was some banter going on about my birthday, and in typical childlike fashion, I let slip I'd seen my doll. I will never forget my mum's reaction. She took me straight to her room, took the doll, and screamed at me, that as I had done such an unforgivable and deceitful thing, that was the last I was going to see of it. Her surprise had been ruined, I had spoilt everything now and after everything she did for me, and gave me, I was such an ungrateful and nasty little girl, that she would give it to a 'poor child' who would appreciate it, because I certainly didn't deserve it. She said she would think about even bothering to hold a party, why should she go to all that trouble for such a horrible child. At that point I was hysterical, sobbing and begging forgiveness; I would never do that again, please give me the doll for my birthday. I remember my granny, too scared after the last episode, walking past to her room, she was crying. I was distraught, to the point of being sick, and my mum told me if I got sick, I would clean the mess up myself. I was sent to bed and remember asking Jesus why I'd been made so bad I was not a nice little girl, I was ungrateful, I did awful things that made my mum scream and shout, and I'd spoilt my birthday for her, and I wasn't going to get my doll. In the days before my birthday, my mum hardly spoke to me, and I tried desperately to make up for my wickedness, maybe there was a chance she would forgive me. If I hadn't learnt by then, I certainly did after this, that my mother never made empty threats. I never saw the doll again.

I knew what I'd done was wrong, and never to do it again, and perhaps the punishment did fit the crime, but a few years on, I also learnt that even if I didn't do anything wrong, I was still punished. I was left then with no guidelines, nothing to measure being punished by, and this influenced the 'victim' label I wore for so many years of my life.

4

I loved school! Firstly because that was where I learnt to read and that was one of my great passions, and still is. I would happily lie in the sun or on my bed and read for hours on end. I lived the books, it was my escapism, and I travelled on 'The Wishing Chair', I Was a part of 'The Secret Seven', I helped 'The Famous Five', and the library despaired when they saw me coming! I was a model child during my early years at school; I was ready and waiting at the car, hurrying my dad up, so that I could go to school! I loved writing essays, and let my imagination soar, I won prizes for my essays, and I was always in the top three of the class. My reading was so good, that I remember my parents showing me off to their friends. They would make me read something from the newspaper when I was about six, and I loved these moments. I was doing something that made them proud, that fuelled my desire for acceptance, and I worked as hard as I could, I wanted to hang onto this approval.

My report cards were outstanding, apart from the standard 'talks too much in classes'. I attended the Catholic Convent that my mother had, and was mainly taught by nuns. There were some civilian teachers, but it with the curiosity of children, the nuns fascinated and scared us. We spent many hours speculating on what they wore beneath their habits, whether they ever laughed, and if they had hair, and if so what colour and type, they always wore the typical nuns veils of their order. There was also the amazing fact that they were all married, and married to the same man—Jesus. How did that work out, could that be legal, and is so how many times had he been married and how many wives did he have? We tried to imagine what the weddings were like; were they the loud lavish drunken affairs that we had all been to, not possible it seemed. We eventually concluded they must have been secret ceremonies held in dark places. At times, when someone was volunteered, normally me, we asked these questions, and they were met with a quiet smile, and gentle sigh. Nothing more, they lived in such a mysterious world.

I was a popular little girl for a number of reasons. Of course I had the best toys in town, but I was also very outgoing and fun to be with. I had already begun to understand the kind of person I needed to be for people to respond to me. I was mischievous without being malicious, and always went out of my way to help the underdog or the bullied. I could be quite formidable too when it came to dealing with other bullies, and I wasn't afraid to stand up for myself or for anyone I felt couldn't stand up for themselves. I suppose this attracted the more vulnerable to me, and I liked being their champion. I could be loud, I laughed a lot, and I had the ability to make others laugh, I was quite the clown. It was only me that knew the real person underneath this all, the shy, sad little girl, with no self-esteem whatsoever.

I did what most clowns do, always laughing, and happy on the outside, quite a different picture from the real one inside. My parents had always told me how important it was to have a 'good personality', so it was important I had one, again, I was trying to earn their affection. If that is what was needed, then that is what I had to have. In truth I had very little self-confidence, and I overcame this by pretending to be the person my friends saw. A lot of them envied my outgoing personality, if only they knew, sadly, I didn't even have the self esteem to be who I really was.

During those early school years, I was the perfect student, I excelled at school, at sports, swimming, tennis and netball were my favourites, and I was in the school team for all of them. Life seemed to be settling in to some sort of routine for me, and I was comfortable with it, until the year that changed so much for me, and set me on a very sad, lonely, challenging path. So much was destroyed in that one year.

I was ten years old going into Standard Four, and my teacher was a lady called Mrs. Black. I thought she was beautiful, tall and elegant,

18

and although to me she was 'quite old', fairly translated, old, being anyone over the age of twenty, she was probably in her late twenties. I so badly wanted her to like me, that if she had told me to jump out of the window, although we were on the second floor of the building, I would have done it gladly. I was excited about this year, I was going to be the star pupil, and really try to come first in class. At this time in my life, I loved learning, anything and everything; it gave me pleasure and excited me.

From the beginning, Mrs. Black singled me out, what proud moments those were. I was too naïve to recognise the sarcasm and derision in the dialogue, and glowed in the light of her attention. My best friend at the time, Mandy sat next to me, and although she had a reputation of being something of a rebel, we made a pact to be best in class together. Soon after the year began, we were moved by Mrs. Black from our desks in the centre of the class to the front, right under her desk. Did I feel important or what. I know it was my immaturity that prevented me from recognising the malice and contempt that was behind this action. Mandy and I continued to be best friends within our wider circle of friends, and we spent most of our free time together. Virtually every weekend we stayed at each other's homes. My mother encouraged this friendship as Mandy was the daughter of the current Mayor; hence I was seen with the right kind of people. Uncle Jimmy, as he was known to me, also owned a bakery and a corner shop. What a bonus, an endless supply of cakes, and our own walk-in, free of charge 'tuck shop'. Obviously I was doing the right thing, and I began to feel that I could begin to live with being tolerated, although, things had improved with my parents since my friendship with Mandy, and so I began to believe that my relationship could and would improve with my mum, there seemed to be only one way, and that was up. I began to draw closer to her, trust her with my little girl secrets, and try to be her friend, she responded, and it felt like I was going to achieve that warm fuzzy feeling I wished for. She was going to love me for me now.

I did my homework without persuasion and put a lot of effort into all my subjects. I became anxious when my grades were lower than normal, and when this was reflected on my first report card of the year, my parents expressed their disappointment. 'I'm trying really hard', I told them, they thought it was because I was in a new year and the work was harder, obviously, but I didn't feel it was that difficult, and thought I was understanding it really well. I must digress and explain that the school terms are different in Africa. The school year begins in January, and while there are half terms and holidays through the year, the longest holiday in end November/December, with a three week break in August and September, so it was by April that my reports were deteriorating. There was a rapid descent after that.

It seemed the harder I worked the worse it got. School started to become a nightmare. Mrs. Black singled Mandy and me out constantly, and began using us as examples to the rest of the class of what disobedient and disruptive students were. I tried to tell my parents what was happening, they however only read what was on the report cards, and believed I was doing and behaving as badly as they reflected. I started to dread going to school, and tried to miss days pretending I was sick. I remember eating soap one morning so that I could vomit, and pretend I was ill. It worked sometimes, but my dad was a doctor, so that didn't help much, he could easily see through it. Unfortunately this seemed to confirm for them that I was behaving badly, and they became very strict and unforgiving of anything I said or did.

There were many occasions when I tried to tell them that my teacher didn't like me, and I was working hard, and behaving in class. I was terrified of Mrs. Black. My days were totally unpredictable, and it was so frustrating. I didn't take the attitude that if you say I'm bad, then I will be, I reacted by becoming withdrawn in class, I was too scared to say anything or answer any questions, because I remember her often calling me a 'stupid, stupid girl', when I got the answer wrong, and she would make a joke out of me, encouraging the others to join in. I would sit there fighting the tears; I didn't want her to know she could make me cry. Sometimes it worked, most of the time it didn't, then she called me a cry-baby. Once I desperately needed the toilet, when I asked to be excused she refused. To this day I don't know how I held it in, stubborn pride perhaps; I do however remember that by the time I could go, I was in agony. I told my mom about this, and she said I should have thought of going before class started. I had no one to turn to, only my partner in crime, Mandy. Granny was unwell, and I didn't want to worry her, so I prayed. They were desperate fervent prayers. Dear God, please make Mrs. Black disappear', or 'dear God, please could the floor under Mrs. Black's desk collapse, and she could fall right into the middle of the earth'. 'Dear God, when Mrs. Black gets angry with me, please make her so angry she will explode' My imagination ran riot. I was desperate. I prayed for earthquakes, volcano's, floods, snakes, deadly spiders, anything, just make her go away.

Remember, we were children, and the rest of the class were aware of the situation, and there was no way they were going to incur her wrath, and end up like me. They laughed when she did, at my expense, and slowly my group in the playground began to dwindle. She noted who I played with, and after playtime would remark to them they might become stupid like me, if they played with me. Mandy was also bullied by Mrs. Black, to a lesser extent, but she did rebel, and became sullen and argumentative with her. After much discussion we decided there was only one thing we could do. Mandy and I decided to run away from home. We thought we could stay away forever, but if we were caught, it might make our parents realise there was a problem. We decided where we would go, it was a little hut in the bush about five hundred yards from where Mandy lived, just close enough to her home in case; we were brave, but not that brave. I did wonder if my family would even look for me, or throw a party. We made our list, and with childish practicality the first item was toilet rolls. Neither of us could bear the thought of using leaves to wipe! The rest was of course to fill our stomachs, and most of this consisted of chocolate, good for energy, cool drink, tins of condensed milk, well, milk was good for you wasn't it, in fact, whatever we could find in tins really, and we were clever enough to remember the tin opener! With all these preparations in hand, we decided we would slowly nick the various items out of our respective household cupboards, and hide them, until we had everything together.

My hiding place was under my bed, not very original sadly, and it wasn't long before our houseboy reported to my mum that there were strange things under there, mostly toilet rolls. It only took 'What is going on?' from her, and the floodgates opened. I had this bizarre thought that if she knew I was planning to run away from home, she would realise there was something very wrong, take me in her arms, and let me tell her all about it. Then she would go and confront Mrs. Black, make her apologise, and then go to the headmistress and get her sacked. She would be so proud of me for coping with so much, and we would live happily ever after. In my dreams! I got the tongue lashing

21

of all time, a long and loud version of how ungrateful I was, and those familiar 'poor children' were mentioned of course, and I was literally told to pull myself together. No wonder my teacher was so unhappy, she had this, that is, me, to deal with most of the day.

I thought it might be time for me to go and jump in front of that car in my daydreams. I really did feel so low, and probably more alone than ever before. Fortunately at that time I didn't know it was going to get worse. How could it get worse than in already was, God I was miserable, the only time I enjoyed were those moments just before dropping off to sleep, because I knew I would at least have a few hours respite from these feelings of utter hopelessness and misery.

It all seemed to happen at once.

First there was my birthday. Something I could look forward to, something to help the days go by. I just had to get to the end of the year, and this would all be over. I issued all the invitations, the normal thirty or so, and my mum got busy baking. Every year had been bigger and better than before. I was so excited waiting for all my friends to arrive, the party was due to start at three o'clock, and I waited on the veranda for the first guests to come. I was eleven, and felt all the excitement of that age, all the presents, all the games, all the lovely goodies to eat, and best of all, everyone singing 'happy birthday', whilst I blew out my candles, and made a wish, I had already decided on the wish, and yes, it was to do with Mrs. Black.

My first guest arrived just after three o'clock, Mandy was here. By three thirty, I was getting impatient, where were they? By four o'clock, I was getting scared, why was no-one else here yet? I heard the phone ring quite often, but I wasn't going to leave the veranda. At about half past four, my mum came to tell me no-one was coming, there wasn't going to be any birthday party, most of the parents had phoned with one excuse or another, but what had really come out of it all, was that the parents didn't want their children to associate with me, as they had heard about me at school. There had been a parent teachers meeting, and she had felt it was in the best interests of the parents to be made aware of what a bad influence I was. This was all done, individually, quietly, and of course confidentially. Remember I mentioned we lived in a small town, and any and all news spread like a bush fire, especially this, I was Doctor Stewart's daughter, I was big news, people like bad news, good stuff all the time is boring, and our perfect family finally had a public flaw, me.

My mum was devastated, how could I let her down like this. Her daughter was so misbehaved, that none of her friends were allowed to come to her party. She asked me what she had ever done, to deserve this from me. The holidays were awful. No friends, Mandy and I weren't allowed to see each other, a family that looked at me as though I was the first alien on earth, my beloved granny ill, and to top it all it was winter. In Africa, that means, cold, windy and wet, I couldn't even swim. I spent all my time doing the next best thing for me, I escaped into books again, and I read until the public library ran out of Enid Blyton, and Jean Plaidy.

The new term began, and so it was back to school. Nothing had changed, God and the angels hadn't visited Mrs. Black during the holidays, and sprinkled her with holy water, and she still had the devil on her shoulder. I wasn't back at school long, before Mrs. Black called my mum in, and I didn't know. That was a day to remember, they say when things go wrong, they go wrong. It was almost laughable. I was running across the courtyard that morning at school, tripped and fell, and badly sprained my wrist. The nuns wanted me to go home, but I was in enough trouble as it was, so I refused, and continued with my wrist bandaged, and my arm in a sling. I was supposed to be playing tennis that afternoon, but, as I couldn't I thought I would still contribute, by being ball boy. It was my fault, I was standing too close behind one of the players, and not concentrating, her racket came back straight into my face. I thought my nose was broken, there was blood everywhere, and I looked like I'd been a punch bag. Not to worry, it was time for my mum to fetch me, and sadly I thought with all the injuries I had incurred, it would generate sympathy, maybe hugs and kisses to feel better.

I limped to the car park, and there she was waiting for me. She took one look at me, and told me to get in the car. I was confused, hadn't she seen my face, my arm, didn't she see I looked like I had been worked over, what was happening. I found out soon enough, and of course it was about the visit to Mrs. Black. When I got home I got the full barrage from both my parents. My mother had heard from Mrs. Black about how bad I was, and how difficult I was making things for her. What was wrong with me, why was the devil in me, where was the A student, why was I doing this to them, what were they going

23

to do with me, I couldn't be a child of theirs surely. My mum had been so embarrassed to be told that a child of hers was such a little monster, and all the lies I had told about Mrs. Black being nasty to me, shame on me. Well such bad behaviour had to be punished didn't it! I was grounded, not to leave the grounds of the garden unless for school, no friends, no cinema, nothing, for one year, and at that age a year is a lifetime. I was sent to bed, disgraced. I lay in bed, my arm aching, my face hurting, but none of it compared to what I felt inside. It was the first time I physically felt my heart ache with despair and pain. I have never forgotten that night. I learnt never to trust anyone, if you couldn't trust your parents to believe you then who would. I also learnt that showing love wasn't worth it, only give so much and no more, and I also learnt about my 'brick wall', how to build it around me, so that no-one could hurt me again. I didn't know it then, but there would be times in my life where I would let those bricks crumble, but I always knew how to build them back.

I really thought the punishment would lessen in time, or perhaps even be forgotten; a year is a long time isn't it. Well nothing changed. I was literally housebound for a year, apart from trips to Salisbury with my mum to visit my granny in hospital. The most vivid memory I have of that grounding was to do with a movie. It had been advertised for months, and I so badly wanted to see it. I even the remember the name, it was a South African production called 'Dirkie', and I would have given away my best Barbie's, anything actually, to join my parents and brother when they went to see it. I did beg, I cried, I pleaded, I even said they could punish me for another year, just please let me go with you. I was taken to friends of granny's, Auntie Ellen and Auntie Grace, and had to spend the evening with them, in their dark cold old smelling house, and of course behave and not sulk. I was eleven years old for gods sake, I wanted to kick and scream when they walked out and left me, and when they came to fetch me, they made sure I got a detailed description of how good the movie was and what a lovely evening the three of them had!

What I was never able to understand however, is that during this time, my brother, who was at a Catholic boy's school, was given a caning by one of the priests for misbehaving or not doing his homework or something. I can't recall exactly what the reason was. Canings were considered normal discipline at that time in schools, and not frowned upon as now, and it wasn't an unusual punishment for the boys, I remember my mother was incensed about the welts he had on his backside, and she was in the car and up to the college to complain vociferously about the unjust and brutal punishment he had received. To say she went berserk wouldn't be an exaggeration. She wrote to the headmaster, and my brother was never physically disciplined again.

5

During these years, I do have some happy memories. As I mentioned we didn't have TV, so the radio was our only form of entertainment, apart from card games, Monopoly and other board games, and I remember, winter evenings sitting around the fire, listening to the 'Day of the Trifids'. I used to climb into bed afterwards, and just knew they were out there, but it was such a nice safe feeling snuggled up in bed.

We also went annually to Beira, the capital of Mozambique, and the drive there was an adventure in itself. The road was literally like a roller coaster, and granny and I would sit in the back of the car, and roar with laughter every time our tummies flipped over, as we went over the bumps. It was three hours of non stop tummy turning and laughing. We always stayed in the same hotel, and it had the most enormous baobab tree in the car park. As soon as the car stopped my brother and I were out and up, seeing who could climb to the top the quickest. Then there was two weeks of sand, sea and fun. There was a wonderful ship wreck on the beach, and this meant hours of exploration, looking for the hidden treasure, and just sitting imagining what had happened.

In hindsight, I think I was a lot like a family dog. I accepted my life; I was fed, clothed, sheltered, and even got the occasional pat on the head. Whatever negativity was levelled at me I took it in my stride, slunk off to lick my wounds, but inevitably came back, tail wagging, constantly on the lookout for some more scraps of attention and approval. Those scraps sustained me most of the time, and although I never expected or asked for more, I was quite prepared to roll over, play dead, and even jump through flaming hoops for an extra pat or two. When I look back, I realise the blueprint of my life had already begun, a perverse and self-destructive pattern of accepting scraps of affection, not believing I deserved any more, and the more remote people were to me in their affections, the more I craved it, and the harder I tried.

Anyway, let me get back to the story of my life. My dad, being a doctor, had all sorts of medical literature about, and sometimes, to scare us and each other, my brother and I would page through them. There were the most horrific pictures of unspeakable diseases and deformities, and I would seriously count my blessings as well as increase my 'Hail Mary's' in my prayers, which I did religiously, forgive the pun, every night so that I didn't contract one of these flesh eating diseases. The scariest of them all didn't really have any pictures, it was spoken about in hushed voices, as if verbalising it loudly you could become a victim of it, it was debated, denied, deliberated and feared by all, feared most by my granny, who was terrified that she would get it, was that a premonition? Not much was known about it at the time, less was known about how you got it, and anyone at any time apparently could get it although it was not contagious, it was cancer, and my beloved granny got it. From the outset, my brother and I were told as little as possible about her illness. I'm not sure that this was to protect us or distance us, whichever, it didn't help being constantly misled, and worst of all being given the luxury and comfort of hope, when most certainly there was none.

Granny had apparently had some health problems, and had to have surgery. When they opened granny up, she was 'riddled' with cancer, and there was nothing to be done, but stitch her back up, and let the disease and time take its deathly toll. During this time she was in a hospital three hours away, and I would travel by car to see her with my mum. All I was told was that granny had to have an operation, and would be home soon. We did bring her home eventually, and I was dismayed that she didn't look like the operation had made her better at all, she seemed more ill than when she went. I constantly questioned my mother about granny's deteriorating health, and was always told it was just taking time for her to get well. I believed my mum; I believed she would get well. I still don't fully understand the reason behind all the lies.

Perhaps she thought I was too young to understand! She didn't think I was too young to look after granny when I came home from school. I would rub her back and feet, hold the bowl for her whilst she heaved and vomited, and then clean her face and mouth with a damp facecloth. I would sit for hours and hold her hand, watch her while she slept, and try to make her eat. When I wasn't in her room with her, I would stay close by so I could hear the small bell she kept beside her bed. When I responded to her bell, sometimes she needed help, at others she just wanted to see me. There was no swimming, playing with friends or leaving the house during those months. My darling granny was going to get well, and I was going to help her do that.

My mum continued to work during this time, and took over seeing to granny when she came home, for the rest of it, I was granny's sole carer. I watched her literally wither away, she ate less, she vomited more, she moaned with pain, and then I knew in my heart, I knew she had that awful new disease called cancer. I confronted my mum, and after days of denial, I suppose she realised that I wasn't quite that stupid, and my brother and I were summoned for a serious talk. That's when we were told that granny did have cancer, and yes, she was going to die. My heart ached, but I remembered Jesus and Mary and God. Don't forget I was attending a Catholic Convent, and granny was a staunch Catholic, so I had certainly heard my fair share of the miracles that were performed, and I knew my bible, and didn't it tell you that Jesus could even raise people from the dead, and make the sick well, faith could move mountains, well surely this was simple then. If he did all that, then making my granny well was an absolute doddle. Thus began the most intense, fervent and heartfelt prayers any child ever said. I prayed night and day, I said more rosaries than all the nuns at the convent could have done. I bribed, promised, begged, and wept for Jesus to save my granny. I remember being so tired because if I dozed off before finishing the hundred Hail Mary's I had set me as a suitable target for healing, I had to finish them in the morning before school. When that didn't seem to be working, I prayed on my knees until they went numb, I even thought if there was somewhere I could get a hair shirt then I would have worn one twenty four hours a day, just make my granny better. She was the only person I felt truly loved by, and Oh, how I loved her back. Jesus wasn't listening.

My mum's two sisters came to see my granny intermittently during her illness. My aunt Edith had just given birth to twins, a girl and a boy, and she was also going through a difficult time in her marriage, so I think that had a lot to do with the infrequent and brief visits. My other aunt found her mum's illness difficult to deal with, and she kept her distance. During this time Christmas came, and granny was desperately ill, but she managed to get into a wheelchair and join us for lunch. She couldn't eat, and couldn't sit for long, but she was there. She was so frail and thin. It was at this time that she guessed she was not going to get better, and kept asking my mum if she had cancer. My mum took the decision not to tell her, whether to protect granny from her worst fear or to protect herself, I don't know. I think she may have been afraid of the emotional and mental burden that might follow if my granny knew her worst fear had been realised, and she needed to keep herself safe from what may have followed had she confirmed granny's suspicions. I do know that all my life I have been told of the sacrifices my mum made looking after her mum, when her sisters wouldn't or couldn't, and the terrible burden she bore with her 'secret'. I don't know if granny died in hope or despair, but she died without confirmation of her illness.

My other grandma, my dads mum, also became ill, she had a bout of flu, which progressed to pneumonia, and she died. It was the first time I had ever seen my dad cry, and I went through a tumult of emotions. I did not have the bond with my grandma that I did with my granny, and I was sorry she had died, more sorry for my dad than anything else, and in my child's mind, I felt guilty that I didn't feel more sadness at her passing, my priority was to make granny better, and all I had was prayer and hope.

My granny took a turn for the worst one night, and my mum called an ambulance. Granny was terrified, she didn't want to go in an ambulance and she didn't want to go to hospital. She said that if she went, she would not be coming back. The last time I saw my granny, was as she was being taken out on a stretcher. At the time I didn't know I would never see her again, but I was so scared. I walked beside the stretcher as they took her from her room, and I held onto her hand for as long as I could. I stroked her hair and face, and kissed her, and told her how much I loved her, and then they put her in the ambulance, and I never heard her voice or felt her touch and love again. I don't remember how long she was in hospital for, I know it was only days, but much as I begged and pleaded I wasn't allowed to go and see her. I remember my mum coming back one of those days, and she was sobbing. I knew my granny had died. I didn't get to say goodbye.

The funeral arrangements were made, and again I begged and pleaded, but I was too young to go to the funeral, funerals were not meant for children. I was often reminded by my mother, that her mother had died, not mine. As in the past there was always this undercurrent of identification and confirmation of my role in this triangle, my mother, her mother and me, and the boundaries were rigid in my mother's eyes, and not to be overstepped. I often think now, how different things might have been if she had applied her rule later on in our lives, when another triangle emerged The differentiation and the naturally observed boundaries in roles of grandmother, mother, and daughter didn't apply then however, because then she became the grandmother. I digress, that is much later on.

Watching someone you love dying, isn't meant for children either is it, however I did that, but I was denied all closure, and it broke my heart. What would granny think, that I hadn't come to see her on the edge of life, and not even in death. I don't remember my parents spending much if any time with me during this time. I know they were dealing with their own respective and joint grief, so I had to deal with mine. My grief came in the form of a gut wrenching pain in the vicinity of my heart, and the emptiest feeling I had ever had. If I'd felt alone before, it was nothing in comparison to this. I cried myself to sleep, and then woke up crying, I couldn't stop, and I didn't know how I was going to live without my granny.

After the funeral, family and friends came for the wake, I was anonymous to them all. They were so wrapped up in their feelings that no-one acknowledged or even remembered how close I had been to her, and the months I had spent caring for her. I was eleven years old, and had witnessed all her pain and suffering, something my aunts had not seen. When they visited, it cheered my granny up, and for the time they were there, it seemed she could keep her discomfort at bay, they never saw her as I had. My granny had given me little bits and pieces, trinkets and a small statue of Christ on the cross, during her last months, and we kept them on her dressing table, so that they were' ours'. I still had not taken them from there, as it felt the longer they stayed on that dressing table, the more I could try and imagine my granny was still here. I saw my aunts and mother go into granny's room, and stood by the door to watch. They started to take everything that was hers, which was not much really, including 'our' things'. I went in to explain that granny had given those to me, and was told to 'get out', nothing was mine, they would decide what I got to remember her by, and that it was nothing to do with me.

I learnt more about greed, guilt and injustice in that moment than in any other in my life. The people that were crying the loudest and longest after her death, had cared the least during the last months of her life, and yet they could just take away what had been given to me. I was dismissed like an annoying bee buzzing around the honey pot, and the difference between an eleven year old child and the adults was that I wanted what I had been given, because the value to me lay in the giver and the giving, not the value of the gift. I did eventually get my granny's rosary and the little statue, both of which I still have, and that was enough, but again my mother had let me down, she had felt the same way as her sisters, that it was nothing to do with me, she was after all their mother not mine, words that were to become very profound in my future.

There was something else very profound that I lost at that time, my faith in God. I didn't know it at the time, but the demise of my child-like faith would be the beginning of a belief and faith so strong and unshakeable it has and is my companion in life.

It was also at this time that I had my first spiritual experience. It was a short while after my granny died, I can't remember how long exactly because at that time, the days and weeks were blurred with grief. I'd crawled into bed early as usual, so that I could have my 'quiet time' where I relived time I'd spent with my granny. My bedroom was quite a distance away from the rest of the house, and there was a door between the living area and bedrooms, which I'd closed. I was startled out of my daydreaming when I heard coughing, I easily recognised that sound, it was my granny. Without thinking, I rushed to her room, and as I opened the door, there she was, lying in her bed smiling at me, just as she had done so many times before. If at this point you are thinking of all the logical and practical reasons as to why I saw her;

31

my grief, still dreaming about her and half asleep, a vivid imagination, a desperation to see her again, everyone else thought of those
too, and no-one would believe me when I told them anyway. I did see
her though, and I started to walk towards her crying with relief, she
was back. Then she was gone, and her bed looked as it had for weeks,
neatly made and very empty. I couldn't go into her room for a long
while after that, it was too painful. I did however, often, and always
when I was alone, hear her little bell, and I knew it wasn't because she
needed help anymore, but somehow she was telling me she was still
with me.

6

It was back to school, and into a new year. My final year in junior school and after last year's experience I wasn't happy. My class teacher was the head teacher of the school, and she was a nun called Sister Alfreda, I didn't know what to expect, but I was prepared for the worst. I was going to try my best, still always looking for approval, and in the hope that maybe I would disprove Mrs. Black's feedback on me. Because of my previous reports, I was told to sit at the front of the class right under the teachers' nose, and that felt like a really negative beginning. My classmates were still very cautious around me, as they had been warned off by their parents, so I didn't really have any incentive to become distracted in class.

I worked quietly and steadily, and kept a low profile both at school and at home. I think a lot was to do with grieving, I didn't really understand the concept of the word at that age, all I knew was that there was one enormous hollow feeling in side, the space that used to be reserved for my granny. I secretly hated all the masses and religion infested assemblies I had to attend, I hadn't forgotten how Jesus and co. had betrayed me.

It came to end of term exam time, and I surprised myself, and everyone else by coming first in class. This proved to be more than just a boost to my confidence, it prompted my teacher to request my previous year's papers and results, as she had some recollection that I had stood out as a dire, beyond redemption pupil. She decided to look a bit further back, and saw a grade A student decline to a grade 'Z' during one year. On further investigation of all my class work, homework, essays, and exams that year, she found in fact that I had actually achieved far higher grades than they had been marked, and to cut a long story short, that was when Mrs. Black was called in to explain herself, and I believe it was at that point that she suffered a breakdown, and confessed to contriving the low grades because of how she felt about me. I suppose, on reflection and with how today's schools are governed this wouldn't and couldn't happen, but at that time a lot was based on trust and integrity so checks were seldom made to verify a teachers report on a student.

I was 'redeemed', I was applauded and apologised to, by the headmistress, and lo and behold, there began the revival of a long dead sparkle in my mother's eye. I was teachers pet, top of class, and instantly hit a high in the popularity stakes with my classmates. Everyone wanted to be my friend, and I was invited to ALL the birthday parties, my diary was fit to bust with all the social engagements. When I tried to talk to my parents about it, I was told that they had no reason to believe me against a teacher, they had made a mistake, and leave it be, these things happen, and it's all part of growing up, it was alright now wasn't it? It was also at this point I was told, that parents aren't perfect, they make mistakes. How could it ever be alright, I had lost a year of my childhood, and I had lost my trust in the two people I should have been able to trust most?

I was rewarded for my good grades however, and my mum suggested I might like a puppy, and wouldn't I just love a Corgi. I didn't know what a corgi looked like, but my mum insisted I would love it, so yes, I would like a Corgi. I'd grown up with dogs, and I did and do love them, and a puppy of my own would be great. It was only later I realised that the Queen of England had corgi's, so that's why I would like one so much. My mum was on a mission, and eventually we found a corgi pup in the newspapers, just one problem, it was in another town about five hundred miles away. There ensued numerous phone-calls, and where there's a will there is a way, arrangements were made for us to collect the pup from Salisbury about three hundred miles away, and his, mode of transport was going to be a Hunter fighter jet, as his owner was a wing commander in the Rhodesian Air Force. During the numerous conversations, my mum became friendly with the pups owners, and although we didn't know it at the time, this was the beginning of a life long friendship, but more heartache for me.

I had always loved my food, but it was at this time, that I began to comfort eat. I had never heard the term before and it is only retrospectively that I recognise it for what it was, and can give it a name. I remember it felt as though I had this huge empty space inside, and food seemed to fill some of that void. I say only some, because try as I might, I could never quite get rid of that emptiness, so I tried harder, I ate more. When I ate something, it gave me pleasure, somehow made me feel happy, and I liked feeling like that, so it seemed to make sense, that the more I ate, the better I would feel? I just couldn't fill the hole though, and unfortunately as my appetite increased, so did my size. My mum noticed my growing girth, and my gorging, and she suggested putting me on a diet, and cutting down on the size of my meals. I did have less dished up for me, which I resented, so I began sneaking food, and consequently I ate more than ever. I know now, that a lot of eating disorders stem from control issues, and I remember feeling, that the comfort I found in eating was not going to be taken from me, and the harder she tried, the more I ate.

I was often berated at the dinner table, when I would ask for more, and I was told I wasn't a pig, so I shouldn't eat like one, and of course kids will be kids, and my brother latched onto this, and I became 'piggy'. My dad often said that if I continued like this, I would never get married, because men only liked women who 'looked after themselves'. He would use my mum as his example, as she was constantly watching her weight, and was very conscious about every aspect of how she looked. The worst thing about all this, was I knew that this was all self inflicted, this was the reaction to my overeating, I was responsible, but I couldn't stop. Eating made me feel briefly happy and comforted, but it also made me feel guilty, I felt sick , I was angry at myself, I hated how I looked, I felt embarrassed, but I couldn't stop.

It was also at about this time, I started to become aware of boys in a different way to my brother and cousins. Becoming giggly when one of my brothers friends was around who I thought was nice, and as my friends were all knobbly knees, elbows and ribs in their little bikinis, I became increasingly shy and embarrassed about how I looked. Of course we had the biggest swimming pool, which attracted all our friends during the long summers, and I became the object of fun with my brothers' friends. There were all the jokes, about when I jumped in the pool, all the water would spill out, but the most hurtful nickname I was given was 'Walrus'. This one stuck, and it travelled. I used to get a lift home after school with a friend, and her house was down the road from mine. During that short walk, all the boys would be cycling home, and as soon as they saw me, there would be a chorus of 'there's walrus'. I know most kids get teased, but this impacted profoundly, because I knew it wasn't about something, I couldn't help, but something I could. I frequently arrived home for lunch in tears, and my mum would confirm my thoughts. 'No need to get upset about it, Cheryl, you need to do something about it, if you don't like being teased, stop eating so much'. So began the first of my inner war's I craved food, and I hated it, it was my friend and my enemy, but I couldn't stop. Every night I would get into bed, and tell myself, what a bad girl I'd been for eating so much, and I would promise myself I would stop tomorrow, I couldn't and I didn't, and so my self persecution continued.

There was a lot of talk during that year about what was going on in the country, I didn't understand much because conversation stopped when I walked into the room, and it was all talked about behind closed doors and in quiet voices. We talked about it at school, and it seemed all our parents were worried, about the start of a war, not here surely, who would want to fight with us? I didn't really worry too much about the hushed talks, and conversations stopping when we, the kids walked in, I had far too much on my mind. I was going to big school! It was exciting, I was growing up, it was terrifying. There were two schools in Umtali, one was called Marymount College, and it was the equivalent of a public school here in the UK, and the other was The Girls High School, a government school, they were both all girls' schools. As there was only one school for my brother to go, which was the brother school to the girls' government school, it was decided I would attend there. Fair is fair. This meant that a lot of my friends were going to Marymount, so I felt like a fish out of water.

I had to get a new uniform, and this was quite a chore, as my body was still growing rounder much faster than up, where were those growth spurts when you needed them. Consequently I had to have a tunic about three sizes bigger than my age, and the hem hit my ankles. The waist (what waist?) hung in the region of my knees, and the armholes ended where the waist should have been. There's nothing like a girl looking good on her first day, to boost her confidence. In fairness, my mum did her best with the hem, but the rest of it just had to stay where it was, and looking on the bright side I suppose, was that if in future I grew up and not out, my tunics would last the rest of my schooling days.

Inevitably the day came around, and I decided the only way, was to tough it out, or laugh it off. I did, and if someone laughed at how I looked, I pretty much laughed with them, and when they realised they weren't going to get the desired response, of tantrum and tears, they lost interest. I soon got the reputation of being one of those 'jolly fat girls'. No threat to anyone, and safe and fun to be with, I was always happy wasn't I, such good fun to be with.

I surprised myself at how quickly I settled in, and I quickly made friends. Sadly though, a lot of this was to do with who I was, that is, the daughter of Dr. and Mrs. Stewart. Everyone's parents seemed to have informed their daughters I was good company to keep. I suppose in this instance it worked positively for me, and as we all do, out of the wider group, I found my best friend. Her name was Jane. She was from a Greek family who farmed outside the town, hence she was a boarder. Jane was absolutely beautiful, and she was thin. She was blessed from the top of her head to her toes, and I worshipped her. I couldn't understand how the prettiest girl in the school wanted to be my best friend, and I felt there must have been some sort of ulterior motive. We were inseparable; my parents approved of the friendship, and got permission from her parents to sign her out for weekends, which we spent, joined at the hip. We confided in each other, and spoke about absolutely everything. We giggled about boys, and Jane would tell me about her first kiss, and snog. More to worship, the closest I'd got to a boy was my brother, don't forget, I was short, round and had zero self-confidence, and the object of taunts and derision amongst my brothers friends.

During the school holidays I would stay on her parents' farm, and they were very happy times. I experienced a sense of freedom too, because it was very unusual that I was comfortable away from home. This sounds completely irrational, why would I choose to stay in the very place I experienced so many anxieties and uncertainties. I was simply terrified of anything new, any changes, be it my surroundings, my room, my routine. This was so good for me. Jane's mum and dad adored their beautiful daughter, and when I was there I basked in her shadow. It was a new and wonderful feeling. In their eyes Jane was an angel, and they treated her accordingly, and even though I only benefited from the 'fall out', it was enough.

I also had the most enormous crush on her older brother Simon. It was safe to feel that way, because I was his kid sisters' fat friend, so I could fantasize to my heart's content, knowing that was all it was and ever would be. My imagination ran riot, down to him swearing undying love, marriage proposal, and living happily ever after. Jane and I would climb on the motorbike and spend hours riding on the dry dirt farm roads, just for the fun of it. One day Simon offered to teach me how to ride the motorbike, and I was thrilled and terrified. So much to think about at once, driving it as if I'd done it all my life, he would be impressed, and of course mentally transforming myself into a slim gorgeous blonde creature that would take his breath away, as I flew across the land, wind blowing through my hair, tight black leather suit skimming my curves. Aaaargh help!!! Dream over, reality kicking in rapidly, Simon screaming at me to brake, no, not the throttle, the brake. What brake, I'm twisting the handle aren't I, why is it going faster, and now I'm dragging Simon behind me! My hero, hanging onto the back of the motorbike, and being whipped about, whilst I'm swinging this monster machine around at a rate of knots! Oh my god, where did that tree come from! The tree leapt at me and joy of joys, I did end up close and personal with Simon, even if it was a foursome including a tree, smoking motorbike, and him battered, bruised and semi-conscious. Jane and her younger brother were no good at all in untangling us, they were rolling about on the ground, unable to even breathe, and they were laughing so much. Jane even wet her knickers. To this day, I have never tried to ride a motorbike again, and the next time I was due to go to the farm, Simon tried to run away from home.

This boy thing was becoming more and more fascinating, and I decided it was time to go on a diet. Ideally I wanted to change my face, my hair, my height, my feet, everything really, but a start, would be to shed some pounds. I spoke to my mum, and she was so supportive, within twenty four hours it was organised that I go to Weight Watchers with my aunt!

I was committed to this venture, and it paid off. I exercised enormous will power, as it was at a time, when you didn't have all the diet aids, and 'low fat' options on anything and everything, and it was really hard. My motivation was to be 'normal', and, to try and look a little like Jane. At least have a similar body; I couldn't do much about the rest. I suppose to me then, she was the equivalent of the young thin 'have it all' models we see on magazines nowadays. I thought if I could get thin, I could have it all too! Childishly, I fantasized that if I was thin, my parents would love me more, and sadly, I think my mum did have a different attitude towards me. Perhaps her ugly duckling had some swan potential after all. I think she felt that there might yet be hope that I could pin that aspiring doctor or lawyer down some day, if I continued this way.

That aside, it was the whole image thing. It was already becoming hugely fashionable to be thin and beautiful, and some of the other larger girls began dieting in their own fashion. Forced vomiting after eating, now known as bulimia, became common practice with a lot of them. The dire implications associated with this, was relatively unknown and unrecognised at that time, and those that practiced it actually thought they were quite innovative and clever about their method of dieting. Fortunately, or unfortunately, as I thought at the time, it was not something I could do, I hated putting my finger down my throat, and the gagging, and then eventually, after literally sticking my whole hand down my throat, getting a result, which was a bitter burning, revolting mess shooting up my throat and out of my mouth, and it stank. It was a noisy business too, and there was an awful amount of careful planning, and sneaking about associated with it. Once the disgusting deed was done, with much flushing of the loo to conceal the retching noises, I had to sneak into the bathroom to clean my mouth and teeth, still gagging because bits of food stuck in your teeth, and my throat felt like sandpaper for hours afterwards. So that meant I had to do it the hard, long and sensible way, which I found really tough. It wasn't just that I had to stop feeding my enormous appetite for food; it was being unable to satisfy my emotional needs, to try and fill the hollowness inside. To try and cope with this, I held an image of Jane in my mind, and fantasised that everything would change for me, as my body shape changed, and every time I stood on those scales, and dropped another pound, I did feel elated. I started to realise I was in control of something for the first time in my life, my body, and it felt

39

very powerful. I wasn't aware of it at the time, but this was the onset of a self deluding lifestyle, that if you look good, you feel good, and you are valued accordingly.

I set personal standards, that were very high indeed, and I became my own worst critic. I was a harsh disciplinarian, self debasing and my own worst enemy. I didn't need criticism from anyone else, I did that well enough, and strangely, the more I achieved, the harder I became on myself. I responded to any pain, both emotional and physical, as though I deserved it. This was a pattern I would follow for many years, and eventually, it engulfed me. If people in my life degraded me, it was because I deserved it, I didn't look good enough, I'd gained weight, my hair needed styling, and basically I gave them carte blanche to abuse me. There came a time years later, that I did let it all go, and I couldn't care less about anything, but that was only when I succumbed to an artificial euphoria, which instigated the darkest deepest pit of my life. That is much later on during my journey in life though, so enough digressing.

Soon, my school tunics were loose, and hung on me like a sack. I could just about wrap my belt around my waist twice, and I felt good! Friends and family remarked on my new look, and I was able to wear the same clothes as Jane, and feel really good in them. In fact we could even borrow each others clothes, and of course I preferred hers to mine. During this transition, my circle of friends had increased, not that I think it had anything to do with my changing appearance, I became more confident, and some of the real me was emerging. It was apparently a less brittle and sensitive butterfly emerging from the cocoon, and it attracted people.

My circle of friends, most of who were boarders included Dana, Margaret, and Tracy. Do you remember the corgi pup that was flown in to us, well Tracy was the daughter of the breeders, and because of the dog we met. I suppose if it hadn't been for that connection, we may never have become friends, because we were such different characters. Perhaps it may have been an 'opposites attract' scenario, and we might have still have developed a friendship, somehow I don't think that would have happened. However we came together though, I grew to love Tracy like a sister, sadly though, at the same time, unwittingly, she became my worst enemy. Tracy was very plump, wore glasses, and she was shy, studious, and an all round 'good girl'. Boys reduced her to fits of giggles; in fact pretty much anything reduced her to a giggling wreck. Her dress code would have been fine ten years earlier, but she didn't want to move with the times so to speak, and was rigid about wearing tent like, shapeless florals. She stood out like a sore thumb in our crowd of make up experimenting, flash nail painting, and funky hairdo young trendsetters.

I cringe now when I think of the killer pink hot-pants, white shiny plastic knee high boots, and of course the tights, but at that time, we thought we were hot! Denims or jeans were in too, and Tracy vowed she wouldn't be seen dead in a pair of trousers, let alone jeans. She was really pretty, but didn't think she was, and no amount of persuasion would induce her to use a scrap of makeup. From the day I met her, her ultimate ambition in life was to get married and have lots of babies, and at thirteen she already looked and behaved like a little mother. Tracy kept us in line to some extent, and she was the sensible practical non adventurous stabilising force we often needed, but seldom acknowledged. We did tease her for her old fashioned attitude and outlook, but we all loved Tracy, and someone really loved her, my mum. My close friendship with Jane was starting to concern my mum, I didn't know why then, but now I believe she felt threatened. She didn't want anyone else having that sort of emotional affect over me, and Jane became a 'bad influence'.

As boarders, my mum had to get permission from the respective parents to take their child out for the day, and my friends' parents were only too happy for their daughter to spend time at our home. Sometimes they went out with other friends, but I had a fairly regular group that came to us every Sunday, in particular Tracy. She didn't have anyone else on her list to go out with, and my mum wouldn't let a Sunday go by, without Tracy visiting. I know Tracy met her needs as a daughter, she gave my mum what I didn't or couldn't, she was the daughter my mum wanted, and I say I know this, because I was told often enough. 'Why can't you be more like Tracy?' she would say to me and to us both, 'Tracy is like another daughter to me, the sort of daughter I always wanted'. Tracy had a difficult relationship with her mum, and she loved the attention and approval she got from mine. The feelings they had were mutual. My mum would tease me when Tracy was there, she would put her arm around her and hug her, and always it was, 'I wish you could be more like Tracy, she's a lovely sensible girl, she has the right attitude in life.' I remember taking ages to pluck up the courage to challenge my mum once, and asked her 'do you love Tracy more than me', I remember she smiled slowly at me and took her time with her answer, I was in agony, and it must have showed, because she stopped smiling. Then she said 'I wish you could be more like Tracy, but I love you too' I felt like I'd been thumped in the chest, I couldn't breathe, and that old familiar pain in the region of my heart was back. She loved us both the same! If she could love a virtual stranger the same as me, that felt like I was so disposable, anyone could replace me, and they didn't even have to put any effort in. Their only criteria would be to be different from me.

I ran to my room, and sobbed, and when my dad wanted to know what all the fuss was about, my mum told him I was being over dramatic again. I had asked a silly question, so she had given me a silly answer, of course she loved me best, and I wasn't to ask such stupid questions again. And then she began to cry, and ask what she had done, to deserve such a nasty child. A child that would question her love as a mother, how did that make her feel, after everything she did for me, and true to form, my dad then gave me one of his very painful lectures on my ingratitude, and cruelty. I was left feeling enormously guilty, confused, and horrible, and spent yet another night wondering why I was such an evil person, that I would hurt my parents like this. I never told Tracy what had happened; I didn't want to give her any more power than she already had. I didn't hold Tracy responsible either, I still loved her. It was my entire fault anyway; I'd asked a stupid question.

7

On one winter Sunday, when for one reason or another it was only Jane and I, we went to the movies, and I met my first boyfriend. Although I considered myself as relatively cool, when it came to boys, I was totally un-cool. Jane and I had spent hours deciding what to wear, put a bit of make-up on, decided we looked ok, and hit one of only two movie theatres in Umtali. I'm not sure why we chose this particular one, it was called the Vaudeville Theatre, and it wasn't the better one of the two, in fact it was quite a dive. I think it was the movie showing that day, must have been one we wanted to see, there again, everything happens for a reason. We bought our tickets, and joined the queue for a coke. There were two boys standing behind us, both in school uniform, and they seemed to be talking about us. Of course this sent us into blushing whispered giggles, much tossing of hair, and pretending we didn't know they were talking about us, as we were so busy talking ourselves. Do you remember doing that, saying to your friend, 'talk to me, so it looks like we don't know they're there,' or pretend you were so involved in your more than normal chat, that you had absolutely no idea, someone was eyeing you up. If conversation ran dry, and the queue took longer than it ever normally did, the walls became fascinating, and the tatty posters were especially interesting. Look anywhere, but behind. We bought our cokes, didn't touch anything else, none of the normal popcorn, or big bag of pick and mix, we didn't want to be seen as childish now did we. We were woman about the town, trying to look seductive and alluring sipping our cokes, and probably looking exactly as we were, two young girls, flushed, awkward, giggling, prattling about nothing, and moving very purposely to the entrance of the theatre.

We took our seats, and minutes later, there was a shuffle in the row to let others in. It was them! Oh my God, what to do, don't appear flustered, don't giggle, blush if you must, the lights were low, it didn't show, thank goodness, I was the colour of a beetroot. One of them ended up sitting next to Jane, and the other on his friend's side. I appeared to have missed out. Jane was just about sitting on my lap though, and if the arm of the seat hadn't prevented it, she would have been. As it was, her shoulder and head were stuck to mine. We didn't see much of the pre intermission stuff, and as soon as we could, when the lights went up for interval we were up and running. The chap on her right had said 'hello', and apparently the other one had looked around towards me, this was all very thrilling! When we emerged from the loos, looking the part of sophisticated young woman, there they were. All sense of decorum disappeared, and we dissolved into giggling whispering wrecks again. This was not going well, and it got worse, they came over to speak to us, such turmoil of confusing emotions. They introduced themselves, one was Alex, and the other's name was Steve. I thought Steve was really nice. Jane told them her name, and I managed to eventually squeak out mine, and then we (more they actually) talked about our respective schools, they were both boarders at our brother school. The buzzer went, what a reprieve, time to go back in, and an opportunity, or so I thought, for me to gather my wits. When we got to our row, Steve asked if he could sit next to me, and the seat was heaven sent, as I literally fell into it in a disturbing combination of sheer terror, and extreme ecstasy, my little heart was thumping and I broke out into a very unattractive cold sweat.

Once during the movie his hand brushed mine, and the tingle went from my toes to my hair follicles, thank goodness he didn't actually hold it, goodness knows how I would have survived that. It was the longest and yet the shortest movie I have ever not really watched. My eyes were aching with the effort of looking at him sideways whilst trying to appear that I was absorbed in the film. Every muscle ached from sitting dead still, in a ladylike fashion (no legs draped over the front seat today), and my throat was dead dry from excitement and mostly not drinking my coke in case I burped. It was worth it though, and when after the movie, Steve asked if he could call me, and would I give him my phone number, I thought I had died and gone to heaven. This was how I met my first boyfriend. Over the next week, he did call, and he came to visit me at home. My parents met him, and I was in the planning phase of our wedding, how many children we would have and everything else that went with it. I was in love. School days passed in a blur of serious discussions about this thing called love, notes being passed to and fro in class, and the biggest subject of all, was that I had never snogged anyone before. You know, using tongues! I was way behind most of my friends, and I sought out their expertise and advice. How do you do it, how does it start, and what do you do with your tongue, so many questions, and so many different answers. The wiser ones all said, don't worry, it will come naturally. We had kissed on the lips, and I was quite happy with that, this tongue thing was quite daunting, but also felt like it could be deliciously exciting. Once a month there was a movie in the school hall, which was mainly for the benefit of the boarders and it was also the opportunity for the girls to invite friends, be it brothers or boyfriends. Steve invited me, and my friends arranged we would all sit together in the two back rows. Most of them, apart from Tracy had boyfriends, and they knew how to get around the monitors, when to sneak that kiss, so they were also there as my advisors. They all said 'the kiss' would happen that night, and that meant sleepless nights for me, swinging between imagining the ecstasy of it, dreading it, what if he didn't like me anymore after he kissed me, what if I was useless, so many anxieties.

The night came, we were all seated, it was half way through the movie, and I had friends to the left and right of me, in the row behind and in front, what an audience. This didn't provide me with a comfort zone, it terrified the life out of me, but I had convinced myself, that there was really nothing to it. I could do this, just open your mouth slightly, move your tongue around a bit, and stop, what was so hard about that? The moment came, guard duty for the monitors, whispered 'now' down the row, and Steve's head, and everyone else's for that matter turned. Steve's head turned slowly towards mine, blocking my view of everything in front of me, his mouth met mine, his lips parted, and then the feeling of his tongue in my mouth, it was lovely, I moved my tongue around his, gently, not too much, but enough to participate in the kiss, oh wow, so this was what it was all about, lovely softness, wetness, a tingly feeling, and as though I couldn't breathe. Oh shit, I couldn't, how did they do it in the movies for so long, I was suffocating, I couldn't breathe, I would last as long as I could before I passed out or brain damage set in, they had snogging contests didn't they and people did it for hours, I couldn't break off before he did, he might think I wasn't enjoying it. Oh please stop kissing Steve, for god's sake stop, I'm dying here, I started thrashing about, and he must have thought he'd hit all the right buttons but panic started to set in, and I ended the kiss with an almighty shove in his direction to dislodge his mouth from mine, and sent him sprawling into the person next to him. There were gasps from all round, but no bigger intake of air than my own, I was like a fish out of water, and when I was able to speak, I hissed to my so called friends, 'nobody told me you can't breathe during a snog', 'what do you mean you can't breathe?' Jane asked, genuinely perplexed. 'Well your mouth is covered, so how are you supposed to breath', I was really miffed now; they were indicating I was completely stupid. Jane said two words and everyone fell about in total hysterics, I did too, when I heard them and realised how stupid I had been. 'Your nose' were those two words, 'you breathe through you're nose.'

It took months for that story to wear off, and it spread like wildfire, the whole school heard about my first snog, and 'breathe through your nose' became a turn of phrase used for anyone being a bit dim. I survived it quite well, mainly because Steve didn't run a mile, and I was a quick learner once I knew the right technique, and we spent many happy moments practising. By now, I had just about set the wedding date. My mum tolerated Steve, but wasn't over enthusiastic as he didn't come from the right type of family. His family were farmers, and whilst that was a noble and worthy role, it wasn't quite the doctor, lawyer, mayor, prime minister, ideal match she had in mind for me. None of this really worried me too much, as its amazing how young love can carry you along on white fluffy clouds, days are brighter, people are suddenly nicer, and those rose tinted glasses work miracles.

Well, as they say all good things must come to an end, and it did. My relationship with Steve came to an abrupt and cruel end one day, when I was told, by someone I knew only vaguely, that Steve was waiting to meet me on the hockey pitch, an unexpected and unplanned visit. I ran there, Heathcliffe and Cathy from Wuthering Heights playing through my mind; saw his blonde head in the distance, slightly lowered, and his back to me. I stopped to tidy myself, and organise it so that my hair would be blowing delicately in the breeze, face glowing with love, and a not so eager languid stroll to meet him. Then I saw the brunette head close to his, he was kissing someone else, and that someone suddenly looked up and saw me. I was frozen to the spot, Steve then turned, and looked at me in horror and surprise, and I realised that the person who had told me he was here, knew what I would find. So much for these do-gooder, worthy types, I didn't really want to know. What the eye doesn't see the heart doesn't feel, and right now my heart felt like it was being put through a shredder. Fortunately I didn't let my true feelings show, which would have been charging the two of them like a raging bull elephant, and inflicting as much physical damage as I could muster, on both of them. I simply turned and walked away until I was just out of their line of vision, plonked myself down, and sobbed my tattered heart out.

The days and nights that followed were typical of the young broken hearted. Nobody was nice anymore, those soft fluffy clouds had become thunderheads, days were dark and gloomy, and the spring in my step, had become a shuffling drag. My mum's input was, 'he wasn't good enough for you, anyway there's plenty of fish in the sea' or 'you are far too young to know what being in love is all about, so get on with your life' and, 'you have plenty of time for boys, concentrate on your schoolwork'. When we are young, I believe our capacity for healing is much greater, and faster, and as soon as I got the next note from a prospective admirer bearing SWALK (sealed with a loving kiss), on the envelope, I perked up considerably. Life moves on, so time to move with it.

8

During the next year my friendship with Jane ended abruptly. It was one of those childish things, when someone says you have said something that you haven't, and it all gets very nasty and bitchy. Dana, even at that age, enjoyed playing with people's emotions, and decided the demise of Jane's and my friendship would make good entertainment, and obviously Jane must have felt it was time for a change too, because she chose to believe what Dana said quite easily. One day we were best friends, the next I was out in the cold, no explanation was offered for a long time, I was just cut off by both of them. I was shocked, confused, and more gutted than I had been in the ending of any of my relationships with boys. I still adored Jane, and I remember going home, eating, or not, and straight to my bed. I was grieving, I didn't understand what had happened, and it was so sudden and final, I didn't really know what to do with myself. Locking myself away, shutting off from the world was my way of surviving this. This had been more than a friendship for me, it was the closest I had allowed myself to get to anyone besides my granny. The only other person I had trusted enough to open up to. I had adored Jane; she had been my confidante, my best friend, my support, and my strength. I had put her on a pedestal, idealised her, and developed myself around being like her. In a way, I felt I had lost part of my own identity, I felt incomplete. I felt confused. During this time, I understood that perhaps, before I'd lost weight and become more confident, I hadn't threatened her admiration and attention, I'd changed, and Jane's vanity was in jeopardy.

I was left to grieve on my own, my parents couldn't understand the depth of my grief, they thought it was abnormal to feel that way about a 'friend', and they mentioned their concern about my strange and too intense sadness. Their concern was not for me, but about me, this kind of behaviour did not fit their criteria of emotional stability, I should cut the dramatics, and pull myself together.

In retrospect, I spent most of my life feeling emotionally confused. There were times of what I considered great kindness. When my mum took me shopping, bought me new clothes, and always told whomever we met, that we were 'best friends' just like a mother and daughter should be. This led to a warped concept of friendship, love, anger, sorrow and just about any other emotion we experience. My experience of it all was that as long as you conformed to the other individuals ideals, and met their needs, then you would benefit from their kindness. It gets more complex though, because what I considered kindness was realistically how normal people who like and respect each other behave anyway. For me, it was rare, and therefore a treat or a reward, and something I had to work for. If and when my natural emotions emerged, be it sorrow or anger, the lecture ensued. The one my father always gave, that always began 'I don't know where you came from, you can't be a part of me, because I am not malicious, or your mother, because she is an angel', and on and on. I witnessed then, and still do, the compassion, kindness, and sacrifice my mother gives her lifelong friends, sisters and extended families, and this somehow only enforced my sense of confusion. What was it throughout my life, about my parents relationship with me, that they could not or would not extend this to their daughter. I have always therefore speculated on my exact origins. As I became more confident on listening to my soul, gut feeling or instinct, what ever name it goes by for you, the concept that there is ambiguity surrounding my birth becomes more profound. I do recognise that even now, I would prefer to discover that this was the case. It would explain everything, and in a way justify their behaviour to some extent. This would be easier to understand, and I believe less painful, as I know that my appearance indicates one of my parents is biologically implicated in my birth. This does however lead to enormous speculation on the impact this would have had on them in their relationship, and the destructive fall out on the entire family.

Again, I digress; however, I feel it is important to substantiate the negative emotional foundation, and uncertainty, that was the essence of my being.

The next brief chapter in my life only serves to reinforce my feelings that all was not quite what it appeared to be. A family from elsewhere in the country had moved to Umtali, and the woman was working with my mum, in a different department entirely, but the same organisation. True to form, my mum took the opportunity to extend her friendship, and in turn introduce her to the local community. Because there were two girls in the family around my age, who would be attending the same school, I was therefore expected to extend the same courtesy and we were going to tea. Simone, who was one year younger than me, and Stephanie, a year older, became firm friends of mine over the next few months. My mum became good friends with Joan their mum, and I spent some very enjoyable weekends with the family. Dexter, their father was the curator of the local museum, and an extreme enthusiast in flora, fauna, and wildlife, in particular birds. Most of the time I spent with them, we went out into the bush, the forests, all over the countryside really, and spent days tramping after him, whilst he discovered new species and revisited old. There were wonderful picnic hampers, and another opportunity to experience family life, totally different to my own. Joan and Dexter, were very tactile, and often we would see them kissing and cuddling, which was so gross, it was ok for us of course, but old people, and especially someone's parents, yuck!!

One night I spent at their home, I had quite a bizarre experience. I woke during the night with a distinctly uncomfortable bussing, flapping noise in my ear. This was actually 'in' my ear, and it was quite deafening. I woke Simone close to hysterics, who in turn called her parents. By this time I'd imagined that my ear was imploding, I had a deadly unknown flapping in the ear virus, and I was quite certain, a slow and painful death was imminent. Simone's dad had a look in my ear, and gave me the diagnosis. I had a moth in my ear. Well the good news was I wasn't close to death; the bad news was how we get it out! Obviously the moth was totally distressed too in this strange environment and it was clearly demonstrating its anxiety, which in turn made it extremely uncomfortable. It sounded and felt like I had a pterodactyl in there. Strange how the most simple solutions, always take the longest to realise. Dexter tried tweezers which only made the moth and I more hysterical, and then he felt I should perhaps go to the A&E which terrified me, and then someone mentioned shining the torch directly into my ear, and hopefully the moth would be attracted to the light, and fly out. There I lay, torch fixed to my ear hole, vehemently praying for the moth to go towards the light, and wondering why Simone and Stephanie had pillows glued to their faces, their bodies shaking, and muffled noises coming from the pillows which might have been laughter! Surely no-one could find this funny, this was serious wasn't it? I could spend days with a frantic moth in my ear, and then have a deceased moth in my ear. What could be funny about that?

It worked and that desperate little moth, must have done a u-turn in my ear, and squeezed its way out, it rested on my lobe for a moment, probably thanking its little moth God, whilst I thanked mine, and I am sure deciding never to go into unexplored caves again.

Stephanie and Simone had sleepovers at mine, and we met at school break times. We were a close threesome, until one day it all came to an abrupt and ugly end. My mum came home from work, clearly distressed, and for a few days there were hushed conversations behind doors, phone calls and all sorts of secretive goings on. Things appeared quite strained and there was an unusually tense atmosphere between my mum and dad, and any questions I had about it, were answered with 'this is nothing to do with you'. Well it turned out it certainly impacted on me, because I was told by my mum and dad, that there had been a 'disagreement' between Joan and my mum, she had actually been spreading nasty vicious rumours at work, and mum would not have anything more to do with her. I wasn't invited back to their home, and they weren't invited to mine. Although we still met at school for a time, and shared dramatic notions of our friendship being thwarted by our parents, we were also respectively loyal to our parents and it became difficult to sustain, and not long after one or other of us didn't turn up at break time, and the relationship dissolved. I know that Simone and Stephanie knew what it was all about, but it was some years later, after persistent questioning that my mum told me what had happened. Apparently the 'rumours' were about my mum having an affair with her boss. I understand this was not only based on conjecture, but that they had been seen in an intimate embrace. Of course it was vociferously denied by my mother, and although a difficult atmosphere hung over our home for sometime, it has never been spoken of again.

There was also within the same period an unusual incident concerning my dad. I was woken in the early hours of one morning by loud voices, one a strange woman's. I got out of bed, put my dressing gown on, and went through to the lounge. There were two policemen there, and a strange woman who was very distressed. She had bruises on her face, and had obviously been crying, but even in that state, she was very attractive. Tall and slim, with long blonde hair, she was clinging onto my father. When I was noticed, I was asked to go and make tea, and whilst in the kitchen, I could hear raised voices, along with more crying from the woman. I took the tea through, and was sent to bed. The following day, you could cut the air with a knife, my parents were civil to one another, and tried to behave normally, but it was obvious even to me, that all was not well. The explanation I was given, was that the lady was a patient of my father, and had been in a violent argument with her husband. She became frightened and called the police, and asked them to bring her to my father. I suppose with all the reading I did, I had a vivid imagination, but I wondered what had instigated the argument, and why it had become violent. Most of all, why would someone in that state not go to a friend or family member, but ask to be taken to their Chiropractors home, and in the early hours of the morning. This also became one of those incidents that were never spoken about again.

Both of these could well be what I was told, somehow though, as an adult and with the hindsight of experience, perhaps my parents' perfect marriage had its challenges after all.

9

It seemed it was relatively quickly that I made new friends, and they became the group that I would spend the rest of my teenage years with. Their names were Sarah, Sheila, and Judy. Sarah lived two houses up the road from me, and Sheila and Judy about a twenty minute walk away. My boarder friends continued to spend Sundays with us, and we all either got together mainly at my house or went out together. We had some great days, we changed boyfriends regularly, and sometimes we went out with one another's exes. This created much comparing of notes, how well did he snog, how many notes did he write, how many times he called, and so on. Although at the time, we felt we were in love, none of these relationships lasted long, weeks at the most, and if it extended into a month, well it was really getting serious.

Just about all of us started smoking. It was so grown up, and although it took many attempts, coughing, retching, nearly passing out, we were determined to master this sophisticated art. Most of our pocket money went on cigarettes, and the quantity we wasted in those learning days was phenomenal, but we persevered, and became successful and accomplished smokers. We sneaked a fag, whenever and wherever we could, the more daring the better. We hid in hedges, walked miles into the bush, climbed trees, and at school the normal places like behind the bicycle shed, the hockey pitch, and hiding in drainage ditches. One night my friend Sarah was sleeping over and we waited until we thought my parents were asleep, and lit up. Within seconds, there was a knock on the bedroom door, and in the minute it took for me to open it, we had opened a window, sprayed half a bottle of perfume, and chucked our fags into the small bin. My mum had gone to the loo, and seen the light on, and thought it was time we went to sleep, I tried to keep her at the door, but her nose decided the room was on fire, and her nose was close to being right. Flames had begun to shoot out of the bin. It was really a bad idea to just dump them in there with tissues and such. I tried all sorts, 'we decided to light a candle', and we were 'playing with matches', which might have worked, if the cigarettes hadn't been in clear view on the bedside table. I was told 'we would talk tomorrow'. What that actually meant was, my parents would talk, I would shut-up and listen to what punishment was dealt. This would not be a two way conversation, I had been caught red-handed, literally, after trying to beat the flames out with my bare hands, and it was time to suffer the consequences. What happened the next day however, shocked me to my core, and imbalanced me for weeks afterwards.

Sarah went home in the early hours, after we spent a sleepless night, imagining my punishment, which at the very least would probably be ten years in solitary, so much for a friend in need!

When we were seated, my parents said that as they knew I had been smoking, (so much for all the toothpaste, perfume and deodorant) they would prefer it if I smoked in front of them, openly and honestly, and not behind their back. I was speechless, and my mouth kept opening and closing, like a fish out of water, I couldn't stop it, until I actually held my mouth closed with my hand. Had they been abducted by aliens, and these were replicas of my parents, what was going on? It was quite a while before I could talk, and all that came out was 'What?'. They actually looked very smug and were exchanging 'aren't we the clever ones' looks, as they repeated themselves at least twice more, and I considered asking for it in writing, in blood would be even better. I couldn't believe my luck, no grounding for a year, none of the 'I don't know where you came from' lectures, just the two of them sitting there, asking me to rather smoke openly and freely, than sneak about. I was still sitting in a zombie like state, when my father offered me one of his cigarettes, and I had to grip onto the arms of the chair, to avoid sliding down onto the floor. The smug look, was now becoming very pronounced, and uncertain about what was actually expected of me, I accepted the offer, took the cigarette, the light, closed my eyes, inhaled deeply, did my best trick of blowing the smoke through my nose, and looked at my parents. Smug was starting to slip, and frowns were becoming visible, smiling mouths became set lips, so I decided they wanted to watch me enjoy my cigarette, and I smoked it with vigour and exaggerated pleasure. They got up and left the room at that point, all stiff and rigid, and I felt confused, but very happy. Wait until I told my friends, which I did in no time at all. The phone lines were buzzing, and in no time at all, the whole group was there, and we were all smoking up a cloud. They couldn't believe how lucky I was having such modern parents, didn't they just wish theirs were the same.

From that day on, there was a certain tension present every time I had a cigarette, however, it was different when the crowd were over puffing away, as they always mentioned how wonderful Dr and Mrs. Stewart were, and they wished their parents equally understood. At those times, my parents, brushed it aside, with their modern attitudes to 'the youth of today', and although, in their day, it would have been considered unforgivable, one had to move with the times, and so on. Eventually, I challenged my parents about why I'd been given permission to smoke in their company, when it blatantly infuriated them. They explained their motive had been to remove the excitement and mischief from illicit smoking; therefore there would be none or little incentive to continue. They had misunderstood my smoking, of course there was a large element of excitement and secrecy initially, but subsequently I had become addicted, so this had really backfired on everyone. I was surprised about this really, as my dad was a smoker, and yet their perception had been, I was doing it to be one of the crowd, which was a fair judgment, and to wind them up, which they constantly reminded me was my sole purpose in life. Consequently, it went from having the occasional quick puff, to becoming a regular smoker. My parents had set aside their principles, and played psychology, which had achieved the adoration and admiration of all my friends, although I don't believe we achieved anything really positive from the situation. Sadly, even after experiencing this failed experiment, they were to repeat it, only the next time it was with alcohol.

My last two 'schoolboy' boyfriends, made life entertaining and fun. I was fourteen going on twenty four by then, knew it all, and thought I had the T-shirt. I met Paul at a disco, he asked me to dance, I thought he was really cool, and we boogied and eventually slow shuffled the night away. I, and most others had heard of him, and he was known to be quite a rebel. 'Rebel' in those days, was someone who swigged the occasional beer underage, smoked, and had an 'attitude'. He was sixteen, and he had his own motorbike of sorts, a sort of put together contraption, which made a lot of noise and pollution. He was super-cool, and of course the absolute opposite to my parents' ideal young man, which made him all the more appealing. He gave me my first love bite, and when that happened, I was close to ecstatic collapse, it was so thrilling, and I felt so wanton. I remember the morning after the night before, desperately trying to find foundation to cover the very vivid bruise on my neck. I couldn't get away with a high-neck anything in temperatures of forty degrees, so instead I had this more than obvious splodge of concealer on my neck, and it was quite a badge of honour amongst my friends. Not, understandably, with my mother though. I had already been given the lecture about going out with people beneath me, particularly one with such a reputation, and now sporting this disgusting Alex, what sort of young woman was I anyway. At that point in my life however, my reputation amongst my friends was more important anyway, so I sashayed about, flashing my semi concealed Alex of love about, to all and sundry.

One day Paul came to visit me at home. I had just got back after school, and we were talking outside on the driveway. He had his motorbike with him, and was straddling it, smoking a cigar. Being Paul, he always had to be different and more outrageous, hence the cigar. My parents arrived home, and my mother's distaste was ill concealed, they had met him, and barely tolerated him. He greeted them politely, and her retort was 'Paul, what on earth are you doing smoking a cigar at your age, what are you going to do when you are older?' His poker faced and immediate response was, 'smoke a bigger cigar, Mrs. Stewart'. Well, my mum's face was a picture, I fell about in total hysterics, and even my dad beat a hasty exit, a smile playing on his lips. Needless to say, that was the beginning of the end of that relationship, as any future dates with Paul were very difficult to achieve without the doors of hell opening.

My other boyfriend was also called Paul. I knew he had been born to older parents, and that they had immigrated from Switzerland, but I never met them. He drove a red VW Beetle which was his pride and joy, and he was a phenomenal dancer. He taught me how to do all the dances from movies like Grease and Dirty Dancing, and when the soundtracks were played at our local disco, we cleared the floor. It was one of the extremely rare occasions that I felt confident, and I will always remember those very special dances with gratitude and great pleasure. Paul's sole purpose in life seemed to be taking my virginity, and the more I resisted, the more obsessed he became. I was adamant I would be a virgin bride, and I really hadn't given him any reason to believe any differently, nor that I was considering him as anyone permanent in my life. As regards, sexual activity, my boundaries at that time, were snogging, and in moments of major hormone turmoil, allowing a quick feel of my breast, and that was always over my bra, not under it. I think I must have been a major challenge, and regardless of his frequent promises that he would be the best first lover for any woman, he never achieved anything more than what I mentioned. Frustration set in, and we had an on off relationship for a while, and eventually he left to study watch making in Switzerland. I didn't see him for a number of years, where, upon his return he played his trump card, or so he thought, but that's a little further in the future.

During the school holidays, I often spent a week or two at one of my friend's farms. As they were term boarders, it was the only opportunity for me to share their home life with them, and meet their families. We had some wonderful times, and when I spent two weeks on Margaret's farm,. They had a farm in an area called Sabi, and it was just mile upon mile of bush land. Nigel, her brother drove the farm land rover, so we would climb on board early in the morning, find a dam or waterhole, and swim, always keeping a watchful eye out for crocodiles, and careful to spot the ever present snakes. We always had a rifle with us, and I started to learn how to shoot. The farming communities were very close knit, and families would meet at a local clubhouse for get-togethers regularly. Most of the farms were quite remote from each other, with vast distances between houses, and it was quite an isolated existence. Anxiety and fear was setting in amongst the community, as early conflicts with the rebels were swiftly becoming more than that, and there was more and more talk that we were heading rapidly towards war. There were problems with cattle being mutilated, and outbreaks of mysterious barn fires, and more frequent incidents of vehicles being fired upon.

We were at war! For the next six years of my life, war was in the background and the foreground. It wasn't just a remote part of our lives, it enveloped our lives. The town I lived in was on the border of Mozambique, which was a rebel stronghold, and our forces took over the town. Schools became barracks, there were more army vehicles, with names like Rhino, and Crocodile, than cars, and camouflage uniforms and FN rifles, were more visible than civvies.

Landmines were planted in the mountains along the border, and every time we had a thunderstorm or heavy rains, mines were set off, by the sliding mud, and after a while we became used to the deep boom of a mine exploding. Helicopters and Hunter Jets were frequent visitors in the skies over Umtali, mostly on training exercises or reconnaissance at that time. There was an overwhelming sense and smell of fear, and this existed for both black and white. This war was not a war of colour, as external propaganda suggested, and whilst I choose to desist from politics of any kind in my story, it is important to understand that we were all afraid of the rebels. They were communist trained in Russia, and China, and many young black males were kidnapped from their villages, and taken away for brutal and intensive training. African mothers and fathers were left bereft and grieving at the loss of their sons, and our cook and gardener spoke often of the terror in their locations. Their houses were set on fire, people 'disappeared' and others were taken into the streets and cruelly beaten, if they did not concede to .become a member of the rebel's political party. The intimidation on these people was cruel and merciless.

It became law that any white male sixteen years or over would be enlisted. They were entitled to sit their O level's but any further education, 'A' Levels, college, apprenticeships, or university had to be postponed. The only way to avoid going into the army was to leave the country, and many people did, to protect their sons. There was six weeks of intensive training, and then they were sent into the bush, kill or be killed. Then followed years of six weeks in, two weeks R&R. (rest and recuperation) These were boys only a couple of years older than myself, and after their six weeks training they were different, after their first bush tour, they were strange men, the boy and the boyhood had disappeared.

They didn't talk much, never about their bush tour, they didn't laugh, they woke screaming from nightmares, they ate, drank, and slept when they could. They cried easily and often, they swore as they never had before, they were angry, they were confused and had lost their sense of reality. Humanity had betrayed them, they witnessed unbelievable cruelty and brutality, they became cruel and brutal to survive, they lost their faith, and they died inside, so many boys to men, so many tortured and confused young souls. Life lost its value; they witnessed so many lives taken, and became killers too, from schoolboy to trained soldier in six weeks, from classroom to hell. Some went mad, some committed suicide, many went by the motto, 'live for today, tomorrow may never come', and it was one we all adopted.

We lived by extremes, and did everything in a frenzied sort of way, always as if it was the last. Whilst this gave us a sense of living life to the full, there was a dark side to this frantic lifestyle. We all had to grow up very quickly, and as the people our young men came home to, we adapted and adjusted to this sense of loss, lost youth, lost innocence, and so much loss of life. One of the first to die in this war, was a childhood friend of mine, and the son of my parents great friends. Gary was eighteen when he was killed, and I remember the disbelief I felt, and trying to come to terms with his death, and the terrible grief that wracked his family. Until his death, we were all cocooned in some artificial sense of false security. I know because he was amongst the first to die, it was a great shock, you somehow don't expect it so close to home, to someone you know, you just expect them to go on as you do, grow older with you, and suddenly they are gone, and you realise that being a teenager is no protection against death. I remember at that age believing I was invincible and indestructible, I believed our lives had just begun, someone of forty was old, and there were so many years ahead, so much still to do, and to see. In your teens, time is on your side, time is your ally, it passes leisurely, a year stretches ahead of you, and it takes so long for Christmas or your birthday to come around. As I grow older, time races and rushes by, it has become my rival, and Christmas is evermore rapidly upon me. How time has accelerated over the years. When you are fourteen, old age and dying were the natural combination weren't they. Not any more, it was time to accept that death didn't honour age anymore, and natural causes would become the exception now, no longer the rule.

It was also at about this part in my life that I became invisible to my parents. My brother was called up, and life revolved around the television, and the telephone. Gone were the days where I could chat for hours to friends, the line had to be kept clear, in case of a call. Life revolved around Andrew's brief visits home, and that was when we returned to normal. While he was in the bush, we endured a zombie like existence, hushed conversations, it was as though to talk normally was somehow disrespectful, and no laughter, that was taboo. How could we be seen to be happy, or normal, when he was living through hell. Well we were too in a way. It felt as though we needed to share this hardship and misery, this was our contribution, our sacrifice.

My mum and dad were absorbed in their concern for him, and whilst I understood this, I missed him too, and I didn't want my brother to die, I didn't really exist. There was nothing important anymore about my days at school, my report cards, my friends, and even though I still talked about it, invariably to myself, it allowed me to fantasize that I was being heard, and I even began to respond to me on their behalf. It would go something like this, imagined parent 'how was school today Cheryl,' me 'Great, thanks for asking', 'did you do any sport', me 'yeah, actually I've been chosen for the tennis single semi finals', 'wonderful, well done', me 'thanks, maybe you could come and watch', and then really outdoing the imaginative thing 'of course darling, we'd love to be there'. Well, it gave me the odd illicit giggle.

I tried so hard to understand how they felt, I was a teenager though, and selfishly wanted things to be as near normal as possible. I didn't like this enforced disappearing act, as though along with my brother's physical absence, I had also somehow vanished into the ether. So many times, I wanted to stand in front of my parents and shout 'Hello, I am still here, can you see me'. I'm not sure that they could see me, I had become invisible, it was easier that way you see, they didn't have the energy or reserves for me, their capacity for emotion was depleted, it was winging its way across the land to my brother.

My dad became the warden for our suburb, and this took up whatever little spare time he had. He took his role very seriously, and I think it took him back to the years he spent in the navy during the 2nd world war. There were frequent exercises, mock ups of bomb attacks, and we all volunteered as victims. At that time, it was fun to be band-aged up, and pretend to be mortally wounded, the reality was to come, and it wasn't funny at all.

As far as boyfriends went, I certainly did pick them. One of the strangest was Keith. Sheila and I went to a disco one weekend, and met two 'older' men. Keith and Paul were in their mid to late twenties, or so they said, but I think they were older, although we took it all in, hook, line and sinker. We also lied however, and our fifteen jumped miraculously to nineteen. They weren't in the army, and even that didn't rouse our suspicions, they fed us some line about having done their national service, and were now on a 'on call' basis. We were so gullible! That however, didn't stop me from falling for Keith like a ton of bricks, he seemed so sophisticated, mature and experienced in the ways of the world. They lived in Salisbury, the capital, which was about three hours drive away, and was the big city. This made them even more alluring, we were country bumpkins, and here we were with two city boys, wow! It was a strange affair, and I don't mean that in the literal sense, we only met them at disco's or went out to a movie, and afterwards, there was a lot of snogging in their respective cars, and we were taken home. They didn't come in to meet our par-ents, which quite honestly wasn't a bad thing, because I'm sure their actual age would have been easily identified by my mum and dad, and I also didn't want the conversation to steer onto age, what with my deception.

We double dated for some months, and Sheila and I were the envy of all our friends, Keith and Philip, were very attentive, and made the effort to travel down most weekends. They always had loads of cash, and treated us, every time we went out. During the week, there were phone calls virtually every night, and although I had to keep the line free, I was able to chat briefly to Keith, and he always seemed so inter-ested and caring. I never wondered why these two men, were attracted to young teenagers, it didn't occur to me, that it might be because we were just that, very young, immature, and very gullible. They had two young silly girls who thought they were all that and more. It was coming up to my sixteenth birthday, and I had convinced Keith to join the party. I was so excited; I was going to show him off to everyone. A couple of nights before my birthday, I received a call from Keith. He said he was very sorry, but he wouldn't be able to come through that weekend, and would have to miss my birthday party. I was absolutely gutted. I remember feeling very upset, and it was obvious to Keith, this had meant a great deal to me, and I was very disappointed. I felt he had to have a very good excuse not to be there, and it turned out he did, probably one of the best of all time. He was calling from jail, he had used his call for me, I suppose that was reasonable considering, but my face must have been a picture. He was in jail, my jaw had hit my knees, and I was literally speechless. Next question was, for what? Why was he in jail, well I wouldn't have believed it, if someone else had told me, but it turns out, he was in on a breaking and entering charge, theft, and now to the point, he had broken into someone's home to nick my birthday present! How much of this could a girl take, in one phone call. He also confessed that he had actually been on probation, so with this offence, it was a sentence, and he was so sorry, and he loved me, and could he write to me, and then his time on the phone ran out, and I sat holding the buzzing receiver for a long while. I didn't want a birthday present anyway; I just wanted him to be at my party.

Oh my God, how was I going to tell my folks, how was I going to tell my friends, I had been so full of how wonderful Keith was, how special he made me feel, how he had spoilt me, well it was no wonder really, I had been wined and dined probably on money he's stolen. And, you know what, I felt sorry for him, when I received the first letter from him from prison, I wanted to write back, and because I thought I could help him. That certainly caught my parent's attention, and I had a succession of the infamous lectures. I realised it was going to be more trouble than I could deal with, so I never replied to Keith, and worked through the months of ridicule which resulted from the unusual end to my relationship.

10

Over the next few years, so much happened it's hard to remember it in sequence; it all seems to merge into what was a really hard time. The war was escalating daily, and civilians were not exempt from it. I clearly remember the night I experienced my first mortar and rocket attack. I remember waking to a distant boom, and thinking it was one of the mines slipping on the mountain. Then there was another, and this was a different sound, and closer. It was just before 4am, when I leapt out of bed at the same time as the rest of the family, and we all collided in the passageway. Booms were coming now in quick succession, and we closed our bedroom doors, to prevent flying glass. 'What's happening, who's bombing us', I screamed. My mum was screaming she didn't know, and my brother and dad told us to go into the dining room, and get under the table. I couldn't understand why, as there were glass windows right along the one wall, but we ran there anyway. My mum and I crawled under the table, while my brother and dad desperately grabbed the big cushions from the sofa, and blocked the side of the table alongside the windows. We huddled under there, with our dogs, and it was the first time I knew that I could die. I didn't ask 'are we going to die?' nobody could answer that truthfully, it would have been an empty question, and equally empty answer. The most terrifying sound was the whistle, as the bombs flew through the sky, and then the enormous crumps as they exploded somewhere close by. The explosions made different sounds, and my

63

brother knew the difference between the mortars and the rockets, he also knew we would not withstand a direct hit from either. We had gone into the dining room, as it was the only room in the house that had a concrete roof, and that might absorb some of the blast, but certainly not all. Sometimes the house and the windows shook with the sound, and we knew they were landing very close indeed; I was more frightened than I had ever been in my life. I knew during those hours that injury or death could come at any second, and we wouldn't know it, I learnt when you heard the whistle, thank god, because that meant it had gone over you, I learnt when you heard nothing, it might be coming directly at you. I also learnt that the rockets would penetrate just about anything, exploding during their deathly path; I learnt that I might not live beyond this night, and I learnt that I had no control over my mortality.

Just when I thought it couldn't go on much longer, there were new and more terrifying sounds and explosions, and my brother strangely let out what sounded like a victorious whoop. He explained our defences had kicked in and those were our guns retaliating. Our town was in a valley, and we were being attacked and defended from the mountains surrounding us, and the sounds of that battle have never left me.

As daylight slowly arrived, it became intermittent, and then it was quiet. We waited before we crawled out from under the table. My legs were very unsteady, as were my family's', and we must have looked like a group of drunks exiting the dining room. None of us spoke for a while, we needed to confirm we had survived this night, we needed to verify we hadn't just all been in a very bad dream, we needed to come to terms with the fact that we had experienced our first and never anticipated attack, we needed to understand that the war had become personal, it had entered our homes, it had truly invaded every aspect of our lives now. What had been our cocoon of safety had been violated, now we couldn't feel safe anywhere anymore. Then the question seemed to come to all of us at the same time. What about everybody else, friends and family, who was dead, who had survived? Were the phones working?

The phone did work, it rang seconds later, and it was my friend Sarah who lived a couple of houses away. Their neighbour had a mortar in their pool, and just along the way, a rocket had hit one of the houses. Whilst I was talking my dad and Andrew had a look around the garden and sanitary lane, and there was a large crater in the lane. We'd had a fairly close call. Suddenly there was the a noise that sent waves of terror through me, and Sarah and I screamed, as I instinctively threw myself under the bed. It was the massive roar of military jets, sweeping low and swift above us, and I thought we were now going to be bombed from the skies. It turned out they were our Hunter jets on their way to Mozambique and the rebel strongholds. We could hear the distant explosions for a while before the jets returned over us, and then we went to school. Something changed for all of us that day, we were all safe, and we had all experienced a miracle. Hundreds of RPG rockets and mortars, had literally been rained on us, houses destroyed, gardens pot holed and cratered, and roads too, and yet there had not been one fatality. A number of people had shrapnel wounds, but no-one had been killed.

Once the fear dissipated the anger set in, and we knew we would not have our homes and lives destroyed or taken away from us. Nobody was prepared to leave, to find a safer place, we would stay and we would gather strength, and we would adapt to this new way of life. It certainly did become a new way of life. The weekends we would spend up in the mountains picnicking, we still did, except we were armed. The girls were instructed that in the event of an ambush, defend yourself as best you could, but ensure you kept a bullet for yourself. It was considered to be far better to end your own life quickly, than be subjected to the atrocities we heard about daily. The roads we drove on were narrow strips of tar, with dirt both sides, and often you pulled over onto this. Now we never left the tar, landmines were frequently planted in the dirt on the side of the roads, and we also learnt to avoid any animal dung, anything lying on the tar, because the rebels hid mines beneath. When you stopped at a lay-by, you took the chance of mines, particularly anti personnel ones, they often didn't kill, just blew your legs off. We continued our lives as best we could, in a defiant way I suppose. With all the risks attached we were stubborn, and continued to go to our old picnic spots, isolated and dangerous as they were, and we became blasé, take each day for what it was, tomorrow might never come.

The next mortar attack was during the day while we were at school. We had had constant drills in the event of this happening, but this was really of no use to me this time, because a group of us, had snuck away during break time, and were hiding on one of the hockey fields having a fag. There was nowhere to hide, apart from a small ditch, which offered no protection at all, in fact we might as well have just laid out on the field. More miracles, we stayed there for the two or so hours, with mortars landing too close for comfort, but apart from being petrified, we survived that one too. Again there were no fatalities. Sadly, even this however, didn't persuade me to give up smoking!

This was also the year I was writing my O level's and we sent a petition over to England to ask for time concessions to be made, as sometimes our exams were interrupted with drills or false alarms. We weren't given any. We were sixteen, we lived in a city overrun with young army lads, who we partied with every weekend, we smoked, and we also did our fair share of binge drinking, we all lost friends, and friends of friends on a daily basis to the war, but we were so alive. We seemed to experience everything with such intensity, it was almost as though we were all on this mad drug called life, there was so much death and suffering around us all the time, we lived frantically, cramming as much in whilst we could, and there was always this feeling that it could end in an instant. We learnt to say what we felt and meant, because nothing should be left unsaid, there might not be another opportunity, it was not so much a way of life it was more a, 'panic of life,' to fit so much in, to love frequently and intensely, to cry and laugh as you experienced the emotion, it was so honest and open, and I often wish I'd been able to maintain that spontaneity. I couldn't though, because all that 'honesty', in mind, thought and deed, was savagely stripped from me, and left me a hollow empty nothing.

Tracy had now come to board with us during the school terms, and it was like having a sister. Andrew was still in the army, and during this year, on one of our picnics a new person was introduced to our group. Our group consisted of Sarah, Judy, Sheila, Christine, her brother Nigel and his friend Alex. We went everywhere together, and spent every weekend doing stuff together. Most afternoons after school, we would congregate at my house, (don't forget we could smoke there freely), and either enjoy swimming, or simply sitting talking. We shared secrets, hopes and dreams; we looked out for one another we were the best of friends. Nigel and Alex were struggling with their sexual identity, both were gay, but hadn't at that point admitted

66

it to themselves or anyone else. They tried to go out with girls, but it just never worked out, and they shared what must have been a private hell. At that time it wasn't easy to admit being gay, there were still too many negative and discriminatory views around it, and their inner struggle and torment was hard to see and experience. God knows how difficult it must have been for them. When we were together, was the only time I think that they could relax and talk about their feelings and turmoil, and we trusted each other.

Let me get back to telling you more now about the new person in the group. This was rare indeed, to allow a stranger in, but we learnt he had recently moved from South Africa, and his parents had divorced. Nigel had met him, and felt he needed friends and support, and that was good enough for us. His name was Darrell, and he was drop dead gorgeous. All us girls in the group thought he was lovely, and I resigned myself to the fact that the competition was too strong, so I kept my distance, and waited to see who, if anyone of us he would fancy. All the girls tried to attract his attention, and he spoke to them all, whilst I remained at a distance, not being aloof, just realistic Sarah, Chris and Sheila were all blonde, and past experience had taught me, that blondes were more attractive to most men, so I felt it was inevitable that he would fancy one of them. I suppose it was silly to have this preconceived notion that he was obliged to like any one of us in particular, for all we knew, he might have a girlfriend, or just want to make the most of all the opportunities open to him, to meet someone. Girls will be girls though, and it was one of those days, where we all tried to appear disinterested and neutral, but every time he spoke to one of us in particular, the looks that were exchanged were very competitive, and that sort of smug expression, if he actually extended himself to more than a couple of words like 'how are you?' then 'Are you in school?', It was like some sort of competition, add up the scores, how many words he actually said to whom. I know Chris had the highest total at the end of the day, nothing surprising about that though, she was blonde, blue eyed, and knew how to attract men, lots of coquettish looks, wide admiring baby blue eyes, and very feminine and helpless gestures.

I did enjoy just looking at him, he was older than us, eighteen going on nineteen, and he was doing an apprenticeship as a mechanic. He had lovely thick Black hair, slightly long, and the most gorgeous blue eyes. He wasn't too tall or too short, and had a body to die for. He seemed nice, and a lot of fun too, perfect in other words.

There was a disco that evening that we were all going to, and just before we were due to go out, Nigel called me aside, and told me Darrell had said he fancied me. After the shock and disbelief, nerves and excitement set in, actually mad euphoria is probably an accurate description. When I told the other girls, there was a mixed reaction, shock, disbelief and envy; it was only the envy I found particularly flattering and encouraging. I was plagued with doubt however, and even considered that Nigel had been winding me up, I still didn't have much self confidence. Fortunately I had given due care and attention to my appearance, hours doing make up and blow drying my wavy hair straight. My nails were done, and I doused myself in perfume. I wore the jeans I thought contained my 'curves', and had high heels on, not too high though, just to allow for a long leggy look. I was buzzing with excitement on the way there. Mentally I was preparing the casual couldn't care less saunter in, and desperately hoping he would ask me to dance. What if he didn't, what if Nigel was wrong, I would be gutted.

We arrived at the disco, and I spotted him as soon as we walked in. He stood out mainly because of his hair. The army guys always had short back and sides, as did any school boys who were there. Besides it wasn't a big town, and we all knew most of the locals anyway. He came right over when he spotted us, and spoke to Nigel, and we wandered to another part of the hall to find a table and seats. We sat down, and I was already in a state of despair, that it had all been a dream, when Darrell appeared beside me with an extra chair, and asked if could squeeze in next to me. I died and went to heaven in an instant. I won't bore you with all the details, but from that moment on, we were as inseparable as we could be. We saw each other nearly every evening, and when we couldn't, we spoke for hours on the phone. I had a weekly curfew because I was studying for my O level's, but Darrell came to visit early evening, and we spent all the time we could together over the weekend. Poor Tracy, heard nothing else but Darrell this, Darrell that, and given the opportunity, so did everyone else.

His mum invited me to dinner one evening, and my mum insisted that Tracy came along as chaperone. They lived in a modest house with obviously little money to spare, but she was easy to chat to, and

68

approved of our relationship, although she did caution us that we were very young still, and not to get too serious. There was a sense of anxiety about her with Darrell that I couldn't understand. It was as though she kept far too close an eye on him and his activities, I put this down to her being protective, keeping her son close after a painful divorce.

We were about as serious as we could get, and Darrell was the first boyfriend to tell me he loved me, and I loved him back. I knew from the little he shared with me, that he had had a troubled past, he didn't offer any details, and I didn't push for more. I also suspected he smoked marijuana, but never when we were together, as he knew I felt really strongly about drugs of any kind. I was terrified of drugs, and nothing could or would persuade me to try anything even once. I'd asked why they had come here from South Africa, to the back of beyond really, and it was because of the divorce, and his mum had a relative who owned a farm not too far out of Umtali. Apparently this was her only living relative, so it made sense for her to be close by. I trusted him, and loved him, and never thought I had any reason to probe further or doubt anything he told me. My parents neither approved nor disapproved of Darrell, and I was quite comfortable to leave it at that, I didn't expect or ask for me or less, as long as I could be with him.

The war and everything that went with it was always in the background, then again, everything was in the background, Darrell was my focus, and the keeper of every bit of my attention in thought and action. I was happier than I had ever been. I eventually had someone who loved ME, and I loved him in return, and for the first time, I actually began to believe that life could hold happiness and wonder. Everyone knew we were an item, and we didn't go anywhere without each other and in a community where everyone knew everyone else, and what they had for breakfast, we were becoming considered a young couple. Our relationship intensified, and it got to the stage where we both felt that the day or night would come, when the kissing and touching would become sex. I was a virgin, and had the archaic view that I would be one when I got married, but the feelings were so strong, I didn't think I'd be able to keep exercising control. Darrell was patient and never forceful, and he knew how I felt about my virginity. I had always been told and brought up to believe that it was

69

something you saved for your husband, and for all the sophistication we pretended, my group of girlfriends were all virgins too.

My mum had always said that if there ever came a time when I felt 'things might happen', I could talk to her. Rather be safe than sorry and God forbid I became pregnant, that really would have been the ultimate disgrace. I took her at her word, and after days of plucking up the courage I approached her about my relationship with Darrell. I felt embarrassed, and really scared, after all this was not a subject you discussed easily with your mother but I was being a good girl and doing the 'sensible thing', wasn't I?

I had no idea how she would react, and was quite surprised at her control. I told her that my relationship with Darrell was becoming serious. She asked 'what do you mean, serious?' I said 'mum, I love Darrell so much, and I think we have a future together, I want to be with him always. You know you said I could come and talk to you, if I felt that things might happen, well I think now is that time. I want to be with him'. 'What do you mean be with him?' my mum asked? She was really making this difficult; I mean how explicit did I have to be for goodness sake. 'I mean, be with him, really be with him', I said. 'You are with him most of the time, so what's the problem', she replied. 'I mean have sex with him', I shouted, and felt myself blushing from the tips of my toes to the roots of my hair. Shit, this was so embarrassing! I also saw her recoil, and although she made a really good effort to maintain her expression of composure, her face had become rigid, and very pale. Well it certainly was taking the turn I expected, no ways should I have believed that she would allow me to have a sexual relationship; I was probably going to be grounded for life.

All credit to her though, although she spoke through gritted teeth, with this parody of a smile, she said she thought perhaps I hadn't thought this through well or long enough, and then the other one I expected, that I was too young. By now I was in fighting mode, and I argued that I had certainly given it a great deal of thought, and no I wasn't too young, and that I was in love with Darrell. That tipped her over the edge. 'You are just a child, what on earth do you think you know about love, you have no idea what being in love means'?

Why is it that parents think teenagers know nothing about being in love? It might not be the type of 'until death do us part' kind of love, but we don't think that at the time. I think at that age you love possibly more intensely and emotionally than at any other time in your life. You don't have the bitterness, the anger or the fear of heart-break that sadly, some of us experience later in life. It is so less complicated when you are young; your world begins and ends with the person in your life that you love. You don't have bills to pay, children to bring up, a job to go to, it's really just you and them. There are challenges though, which include your parents, your curfew if you have one and studying, perhaps tag pocket money, or lack of it onto that list. Then again, all these are simply background issues, you live and breathe your passion and your love. I also believe that passion at that time of our lives is incomparable. Every touch, every kiss is wonderful. No doubt a lot of that is due to the hormones rampaging through our bodies, but that just enhances everything and anything physical between two young people, who believe they are in love.

I didn't feel I should rant on about what I felt I knew about love, it wouldn't change anything anyway. I just said 'you asked me to come and talk to you, and I have, I thought you might have meant what you said, but obviously you didn't. I don't want to get pregnant, and you said you would help me prevent that. I am worried that there will come a time, when I won't be strong enough to stop, and it will happen.'

I think my mum decided ranting at me was not going to work, so she used the sensible approach. The gritted teeth were still there though, but she suggested that perhaps we waited a little while longer, another couple of months confirmed how we felt about each other, and then the big one! If we really loved each other, we should be able to continue our relationship without sex; surely this would be a true test of our love. I swallowed it hook line and sinker, and when I met Darrell later, I said as much to him. I really thought this would ultimately determine the depth of our feelings. Darrell was quite reasonable about it, and I loved him more for it. What a lovely person, other boys of his age, would probably have thrown a wobbly and ended the relationship. That was after all what we girls were constantly warned about, most young men are only after one thing, and if they don't get it they move on. This wasn't true of my Darrell, he wasn't getting any, but he wasn't going anywhere, I was the luckiest girl alive!

Darrell had become good friends with Nigel and one afternoon Nigel phoned to say they had spoken and were arranging a special evening that weekend. Nigel was going out with Diane, in another of his attempts to deny being gay, but she was nice enough, although very masculine in appearance, dress and manner. Diane would have burping and farting competitions with the boys, try to drink anyone and everyone under the table, and generally just seemed to be in some sort of identity crisis of her own. If she made him happy for now, or worked as a comfortable smoke screen, how she dressed or behaved was really unimportant.

The plan for the weekend was the four of us having dinner at Darrell's house. Apparently his mum was going to spend a couple of days with her relative, so the house would be ours, and it was going to be so cool. Us girls would cook, we could listen to some music, just chill together, no adults, no parents. It really felt very grown up, and like playing house. I was really excited but knew I had some serious persuading to do with my parents, I didn't think they would be too happy that Darrell's mum wasn't going to be there. I asked Nigel, who they liked and thought was a sensible young man, to put my case forward with me, and we spoke to them together. Nigel confirmed that he and Diane would be there and we would leave together at eleven pm, so I would be home just after. I was driving there on my own, and as Nigel lived just up the road, he said he would follow me home. I gave them Darrell's home number, and they were fine about me going. Talk about chuffed, I was over the moon, and spent hours dreaming of cooking in their small kitchen, playing housewife. It would feel just as though we were living together in our own little home for a night, and I felt years older than a mere sixteen.

Friday came, after what felt like years, and I waited for Darrell to get home from work, and give me a call. Nigel, Diane and I all arrived at about the same time, and it was so cool. Darrell organised drinks for us all, gin and tonics, and we put some music on, sat and chatted, and I felt so grown up. Life couldn't be better; this was everything I had always dreamed of. A boyfriend who loved and cared for me, and doing the sorts of things young couples do, my heart was literally bursting with joy, I could look towards the future, and imagine that this must be how it felt to be married, in your own home, and being with person you loved. I was in heaven, and I wasn't going to think about when it came time to go home, at least there was tomorrow, the next day and the day after that. It actually didn't matter, I felt sure that somewhere in the future, I would share this with Darrell, when I was old enough to leave school, get a job, we would be together forever.

We all had another drink, and I remember going into the kitchen with Diane to start cooking. I suddenly felt unwell, really light headed and dizzy, and thought it must be because I hadn't eaten. I went to sit on Darrell's bed, and he came through to see how I was, I was gutted that I was feeling so bad; I had looked forward to this evening so much, and now I must be coming down with something. Whilst we were sitting on the bed, I felt worse, and then I felt nothing at all.

11

What was that banging, my God my dad's muffled voice shouting my name, and he sounds so far away there is banging on a door, slow echoing sounds. I am in a bed, I need to get up and go and open the door for him, why is he stuck behind it? My legs are wobbly, but I have to get to the door, it seems to be far away, and everything seems to be in slow motion, but I am getting there. Am I dreaming, why do I feel so strange. I am at the door, and the banging is so loud, and my dad is shouting so loudly, I must help him, what has happened to him, why can't he open the door. I am at the door, I hold push the handle down, I am trying to answer him, to tell him I am coming, I can't speak. The door is locked; I turn the key, and the door bursts open. My mum and dad are there, what's wrong, what's happened. They push into the room, and I look around to where my dad is going, he is still shouting, why, at what, at whom. I still feel like I am wading through cotton wool, my body feels heavy, and movement feels deliberate, and slow. Then I see Darrell, he is in a bed, why is he there, why hasn't he said or done anything, where am I, and now a screaming in my mind, what is happening, I want to wake up now, I'm scared, please let me wake up. My mum is pulling my dad away from Darrell, why, they like him, why is he angry with Darrell. She is madly picking up someone's clothes from the floor. My dad is shouting, and my mum is telling him to stop, to go out of the room. Then my mum approaches me, with this bundle of clothes, the expression on her face is one of fury, and disgust, why, what have I done, what has happened? She shoves the clothes at me, and she can barely speak, the words spit out 'get dressed' she hisses. What does she mean, I look down, I am naked, apart from some red stuff on my legs. She pushes me from the room, I turn around, look at Darrell, why are you still in the bed, why have you got the cover pulled up to your chin, what is happening.

I try my best to dress, my hands won't work properly, I am still in cotton wool land, my limbs are so heavy, everything feels so slow. We go through the kitchen, to the cars outside. My dad drives his car, and I am pushed into the back of my mums. On the way home, she tells me how badly I have embarrassed her and my dad, apparently it is two in the morning, and when I didn't come home, she had to phone Nigel's home to find out where I was. Now his parents knew, and so would everyone else apparently, that I didn't obey my curfew, and it would be obvious, that I was having sex with a boy. How could I do this to them, after everything they did for me. What did she mean having sex, I hadn't done anything of the sort, I tried to tell her, I hadn't had sex, I had listened to her, we were waiting, I hadn't done anything.

We got home, and I was hauled out of the car and indoors. There was this horrible pain between my legs now, and I was starting to feel sore bits all over. I was escorted to my room, and I managed to tell them I was hurt, something had hurt me. I also tried to tell them that I felt like I'd been drugged, I felt so strange, I was so scared. My mum and dad looked at me, told me to take a bath, and that they were going to bed. Hadn't I given them enough trouble for one night, hadn't I broken their hearts, well they had had a difficult time, and they needed their sleep. No, please don't go, please stay with me, please talk to me, please help me, please don't leave me alone, I feel so afraid, please help me mum, please help me dad. Their bedroom door slammed.

I managed to run a bath, and my head was clearing slowly, the fuzzy bits were wearing off. I got into the bath. I don't know if I can put into words how I felt then. I sat in the water, blood trickling from between my thighs. I had bruises on my inner and outer thighs, and around my nipples. I ached inside, in the same place I usually had period pains, and I felt raw inside. A flash of memory came to me, I remember Darrell on top of me, I remember I couldn't move, I

75

remember trying to tell him to stop hurting me, asking him to get off me, and please don't make me pregnant. This wasn't a vivid memory, it was foggy and distant. I was lucky I suppose, because to this day that is all I have ever remembered of that night. The water was cold now, but that didn't matter, nothing really did anymore, in amongst all the physical pain, the worst was my heart and my mind. In an instant I had to shift from loving to hating Darrell, and the total utter despair I felt about my parents aloofness is indescribable.

I don't know how long I sat in the bath; I only know that when I got out, and went to my bed, it was becoming light outside. I got between the sheets, I ached so much, I got up again to take some pain killers. It was so sore to walk, and I was terrified to pee. I knew the pain killers would help my body, what could I take to ease the agony in my heart and mind.

I heard my parents wake and move around, and suddenly I felt hopeful. I would wait a while and then get up, and they would be there to talk to, to comfort me, to help me work through all this pain. They would hug me, and hold me, and help me heal, and make me feel safe again, they were my mum and dad. Then I heard the front door bang, and they were both gone. I had been left alone; they hadn't even looked in my room to check on me. Why, was screaming through my head, what had I done. I desperately tried to remember any detail of the night before, I always got as far as sitting on Darrell's bed, and then nothing. Did I just get horribly drunk, and allow him to have his way, that didn't fit with the bruising and my only memory. I had experienced enough hangovers in my time, and the way I'd felt from the time I'd been woken, was nothing I'd experienced before. What had happened to Nigel and Diane, why had they just left me there? I'm not sure how long I lay there, but I decided to get up and get dressed, perhaps get a cup of tea. Some time later, I hear my mothers car stop at the top of the driveway, she always parked in the shade. I walked slowly up to meet her, I was absolutely desperate for some sort of contact, anything. She had gone to do her weekly grocery shopping; she had just left me to go shopping. No matter, just throw me a scrap of kindness, and I would be alright. I got to the car, and she was taking the groceries out of the boot. I said Mum, that one word was filled with pleading and need, I needed a word, a touch, a kind look, anything to ease this pain. She looked at me with that familiar contempt and hate, and said 'help me with the groceries'. She loaded me with bags to carry and unpack in the kitchen, and she didn't speak to me again that day. My dad came home some time later. I had renewed hope, maybe something from him. There was, he handed me a pill, told me it would prevent an unwanted pregnancy and that I should count my blessings that he was in a position to provide it for me, and he too didn't speak to me again that day.

In the years since then I have tried to justify their actions. I have thought that perhaps it was an act of defiance. Perhaps that night I just got totally drunk, passed out, and let Darrell have his away, and blocked it all out due to an overwhelming sense of guilt. Perhaps if that was how it happened, then their reaction would be one of anger at my rebellion, and that would make it easier to understand. I have to be honest and say I still sometimes find it easier to remember it that way, and to take responsibility for my actions. I also sometimes find it easier to believe that version, when it comes to Darrell. Did I give him permission whilst drunk, and then cry rape; it would mean that he'd loved me then, and that my friends hadn't deserted me. Those feelings and thoughts were the stronger ones at the time, as Nigel stayed within our group of friends, as did Diane. I think I felt I'd lost so much already, I wasn't prepared to lose more. I got to the point where I didn't know what to believe, and it was easier that the gossip was I'd been caught in bed with my boyfriend by my parents, than anything as sordid as rape. I came to realise over the years, that my reaction to this sordid situation, was a familiar pattern that I would follow for years. It is typical of emotional abuse. I always looked inward, what had I done that had generated the reaction, it had to be me, something I had or hadn't done for these things to happen. Then sadly, I would try and make amends, make it up to the people I believed I had disappointed or angered. I did that now, I agonised for hours on what must have been my wanton behaviour, I had obviously allowed Darrell to believe that I wanted to have sex with him, so what right did I have then to believe that he shouldn't have taken what he felt was his to take. I had given my parents reason to believe I was going to have sex with him, so why should I consider that they would believe my virginity was taken by force, without my consent. Hadn't I also caused them so much embarrassment by them having to call Nigel's family in the early hours, and therefore alerting them to a situation, my parents

77

would hate to become public knowledge, which unfortunately it did. When you come down to it, it really was my entire fault, and why then should I even suppose that they owed me any kindness, what I believed I had to work hard for now was their forgiveness.

Forgive me mum and dad, that I have had my heart and body broken. Forgive me for feeling violated and dirty, forgive me that I wasn't in any state to come home, I wasn't even conscious. Forgive me for expecting you to at least talk to me about it. Forgive me for expecting your concern and love, and forgive me for expecting you to believe me, and when I asked that the police be called in, forgive me for not understanding how very important it was for you, that this 'sordid little mess' did not become public, you refused to even entertain the idea. Forgive me for 'breaking your hearts' and disappointing you yet again, forgive me for crying for so many nights, and keeping you awake, and forgive me for the weeks I came home from school in such a state, because of all the teasing and mockery I had been subjected to all day. Forgive me for feeling disappointed when after begging you to do something at least, you phoned Darrell's mum, and told her that her son had been a naughty boy, and that we were not to see each other again. Forgive me for feeling heartbroken yet again, when Andrew came home for R&R, and you told me I had better tell my brother what I had done. Forgive me for the times I hated you mum and Tracy, when you both giggled and laughed and chatted, whilst I was so stuck in this deep misery.

Finally, forgive me for the many nights I considered that dying would be easier than this, forgive me that I didn't have the courage to follow that thought through.

I created an inner pit. It was like I had this big empty space available and I threw feelings and emotion into this hole, like boulders, rocks and some pebbles. Trust was in there, and this was probably the biggest boulder. This carried all the weight of how I felt about people generally now. At the risk of being repetitive, if you couldn't trust your parents, who could you, trust. I really couldn't trust them to believe anything I said. My 'friends', well not much trust left there, they would all surely at some point or another let me down. Love, well that was second in boulder size, I hadn't experienced much of that lately, and on reflection, this latest situation, for want of a better description, mirrored my earliest experience of rejection. I concluded that the more emotionally isolated I became, the safer I was. Sure, it was a lonely place to be, but as far as I was concerned it was less painful. In addition, I visualised my brick wall, and I could build on it at will, that way I could effectively shut anyone out emotionally. My coping strategy worked, and if I started to feel anything I didn't choose to, I chucked it in the pit. That way I walked, talked, lived and breathed like a normal person, but I didn't have to feel inside. I don't know how I would have dealt with the backlash otherwise. For months afterwards, everywhere I went, people whispered, giggled, mocked or sneered at me. A lot of the boys looked at me as though I was the answer to their hormonal prayers, well I was considered easy now, some were cruel enough to call me a slut. Some of the girls looked at me as though I was something you scraped off your shoe, others with that pitying disgust that communicates their utter contempt. There were the hero worshippers too. 'What was it like?' was the FAQ. (Frequently asked question) 'I don't know' was the FA (frequent answer). Their reaction was dependant on their age, gender, and general standing in the community. My parent's extended families gathered around them, to offer support, sympathy and concern for them, in their time of need. What a terrible time they were having, not only the worry of a son in the army, now a daughter that disgraced them, and put them through all this. My circle of friends were hesitant about being branded with the same iron, and kept their distance, so I wasn't really included in any group outings, for some months. They would call in private, but it took a long while for them to consider being seen in public with me, which meant I didn't really go anywhere apart from school, and the only way I could do that was behind my brick wall, with my pit readily available. The one emotion I couldn't throw away was guilt. It enveloped me. I felt guilty about everything, even simply being alive.

To say that I got over this trauma in my life would be untrue. I don't believe I have ever nor will 'get over it'. I learnt then, as I do now to live with my experiences, and I moved on from the pit, to a pigeon-hole strategy.

When and if I need to draw on these experiences, perhaps to empathise with someone, or as now, to share this story, I open the door and allow the memories in. In writing this book, I will open all these doors, and whilst this is difficult and painful at times, it is also healing.

I carried my burden of shame and pain closely for years, and I had become very skilled at hiding my fears and tears, I learnt to live by the phrase 'cry and you cry alone, laugh and the world laughs with you.' It's called survival.

12

Margaret (Mags to her family and friends) and I were very good friends, and spent a lot of time together. Earlier in the book I told you about staying on her farm with her family, and amongst other things we had in common, we shared a love of sport, particularly swimming. There was an ongoing competition in swimming between three of us. Mags, I and 'Spike' nicknamed due to her spiky fiery orange hair. We were madly competitive, and although Mags was by far the better hockey player, I was better at tennis. We drew a tie on netball and swimming but not without both of us constantly trying to better the other. It was funny really, we seemed to trigger energy in each other, and we could never stroll anywhere together. It would start off as a walk, into a jog, and then a run, both giggling and breathless, when we got to wherever it was we were going.

Needless to say a lot of our time together was mostly energy charged and active, but we also enjoyed all the girly bits too. When she spent the weekend we did the whole make-up thing, listened to all the weepy broken hearted songs of the time, and the only time I ever saw Mags cry then, was when we went to see 'Love Story'. Little did we know at that time, that we would shed many tears together, and for a long while, we would cry a lot more than we had ever laughed? Mags was one of my friends who never criticised or condemned me, and she was relatively neutral during the time I was ostracised by most. She was popular with both sexes, and had a quick humour. What I found special in her was her matter of fact, down to earth attitude to everything and everyone, and it was rare that she had something bitchy to say about someone else.

She spent almost every Sunday with us, and some weekends. She was a boarder at school, and her home, a farm, was in one of the 'hot spots'. Farmsteads in the area were frequently under attack from the rebels, and the countryside was littered with landmines. Mags's parents had decided to attempt to make a new life in neighbouring South Africa, and because of this, Mags couldn't go home for weekends, so she spent the time with us. Because her parents were so far away, they had signed over permissions for Mags to my mum. This meant that if Mags wanted to spend a day or weekend with another friend, my mum had total authority with regard to where Mags went and with whom.

It was the Easter weekend, and my mum had said she didn't want anyone else staying with us, as she and my dad wanted time out, time on their own. I kicked up a fuss because the thought of spending that length of time with just my parents for company did not invoke much pleasure at all. Arrangements therefore, were made for Mags to stay with friends and neighbours of her family. The Smith family. There were four daughters in the family, three who were at school with us too, and Mags knew them well. They boarded at the same hostel, and they were looking forward to her being with them. They had the adjoining farm to the one Mags's parents used to own, and Mags was excited at spending some time so close to her old home. I was anxious about the area being potentially very dangerous, but was assured that it would be safe, and anyway, what about our unconquerable spirit, we would not be driven from our homelands, and would not allow the war to destroy our recreation nor previous way of life.

She stayed with us the weekend before Easter, and as usual we swam for as many hours of daylight were available to us. On the Sunday a number of other boarders were over, and we had our huge Sunday roast, lay about in the garden recovering from our over stuffed bellies, and then swam, until it was time for them all to go back to their hostels. For some reason we had a group photo taken that day in the garden, I still have it. It's a group of young girls sitting together, faces flushed and happy, absolutely no hint of the horror to come. I look at Mags's smiling face on that photo, and it is one of those times when there is such a conflict. Thank God we didn't know what was to come, because I don't think any of us would have believed that something so awful could be experienced. On the other hand, if we had known, we could have prevented the tragedy happening. Fate, it delivers such sudden, devastating blows.

The phone call came on Saturday. It was from one of the matrons at the boarding hostel. The information was sketchy, there had been a terrible tragedy, a vehicle travelling back from a social meeting at the local clubhouse, had hit a landmine. It was believed that there may be survivors, but that had not been confirmed. The vehicle, a small pick up truck was owned by the Smith family, and apparently all the girls were riding in the back, the mum driving, and the dad a passenger. The next few hours were a complete nightmare. I was desperate to know if there were any survivors and if so whom. I couldn't believe that Mags might be dead. Later that night we were given further details. The driver of the vehicle, their mum, had been killed instantly; the force of the blast pushed her into the roof of the van, and broke her neck. The passenger, their dad, had survived with multiple injuries and was critical. The youngest of the five girls travelling in the back, was dead, and her body had been found in the branches of a tree. Two of the other girls were killed too, their bodies found some distance away. Two had survived and were both in critical condition with life threatening and mutilating injuries. One was Mags, she was alive, but just, her legs had been blown off, and at that time one of her arms was literally hanging on by a thread. It was not known whether they would survive the night.

Mags did survive, the other girl didn't, out of the seven, two lived, Mags and the father. The country grieved, our school was in mourning, we had lost three pupils, and another was fighting for her life. I struggled to come to terms with the fact that my friend had lost her legs. Her damaged arm had been saved only due to the absolute despair and determination of one of the theatre nurses. She felt this young girl was already losing so much. Mags had been scheduled to have both legs amputated and her one arm, and this nurse felt that if there was the remotest chance that her arm could be saved, the attempt to save it should be made. She believed there was a blood supply in amongst all the mangled flesh, and defied the surgeon, denying him the necessary instruments when he elected to amputate the arm. Although the injured arm remained fairly disabled, Mags retained both her arms.

Her parents travelled from South Africa, and were with her during the initial critical phase, and I wanted to get to Salisbury, the capital, to see her. I was able to get a lift through one weekend, a few weeks after this terrible incident, and the days and nights before I was due to see Mags were very traumatic for me mentally and emotionally. I had seen people without limbs, but they were either elderly or soldiers. Most were missing one arm, or one leg, and whilst I felt so sorry for them, when you were in the army, you knew the terrible risks, and in the sad tragic fallout of any war, these casualties were not isolated. A group of us would visit one of the victims of war units at our local hospital, and there were so many disabled young men, they somehow seemed to find some courage and comfort in their shared disabilities. I think they found comfort in their shared 'war stories', which always had a sense of heroism attached. Mags however, was isolated in her loss, She was my age, she was a civilian, an innocent casualty of these terrible times.

I just couldn't seem to fit the picture in my mind of my sixteen year old friend, who ran everywhere with me, who loved sport, loved being physically active and challenged, without legs. I celebrated her being alive, I was so happy I hadn't lost her, but I had no idea how she felt. How would and could someone with such a strong love of anything and everything physically active cope with this. I didn't think I could. I tried to put myself in her place, but that's not really possible, because try as you might to imagine it, you know that you still have your total mobility, and it's with a sense of relief that you withdraw from the self induced nightmare. I desperately wanted to see her, and yet I was terrified, we had talked briefly on the phone, and Mags had asked me to come and visit her. I was terrified, how would I react, would I be able to look at her as though she wasn't different, did she want me to, or did she want me to acknowledge her loss. What would I say, 'how are you?' seems inane and artificial, how the hell did anyone think she would be. Would I end up a bawling wreck, weeping on her behalf and mine, therefore she would end up comforting me. I didn't want that to happen, I wanted to be able to meet her needs, in some bizarre sort of way, I felt bad that I was walking into her room, something she would never do naturally again, I wanted to apologise that I had legs and she didn't, I wanted to try and make it up to her, that I was unchanged, unscathed, normal. God I was so scared. I just wanted to be able to go in there, and support her, and I didn't know that I was emotionally capable.

The day came, and I was standing in the corridor outside her room. Visitors had been restricted, as she was still very unwell. Her face was on the front page of all the newspapers, and the outpouring of a nation, shocked at this atrocity was widely reported. The staff at the hospital had had to find another room for the huge quantity of flowers, cards, soft toys and random gifts that were sent in daily. I was shaking, and if anyone had given me the remotest opportunity to run, I would have taken it. I took a deep breath and pushed open the heavy door. Mags's bed was to the right of the door, and whilst there were flowers and cards everywhere, the bed was predominant in my vision. It was hot, and she had a very light cover on, which outlined her body completely, and the outline stopped at the knees. It was at that moment that it became real for me, perhaps I had harboured some ridiculous hope that her legs had grown back. I felt my breath start to catch in my throat, and I didn't want to make any noises indicating shock or horror. I am sure Mags had had to deal with a lot of those reactions. I focused on the familiar face, and she was smiling, I smiled back, the tears welling, and walked across to her, 'I've missed you,' I said, 'and I am so glad to see you'. 'Me too' she replied, as I kissed her on the cheek, and then we cried and laughed at the same time. Her shoulders, face and neck were pockmarked with shrapnel, and there was still a lot of bruising, but I was able to look beyond that and recognise my friend in her eyes and smile.

I sat on the edge of the bed, close to her stumps, and I looked at them and asked 'are you still in a lot of pain?' Mags, smiled again, and replied 'thanks for looking at them; most people try to pretend they aren't there, and they keep their eyes glued to my face'. That was my prompt really, and in a mad rush of bravado, I asked 'what does it feel like, do you still feel as though your legs are there?' It was like a damn bursting, Mags talked about the phantom itching , and how often she woke up and had to sit up to confirm that her lower limbs were missing. She said her left foot was itching right now, so I went to where I thought her foot might be, and made a scratching motion in the air just above the bed. 'Is that better?' I asked. 'Great', she replied, 'now could you do the other one'? It went from there really; she showed me her hand, which was protruding from plaster. It was like a claw, and her fingers rested against her palm. She was due to have months of

85

physiotherapy which would relax it a little, but her arm, which was bent at the elbow, was never likely to straighten, she was still grateful to have it at all though.

She appeared to be dealing with it all relatively well, but I was concerned about the time when all the press visits stopped, the gifts and cards stopped arriving, basically when all the attention died away. That was keeping her mind active, and my fairly shy, never before famous friend, was suddenly in the spotlight nationally, and whilst it was happening, I don't think anyone wouldn't feel enormously special. She was special and always would be, to those close to her, but it wouldn't remain that way with the general population. Another atrocity or tragedy would take the spotlight away, and what then. I suppose it's a bit like the days after someone dies. They are filled with visitors and friends offering sympathy and company. All the funeral arrangements are to be made, time is taken up in all that. It's after the funeral that the empty reality of the pain and loss takes place, and that's what worried me. That day would come when the attention died down, and there was nothing else to distract Mags from the reality of her loss. That was when she would need the most support. We didn't talk about the day it happened during that visit, as time ran away with us, and I felt she would talk about it if and when she was ready. I wasn't going to see her again for a long while, as I had to travel home the following morning, but we promised to keep in touch by phone. I kissed her goodbye, and she said 'thanks'. 'For what?', I asked. 'For being normal' she replied. As I walked down the corridor, I cried. I cried with relief. Her body had changed, but she was still Mags, and I was determined to do whatever I could to support her now and for however long she needed it.

I didn't see Mags for some months, but we were in regular contact, and she updated me on her progress. She had further amputations on her legs, and lost her knees. This was devastating initially, as that meant she lost the flexibility and movement that the knee joint gives, and it also meant new artificial limbs had to be made. This was a very frustrating process, as due to the sanctions imposed on Rhodesia, they had to be made overseas. We managed to giggle about her legs, because Mags could to a certain degree choose her size of feet, and how tall she wanted to be. She couldn't get too over enthusiastic though, as balance and weight were critical factors. She also had to have a breast reduction, because being top heavy created difficulties with her balance. We laughed and cried our way through these changes and traumas, and Mags was enormously brave and resilient.

After months of therapy and recovery, Mags was coming home. She had decided she wanted to complete her schooling before joining her parents in SA, and she was coming to live with us. I was thrilled, I felt it gave me the opportunity to try and help her, or somehow try and make up for the fact that she wasn't with us that weekend. My mum agreed readily to this, and although it had never been discussed, I didn't know whether it was because she ever thought about how different it all may have been, or whether she felt it was her contribution to Mags's recovery. Remember, my mum was always willing to help anyone out, but there was still a lot of publicity, and as soon as it was confirmed that Mags would be staying with us, a visit was arranged for the local Mayor and Mayoress to visit our home, and a photo session was set up for the local paper. I still have the photo.

During our frequent and extended calls, I had noticed a change in Mags, she had become really bitchy, and winged about everyone and everything. This wasn't surprising really, I felt she had every right to feel bitter, angry frustrated, and cheated, I experienced those feelings for her, and I wasn't the one it had happened to. I remember for a long while, every time I got out of bed, out of a chair, just stood, or even walked to the loo, I was conscious that I was able to. Standing, walking, running, something I took for granted, now I had cause to stop and to think how very different it would be if I couldn't.

I counted my blessings so many times those months; I could have made good use of an abacus. I remember, sometimes if I was running, it would suddenly hit me that I could, and that Mags would never run again, and I would slow down and stop. I felt so guilty; I thought maybe it should have happened to someone like me. Mags was such a good girl, she had never given her parents a moments concern, she was a nice person, she didn't have to be told that she was a disappointment and created difficulties and disruption in her parents lives. I felt guilty and I also felt so grateful that it wasn't me, and all these feelings created such conflict in my soul, that all I wanted to do, was try to make up for her loss, and my undeserved blessings.

Mags needed a specialised wheelchair, and they cost a lot of money. Whilst she got a great deal of support from the 'Terrorist Victims

Relief Fund', it wasn't a bottomless pot, so Spike and I decided to do something about it. We approached various teachers, and put our idea to them. We wanted to do a sponsored swim, and try to break the world record for non stop swimming. The idea was accepted, and we got a team of swimmers together, and left it up to the teachers to organise the funding process, and the details around the world record. We couldn't hang about because Mags needed the money as soon as possible, so we had to set a date to start the swim, it had to be during school holidays, and unfortunately, without too many options open to us, it was going to be in winter. Although winters in Africa are not anywhere near as cold as they are in the UK, it still gets very cold, and taking into account we were going to be swimming in an outdoor unheated pool, it really was going to be a challenge. Spike and I volunteered for most of the night swimming, I felt the harder it was for me, the more I was contributing to helping Mags.

It was hard, it was so damn cold, the water was icy, and it made my limbs sluggish and heavy, and no matter how hard I swam to get warm, it didn't happen. We tried smearing our bodies with Vaseline to try and alleviate the cold, it didn't really work, I just ended up feeling like a jellied eel. It also took hours of showering and bathing to get rid of the stuff. I remember swimming length after length of breaststroke with my teeth chattering so hard, I was swallowing what felt like gallons of chlorine water. We didn't set individual targets, because there were too few of us to do that, so we swam until we just couldn't carry on. I remember thinking 'just one more length', and holding a picture of Mag's state of the art wheelchair in my mind, and when I felt I couldn't go on, my mantra kicked in, 'just one more length'. The worst of it was that if your feet touched the bottom of the pool you were disqualified. I was pulled out of the pool more than once, by the supervising teacher, when I'd got to the point of near drowning. God I was really on a self atonement mission.

We did it! We broke the record, and we raised enough for Mags's wheelchair. We were so chuffed with ourselves, and felt this achievement would perhaps remind the rest of the world that we were a country in dire straits and in need of help. That never happened, our record was never recognised because we had been ostracised by the rest of the world. We felt enormously let down, but the real motivation for the swim had been achieved, and that's what mattered. We'd raised enough through local sponsors to get Mags the wheelchair of wheelchair's and that was reward enough!

My life changed when Mags came to stay. I became her constant carer, and because our house and garden was not wheelchair friendly, I had to push and pull Mags wherever she wanted to or needed to go. If she needed the loo during the night, she would wake me, and I would help her into her chair, to the bathroom and onto the toilet seat, and then move the wheelchair out, so that she had some privacy, and move it back in for her when she was ready. Help her back to bed, and fold her chair out of the way. She had nightmares, and I would wake her from them, and sit with her until she could sleep again. I helped her into the bath in the evenings, making sure the water was quite hot, and then get in with her, there was plenty of room for two, and because of course she had no legs. Whilst in the hot water, we would each choose a stump and squeeze tiny fragments of shrapnel out. They come to the surface of the skin over time, and there were always new eruptions. We would collect them in a little bowl, and celebrate when we had a good crop. We had some good laughs in the bath because without her legs to balance and steady her, she would slip and slide from one end of the bath to the other without warning. One minute she was there, and the next she disappeared under the water, I would grab for her, latching onto whatever part of her body was about, some-times her arm, her face or catching her by the boob, and we would howl with laughter when that happened.

There were always visitors. Strange isn't it how the most remote ac-quaintance suddenly becomes a friend, those were the ones that came out of morbid curiosity, to see a living breathing teenage girl with no legs. Shit they angered us, so we decided to give them what they wanted, and when the vultures came to gawp, Mags deliberately dis-played her stumps. We would watch them and pull them apart when they had left. 'Did you see her face, when she saw you, she couldn't look below your waist', I would say. 'And when I wiggled my stumps at her, she nearly fainted', Mags would add, and we were off again, howl-ing with laughter. We did laugh a lot, and not always at other peoples expense. When we wanted to swim, I had to push Mags in her chair to the edge of the pool, and then tip her in. She would then bob up like a cork, steady herself at the side of the pool, and swim with her arms. For some reason we found this enormously funny, the bobbing cork action. I would stand waiting for her to come up, and her body literally popped up from under the water. I'd end up a useless giggling wreck and Mags would have to cling to the side of the pool until her laughter subsided.

When we went to the movies or town, it was fascinating people watching. The only really honest ones were the children. They would stare openly, not out of the corner of their eye, they would point, and shake their parents hand, and in a loud voice say 'Mummy what's wrong with that girl, why hasn't she got any legs?' Mummy would then say in a hushed loud whisper 'don't be rude, don't point and stare, that's not nice'. Mummy however was quite glad for the opportunity to look openly to where her child was pointing, at least she could then have a good look without taking responsibility for it.

With her close friends however, Mags was becoming more and more bitchy and bad tempered towards us. She was petulant and demanding, and would be in her wheelchair, a couple of feet from something she wanted on the coffee table or whatever, and tell, not ask, but tell one of us, mostly me to get it for her. Please and thank you were non existent, and we all put up with it for quite some time, until one day I lost the plot. She was sitting about two feet away, and said 'get me my coffee', well that just tipped me over the edge. 'Get it yourself', I said, 'you can move your wheelchair closer, and do it yourself'. Then I went into a full rant! 'I am sick and tired of your attitude towards us. You treat us like shit, and I don't mind doing stuff for you, but I am not your slave' I shouted. Mags's jaw was hitting her chest by now, but once I'd got going, it wasn't going to stop. 'I know you have lost your legs, and I am so sorry, but along with that you are losing who you once were, don't let them take that as well', I said, not shouting anymore. It was dead quiet, and I continued. 'Mags, you won't always have lots of people around you at your beck and call, you need to start doing the ordinary things for yourself. It really was nothing for you to move your wheelchair that tiny bit, to get your own coffee. Don't disrespect me like that'. In the continuing silence, I was in full flow now, and things I had wanted to say for ages, but had been so worried about upsetting Mags, were coming out, and nobody was stopping me. 'I am not prepared to watch the person I knew turn into this bitch, and not try and stop that happening, and I can't imagine what you have gone through and are still going through, but don't direct your anger and everything that must go with that at people who love you, and are trying to help you', just time to draw a quick breath, and then I dropped the big one. 'Next time, I will take you to the kitchen and it's your bloody turn to make the coffee'. With that I walked into the garden. Tracy looked at me as though her dearest wish was that I would shrivel up and die right there and then, and rushed over to Mags to comfort her. My mum had walked in at the start of me shouting, and matched Tracy's looks and actions.

Shit I was angry. I was angry I'd lost my temper, I was angry at Mags, I was livid at Tracy and my mum, and I felt that oh so familiar feeling 'guilty'. I decided my best option was to stay in the garden and hope everyone would simmer down, so I sat there until dark, and then snuck in. We had a very big house so it was easy to find a way to my room without bumping into anyone. They were all in the tv room anyway. I was starving but thought it was best just to crawl into bed, and pretend I was asleep, I really didn't want the familiar lecture about what an evil person I was, I knew that already, I just wasn't up for being reminded tonight. A while later I heard Mags's wheelchair come down the passage into the bedroom, and she had started to manage getting into bed herself, so I let her get on with it. A while later I was still awake and I heard Mags crying, I was about to go across to her when she said 'Cher are you awake?' 'Yes' I replied, and thought here we go, I'm about to get a verbal hammering. Well the next words Mags spoke shocked me more than her ranting at me. 'Would you mind coming over to my bed please?' She asked. What I thought, she said please, and asked so nicely, what was going on. I literally flew across the room to her bed, and sat with my legs curled under me just where her body ended. She was crying, and I started to apologise. 'No don't say sorry', she said. 'I want to thank you.' God, I thought I must be dreaming, why would she want to thank me for what I said? 'Why?' I asked. 'Because for the first time since the accident, you made me feel normal', she replied, and she went on 'everyone has treated me like a kind of freak, don't upset Mags, be nice to her, poor thing she's lost her legs, and I fell into the role of being this person who couldn't or wouldn't deal with anything other than sympathy and kindness'. I sat quietly and listened as she went on. 'Do you know how shit it is for everyone to be nice to you all the time, even when you know you're being a bitch, it actually makes you feel like some kind of imbecile, you know its fake'. 'Sometimes I've wanted to say to you all, stop, be normal with me, treat me like you used to, I want to be like I used to be, not be treated differently because I've lost my legs, being all sweetness and light all the time is just a constant reminder that you believe me to be different now. I've only lost limbs, not my identity'. I was crying now, and went to give her a hug, forgot the whole balance thing and ended up on top of her. We were doing that crying laughing thing again, and when we had both calmed down, we talked long into the night, about how she had been feeling, how we had been treating her, and how we could work at getting it back to 'normal'.

There was a breakthrough that night, and the underlying tension that had always been there, but gone unnoticed or ignored slowly disappeared. We didn't tiptoe around what we said to or did with Mags, and although we all had to work at breaking our respective habits, we were able to remind each other. 'There you go again treating me like a moron', Mags would say, when someone talked about 'running' away. It's amazing how conscious you become of using words relating to someone's disability, and how stupid you look and make them feel when you try to retract them. That was just part of our process of change, but change we did, and Mags became one of the girls again, no special favours.

13

We were quite evil sometimes, and Mags wasn't shy to use her disability to teach someone a lesson, or to feed two starving students. Mags would come to the discos with us, and we would pop her on one of the chairs and fold and tuck her wheelchair in a dark corner. When she was sitting at the table, nobody could see that she was any different to the rest of us. When the army guys came to ask us to dance Mags got her fair share of requests, and if she felt comfortable enough, she would suggest to them that dancing with her might take more strength and energy than they had thought. She would then push her chair back and show them why, and the decent ones would pick her up anyway and take her onto the floor. It actually looked quite funny, Mags clinging to them for dear life, with the lower part of her jeans flapping about his legs. She would dance for as long as her partner was able to hold her, and then he would return her to her chair. More often than not, she would have a companion for the rest of the evening, and we made some good friends. Most of the young men were in the army, and they didn't stay in one place for very long, so there were always new victims, and there were some real idiots. One guy in particular really thought he was 'all that', and he clearly wasn't, and he seemed to find our group particularly fascinating. I think challenging is more to the point, because most times he asked one of us to dance, we would look at the other, and it was 'no thanks'. Occasionally one of us would take pity on him, and dance with him, but he took this as an indication of undying love, and weren't we the lucky ones privileged enough to be in his company. He was so arrogant, to the point that when we refused his request to dance, he had a particular retort, which was 'what's your problem, you got no legs'. Well that was a red rag to a bull for us; it would be so cool to bring him down. He sort of went around the table with us, asking us in turn at the disco's we were all at, and he hadn't got to Mags yet, we were dying for the time he did. Our opportunity came one night, and we watched him approach. Right on cue, he went over to Mags, bent forwards, and in his best so called sexy voice he asked 'you wanna dance with me babe?', as rehearsed, she didn't let him down gently, she just replied 'with you, no thanks'. Well of course this really dented his ego, and the familiar 'What's your problem, you don't have legs or something?' was out there. We could barely keep ourselves together in those few seconds before Mags dropped the clanger, and how he didn't notice us all staring with our hands over our mouths and our eyes wide I don't know. Mind you when you think about it, he was probably reeling with shock that he had been put down so badly; after all he was God's own creation for woman wasn't he! As he turned to walk away and leave us in a devastating wake of loss, Mags said 'actually, I don't have.' He turned and looked at her as though she was something he should scrape off his shoe, and with a flick of his non existent hair, he asked 'you don't have what?' Mags hesitated for a couple of seconds, just to make sure we got the best effect, and replied 'legs'. He threw his head back with this mouth open 'hah, what kind of fool do you take me for' opened arms gesture, and started to walk away. Oh no, we were going to lose our moment! Mags said, 'Don't you believe me?' and he turned back, bent forward slightly and in this exaggerated patronising tone replied 'Nooo'. And, whilst he was bending forward, Mags pushed her chair back to expose her legs, which of course ended at the thigh, and her jeans tucked under them, made it blatantly obvious that she was telling him the truth. He stepped back in absolute horror, tripped and landed on his butt, and our table literally exploded with hysterical laughter. Mags was laughing so hard, she nearly landed on the floor too. Of course this had attracted a lot of attention, and the arrogant prat sat on the floor with a crowd of people howling with laughter around him, and as he started to get up, I thought he was going to leg it. I must give him credit where credit is due though, and he did exactly the opposite, he went up to Mags, looked at her stumps again, and said shame faced 'I don't suppose you would reconsider, and dance with me?' She did, and he didn't leave her side for the rest of that evening, and he became a firm friend. We discovered he was actually a really nice guy, just had a totally misguided concept on how to attract woman.

I am moving ahead of myself now, but as this story is really about my friendship with Mags, I thought this was the best place for it. About a year later, when we were both at college in Salisbury, and typically broke, Mags came over to my bed-sit one day to scrounge something to eat. I had absolutely nothing to offer, and a day to go before my allowance arrived. We were both starving, so we devised a plan. Wearing the oldest, dirtiest clothes we could find, we drove into the city centre, got her sorted out in her wheelchair, making sure that her disability was adequately displayed, and with her carrying a tin mug, we collected enough money for a feast of hamburgers, chips, cokes, and with some to spare. We didn't really have to do anything other than walk about, and the coins and some notes, just kept dropping into our mug like manna from heaven. We must have looked like a couple of nutters, we were embarrassed, and sort of charged over the pavements, heads down, and just the tin mug extended, but people's generosity was amazing. We had to empty the money into a bag a number of times, and once we knew we had absolutely enough to stuff our faces, we stopped. I think we felt a bit guilty about it, long after our bellies and pockets were full of course, but we made sure we were never quite that desperate again.

Mags went on to get married and have children. The only time I ever saw her walk was on her wedding day, and then she hung up her artificial legs for good. My friendship with Mags was special and unique, and I learnt to appreciate the things we take for granted.

Do you remember Spike, she was our friend who swam for the world record, for Mags's wheelchair. I owe this to her, because she suffered so much. Spike never talked about her home and family much, but the impression we all got was that her home life wasn't good. It was a priority for her to make people laugh, and I had never seen her irritable or down, I don't think she even suffered from PMT, it was important to Spike to lift people, to make them laugh, a lot of the time at her insane and deliberate antics. Spike loved sport and any form of activity probably more than we all did put together, and although she was fiercely competitive, she was a damn good loser too. I suppose she could afford to be, she very seldom came second, or lost anything, and she won just about all the sports awards. She was fiercely independent and consequently her nickname was because of the way she wore her hair, it stood up in spikes around the top of her head, with the back bits long. It was bright orange and she was covered in the same colour freckles, and I never saw Spike wear anything other than scruffy jeans and men's shirts, apart from her school uniform of course, which she just never looked comfortable in. A skirt to Spike was like wearing a hair shirt for punishment.

She was an active part of Mags's recuperation, and because she was mad as a hatter she would sometimes grab hold of the handles of Mags's wheelchair, and suddenly take off at a sprint. Hooting and howling like a mad thing, while Mags clung on for dear life, bumping all over the place, and inevitably they would hit a rock or hole in the path, and Mags would go flying, landing with an almighty thud with Spike on top of her, both of them crying with laughter, whilst we tried to catch up, panicking and flapping like mother hens.

Spike never walked anywhere, she trotted, she seemed to have her own internal energy field. When she spoke, she shouted, when she laughed, it was like car hooters going off in unison, when she yelled 'woohoo' just for the hell of it, birds fell out of the trees in sheer terror. She would come up behind you and suddenly there was this foghorn yelling 'Howzit' in your ear, and a slap on the back that sent many of us to our knees, but it was so funny. Every time it happened to me, although my heart nearly stopped, I was deaf for hours afterwards, and had to get my dad to give me a chiropractic manipulation to put me together again, it cracked me up. She was so totally alive.

About a year after Mags's accident, Spike was driving to Salisbury, and was involved in a car accident. She survived it as a paraplegic. She was paralysed from the waist down. Oh God not Spike, not this crazy, happy wonderful nut that lived life on fast forward. Nothing however, was going to change that it had happened, and when I went to visit Spike in the rehab centre I didn't recognise her. She was so thin and pale, but what was so sad, was that Spike couldn't smile anymore, she didn't want to. When she spoke, it was as if her voice had been paralysed along with her body, it was a whisper. She did something

I had never seen her do before, she cried, and told me she wanted to die. There's nothing to say to that, how do you tell someone not to think that, life is worth living, you can be strong, we'll be there for you, all those inane comments that mean nothing, when you are the one that is going to walk out of there, and go home, and thank God it wasn't you. What made it harder, if it could have been harder, was this happened soon after Mags's trauma, and Spike had experienced the national acknowledgement and attention that Mags had received. The massive outpouring of well wishers, the truckloads of flowers, cards and gifts, and the financial support she was given. There was none of that for Spike, her accident wasn't high profile at all. Even though they now shared a similar future, neither would ever walk naturally again, Spike had to go this alone, if she chose to at all. When I visited Spike, there was one other card in her room, apart from the one I brought, and not a single flower. There wasn't going to be months of reporters, photo's and attention for Spike, or more visitors than she would choose to have, I understood there weren't many visitors at all. She got a column in the local newspaper, and that was it.

Spike asked me not to come back, she said I reminded her of what she would never have again, and I honoured her request. I heard she attempted suicide but wasn't allowed to succeed, and the last time I saw Spike was at an outdoor barbeque some years later. She was in a wheelchair that looked like it had been put together with scrap, nothing state of the art there. She emitted despair and misery. Her clothes were dirty and torn, she was still very thin, and looked unwashed and uncaring, and she was very drunk, saddest of all though, was she was still crying.

During some of the very low times in my life, I tried to remember to focus on the blessings I have. I remember Spike and how such a bright light became dim in an instant, and that she lost everything that had meant anything to her, worst of all, she lost the will to live. There were times in my life, which I will share with you, when I could understand how giving up, seemed so much more reasonable, than going on.

14

Since 'the rape', as I have always referred to it, I had distanced myself from any sort of relationship. Mostly when we went out, I made sure I drank enough to make the whispers and sniggers either seem meaningless or funny, that Dutch courage thing. It was taking a long time for my notoriety to die down, I think it was because I was their distraction from the war, something else to talk about, and of course it was such juicy gossip, me being the daughter of Dr Stewart, and from such a fine upstanding family in the community. I was happy to have the occasional dance, but that was as far as it went, then I would settle myself at the table, and slowly drink the evening away. I really liked what alcohol did for me, it was a pain killer, and it gave everything a soft blurry focus, took away the sharp edges, and muffled the whispers. Then I met Eddie. He asked me to dance, and I danced with him a couple of times, said 'thank you', and went back to my table. He followed me, and asked if he could sit down. I said 'OK why not', and we chatted. He was very easy to talk to, softly and well spoken, with a good sense of humour, and we spent most of the evening together. He'd asked if we came to the discos regularly, and I told him, every weekend. It was our only form of entertainment really, and of course we had a never ending supply of young men. Most of the girls had more than one boyfriend at a time. They were only around for a couple of months, and then were sent away on active duty for about the same time. New replacements or returning regulars came back to barracks, so it was really like having someone at all times, rotating them. This might sound quite harsh and uncaring, but realistically, nobody expected these relationships to last. Whilst we were young and playing the field, having a good time, the young men we met often lived the other end of the country, and were regularly and frequently seriously involved with someone at home, and often married. The war gave a lot of those men the opportunity to live dual lives. They could give a fictitious home address, they didn't have to disclose their personal phone numbers, don't forget there was no such thing as a mobile phone at that time, and the girls they met, they could write to when they were in the bush, as well as maintaining whatever relationship they had back home. It was therefore very rare, that any form of contact outside of what they shared with us in our home town existed. There were some exceptions of course, but there were many more broken hearted young gullible teenage girls, than there were happy endings.

We felt and behaved accordingly after a time. We had fun, we fell in and out of love frequently, but we seldom expected much more. Most of us had learnt by one or more heartbreaking experience. Well, not me. I continued to believe in and trust this deep down feeling that I would be different. I would be the one that met my one true love, and walk off into the sunset, live in the country cottage with the little white picket fence, and have lots of happy smiling children. Nothing wrong with that I suppose, I think we all harbour that hope somewhere, at sometime in our youth, I was at a disadvantage though, and it was in my choice of men. My relatively short time on earth had been spent believing I was a disappointment to my family, that I made people unhappy, and I was ungrateful for all the 'things' I had, and how lucky I was that I was tolerated. I believed you had to work for kindness and love, it was not given freely, and the less it was given the harder you had to work for it. I never felt accepted, I knew I wouldn't be loved for who I was, I would only be loved if I met the needs of others. Generally I had no self worth at all, and I was uncertain about my identity. I was like a chameleon, I changed colour to suit situations and other peoples needs. This pertained mostly to my parents and how I felt about relationships with men. After Darrell, I believed I was soiled goods, nobody had suggested I should feel any differently, and that therefore made me even less worthy of love and affection, let alone respect. I would jump through burning hoops if it made someone like me, approve of me, or perhaps love me.

Eddie and I met again at another disco, and he asked if he could phone me sometime. I agreed, and we became friends. I liked him a lot, he was lovely to talk to, and always so kind and gentle. I was comfortable with him, and didn't feel under any pressure to perform for him, in other words I could be as close to the real me, as I had never been before. One evening he kissed me, and it was nice, a soft loving kiss, and I enjoyed it. There were no wobbly knees, or funny tummy passion to it, but it was comfortable. We saw each other regularly, went out when he was off duty, and he came to visit me at home. He helped my dad build our bomb shelter in the back yard. Most families were building them, because more rocket and mortar attacks were inevitable, and least we would have somewhere safer to go, than in the house. It wasn't likely to withstand a direct hit from a rocket, but when it's your time, it's your time.

Eddie was mature, considerate and treated me with absolute respect, and he obviously knew he had to tread carefully, so it was after a long while that he told me he had fallen in love with me. This concerned me in more ways than one. I knew I wasn't in love with him, I loved him as a really good friend, and I also felt he was too good for me. I felt like I was deceiving him, didn't he realise I was trash, that I wasn't any good for anybody, I wasn't a nice person, and he deserved nice. I tried to tell him, and end our friendship, but he didn't want it to end, and as he was going into active duty for a while, he asked me just to let things be, until he came back. He said he was a patient person, and he would be prepared to wait. I agreed, I thought the time and distance apart would make him see sense, and in the meantime I retained his love for a little longer.

Whilst Eddie was away, I met David. It literally was a case of chalk and cheese. Eddie was an engineer in the army; David was in the Special Forces. Where Eddie was medium height and fair, David was tall and dark, Eddie had a medium build, David was all big muscles and generally a big man, the starkest difference was that when Eddie kissed me it was nice, when David first kissed me, an entire fireworks display exploded in my head. I was very quickly and totally smitten with him, and poor Eddie didn't get his letters as frequently as before.

I was playing the game, one boyfriend at home, the other fighting in the bush, and neither knew about the other one yet. David appeared to feel the same way I did, and we spent hours on the phone declaring undying love. I saw him at every possible moment, and when he met my parents, it is the first time I saw my mum smitten too. She thought he was absolutely wonderful, and in a short while David was calling her 'mum'. He often talked about our future together, and in fairness to the rapid seriousness of feelings and the intensity of the relationship, I told him about the rape. I felt I had to forewarn him that I was damaged goods, if he felt that we had a future together. He was very sympathetic and kind about it, which surprised me, I always expected a reaction of disgust. My mum had always told me that 'nice' boys don't like girls who haven't saved themselves for marriage, worse if they were sullied by something as sordid as rape. Well that either meant David wasn't nice, or mum was referring more to how things were during her youth. As it turned out, both had elements of truth in them. I was able to tell David about Eddie, but conveniently played the relationship down to one of friendship, my motive was to assuage some of the guilt I felt. Well I couldn't be that bad, if I was partially honest, and I know much as I didn't want to admit, it safeguarded things with David, if there ever came a time that they turned up unexpectedly together. I didn't like to admit it, but that highlighted to me whose company I wanted to keep most, and I also knew that out of the two Eddie would by far be the more forgiving. I didn't stop to think that he would also be the one most hurt by the betrayal. I juggled the two relationships successfully for a few months, and I was flying high. Both were such different people, which gave me something of everything. The calm and security of Eddie, the adventure and uncertainty of David, I was having a wonderful time, and so far so good, nobody was getting hurt.

Well it was inevitable, I was out with Eddie, and David, who was supposed to be away for another two weeks, was returned to Umtali on some secret mission in the area. He had phoned my home, and my mum told him where to find me. I saw him coming in, and in a total panic, told Eddie I had just seen a friend, and would be back in a moment. Oh shit what was I going to do now? David saw me approaching, and in his enthusiastic way, he behaved exactly how I had half hoped he wouldn't. I had planned to get to him quietly and whisper to him, to come outside and talk, and then I would have had time to think of something, but it wasn't going to happen like that. He came charging over, picked me up and snogged me as if there was no tomorrow. For a moment I hoped Eddie's attention was elsewhere and he hadn't seen anything, but when David put me down, Eddie was right there, and of course he knew, nothing I could say would make him believe anything other than I had been two timing him. I wasn't proud of the pain I saw in his face and eyes, but God forgive me, in that instant, I didn't want David to know there was more than friendship between Eddie and I. In a moment I dumped everything that Eddie had been to me in favour of David. I introduced them briefly, pointed to where I was sitting to David, and hurried Eddie outside. I think David was too arrogant or confident in my very obvious feelings for him, to express any concern or doubt, and he squeezed my arm and walked away.

When Eddie and I got outside, I didn't have to explain anything, he knew already. I had been cruel and deceptive, and he was badly hurt, strangely I was hurting too. I wanted the best of both worlds, I didn't want to be forced into making a choice, I wanted some of them both, and I did love Eddie, he was a good kind decent person, who really didn't deserve this. He did what was probably the most hurtful thing he could have, and he was justified in doing it. He gestured to stop me from trying to explain, and said 'don't insult me any more than you have already done', and he turned and walked away. I had seen the tears in his eyes, and felt them in mine. Part of me knew that I should be going after him, the rest of me turned and went indoors, and with the resilience and callousness of youth, I drank, danced and kissed the night away with David. I did spare a painful thought or two for Eddie, but it was only later that night, when I was in bed, that I truly did experience that all consuming guilt, and heartache too. I did a lot of 'if only's' too. If only Eddie had loved me less, and then we could still have been friends. If only I had loved him more, then David would never have happened. Eventually I slept, and was woken by my mum to say Eddie was on the phone. It was true, he was too good for me, he said that if I only had friendship to offer, he would rather have that than nothing at all. We spoke for a long while, and I had the opportunity to say how sorry I was, and how bad I felt about the way I had treated him. I was able to tell him I did love him as a very dear friend, and I said I hoped one day he would find someone special who would make him happy. I had the opportunity to thank him for still allowing me in his life, and still being in mine. Thank you God for this, because it was the last time I ever saw or spoke to Eddie, later that day he was called out, and a few of days later, he was killed whilst diffusing a mine.

I'm so sorry Eddie, I still wonder today, if what had happened between us lessened your concentration, and I have comforted myself, that I would just be arrogant to think it would still have been on your mind. Somehow though I have never been able to completely believe that I wasn't in some way responsible for your lack of focus, and over the years that have passed, I also believe, that if I was, you forgave me a long time ago, that's the kind of person you were. Thank you Eddie, you were the first man to show me genuine kindness, love and respect, you and one other gave me measures to work with, sadly I only observed and used them many years later.

Funny how life gives and takes, and how we perceive things. Some would say just bad luck and inevitable, me, I called it retribution and punishment, part of my persecution complex perhaps. I think because of my feelings of loss, I wanted confirmation of love, and I needed to speak to David. He was on R&R and at home on his farm. I had the address from letters he had written, and I eventually got his number from directory enquiries. Sarah and Sheila were with me, and I dialled the number. His mother answered and I asked to speak to him, she sounded very stern, and I heard muffled angry voices before he came to the phone. He sounded very strange and distant, almost angry that I had phoned him. I told him I had just had news that Eddie had been killed, and he was unresponsive. I asked him what was wrong, and I thought I could hear women's voices in the background, one sounding angry, the other very upset. He then told me I had upset his mother and fiancé, and now he would have to explain to them, that I was a friend of one of his mates in the army, because they thought he was keeping a secret girlfriend in another town, and then he thanked me for being kind enough to call and give him the news that someone he knew had been killed, and would I pass on his sympathy. As I said earlier, bad luck, inevitable, or punishment meted from above. I had played the game, and I had lost in a way I could never have imagined in my worst nightmare. I now grieved for two lost loves, in entirely different ways, but grieve I did.

15

I forgot to mention, that I actually passed my O Levels, and it was now time to choose my career. Actually, it wasn't mine to choose, my mum chose it for me. Even though I'd had notions earlier in life to go to University, and study in forensics, become a teacher, or better still, become a chef, the feedback from my parents was that girls got married, and had babies, and boys furthered their education. Besides, there wasn't much faith in my academic abilities communicated, in fact the best career for me and my apparent limited intellect, would be to follow in my mothers footsteps and become a secretary. In all fairness, my mum had said when my O level results came through was that I was 'bright', but lazy. I suppose the mental and emotional trauma during that year, the year of the rape, was 'laziness'.

This secretarial training would as I was told, always be useful to me later on in life, and look at how good my mum was at it. Retrospectively it has been useful, not enjoyable, but useful.

Of course I had to have the best, and there was a top secretarial college in Salisbury, that ran an intensive course that covered absolutely everything a young lady should know. This of course included all the most up to date secretarial skills, but, there was a potential problem. Because of the vast range of subjects, the very high standards, and intensity of the course, you had to have a certain IQ in order to be accepted. Well, I thought that solves that, I didn't stand a chance, why even bother, but my mum wanted me in there, and she agonised over the probability that I wouldn't make it. Especially, as my friend Christine was also applying. Christine was Nigel's sister, remember the one involved the night of the rape. This made it even more crucial that I was in. God forbid, I let them down again, hadn't I embarrassed them enough that night, that they had had to contact Nigel and Christine's parents in the early hours. It would be devastating if Christy got in and I didn't. No pressure then!

We travelled up together, Christy and I, and our two mums, you could feel their competitiveness and tension, I just thought, here we go again, nothing I can do about this one, you can't study for an IQ test. I still desperately wanted to please my mum though, as I always thought there would be some turning point. Something I did to please her, might one day, change how she felt and thought about me, maybe then this was it. Christy and I did the test, and then we waited the rest of the day for the results. My God, I had passed, apparently I had an amazing IQ, and when we called back for the results and to meet with the Head of the school, they all but laid down the red carpet for me, what do you know, I was told I was an extremely intelligent young lady, not just bright, but extremely (they used that word) intelligent and they would be thrilled to have me on their course. Christy was borderline, but was accepted on a probation term to see how she would cope, and my mum glowed all the way back. She said to Christy's mum, 'I always knew Cheryl was very 'intelligent' (not bright anymore), but she's just been lazy'. Oh well, at least I've moved up notch or two in her estimations.

It was also at about this time, that we received the phone-call that was everyone's nightmare. It was the army telling us my brother had been shot. In that instant, I thought my parents were going to die before my eyes, these two dominating, controlling and controlled people, crumbled in a moment, and a side of them I had never seen before emerged. They were helpless. Somebody had to deal with the calls and enquiries, and we had to determine the extent of his injuries, where he had been cassavaked to, and how we could contact the hospital he was at. There wasn't anyone else but me, and I had to shut down my fear, not give into crying too and take over. We discovered he wasn't seriously injured, he'd been shot in the foot, and we found out where he was, and were able to contact him, so that my parents could speak to him. In the meantime, I contacted my aunt to come over and be with my mum, whilst I tried to gather information. This impacted on my dad in particular, I had never seen him so distraught and out of control, and I worried about his health.

My brother and his unit had been ambushed by the rebels, and one of his very good friends had been seriously injured, some had been killed, we had been blessed. My brother came home to recuperate, and it was some of the best quality time we spent together. I had a renewed appreciation of him, and he had been reminded of the importance of being alive. Unfortunately, this situation was the opportunity for me to be tagged with yet another label, 'cold hearted'. My coping and dealing with the situation, was seen as uncaring, and unemotional, and my parents and aunt were aghast at my control. This really worked against me, and when it was deemed appropriate, or if I had misbehaved or upset my mum with whatever teenage girls do or say, a new lecture ensued, how could I be so cold, obviously, the only person I cared about was myself, and hadn't it always been that way. I had always been self-centred, and didn't it show in how little I had worried about my brother after I'd heard he'd been shot. What all this had to do with getting the necessary information for my parents at a time, that they were unable to cope with anything, I didn't know, but it was clear that whichever way I turned, whatever I tried to do to help, was always turned against me. I despaired yet again, and pigeon holed this too, in the growing coop of my mind.

I was however; still excited about going to college, but there were a few months before it started, which was quite cool really. The school year starts in January in Africa, and our main holiday is over Christmas, it's also one of the hottest times of year, so I had a while to spend doing nothing but lazing by the pool, and reading to my hearts content. I hadn't been going out much, and as my friends and I were going separate ways, we decided to go out together as much as we could. That's how I met James. We had gone to one of the pubs, not even a disco, and it was one of those moments when everyone was either in the loo, at the bar or talking to someone else, and I was sitting alone. I was quite happy to be on my own for a bit, and I was enjoying people watching, when a very tall army guy came across, and asked if he could join me. Why not, so I told him it was ok. He asked if I was alone, and I told him that I was at that moment, but was with a group of friends. He introduced himself, and his name was James, he was a big lad, with dark hair, and sported a moustache. He had lovely eyes, and a friendly smile, and I found myself talking and laughing easily with him. The others came and went around us, and I was surprised how late it suddenly was. James had got a lift with some mates, who had left, and there were only a couple of us in my car, so I offered to drive him back to the barracks. He asked if he could stay in contact, and I thought it would be ok, I was going to college soon anyway.

Over the next couple of months, James became very special to me. I was able to talk to him about anything and everything, the rape, Eddie, David, my lack of confidence, absolutely anything. It was mutual, and we developed a very strong bond, which moved slowly from friendship to a relationship. My idea of relationship still didn't involve any intimacy apart from kissing, holding hands, that sort of thing and James respected that. Soon, it came time for me to leave for college, and James and I were committed to keeping in contact.

I was pleased I wasn't going to be on my own, and Christy and I were going to stay in a girl's hostel on the same road as the college. The hostel was supervised to a point, we had to be in at a certain time, but we had regular meals, and the rooms were ok. Christy and I were sharing a room, and we decided which posters and pictures we would take to make it a little more homely. Neither of us had ever been away from home for any length of time, and it felt quite scary too, but ultimately it felt like I was really growing up now and becoming independent.

We arrived along with about another hundred or so girls also staying at the hostel, and it was mayhem. Everyone trying to find their room, suitcases all over the place, and all those female voices along with their families, it was mad. Eventually we were directed to our room, said hurried goodbyes to the mums, and literally pushed them out the room and on their way. Most of the other parents had said their goodbyes in the hall downstairs, so we were starting to feel awkward with ours still there. It's one of those moments, when you really don't want them to go, because then there is no turning back, and your link with home and everything that goes with it is gone, but likewise you really don't want them hanging about, otherwise you are left with zero street credit. All the other girls looked confident and excited, no tears and trauma, no clinging to mummy, so there were no ways we were going to be any different. I remember feeling quite brutal in my goodbyes. It went something like, walk into the room, put all the bags down, turn to my mum, and say 'bye then mum, I will call you soon'. I think a formal handshake would have been appropriate with that sort of farewell, but I was enveloped in this big hug, and she was dabbing her eyes. I'm not sure whether she was following Christy's mum's lead, as she was literally sobbing on Christy's shoulder, at which point, I rushed to close the door so no-one could see this totally unnecessary display of emotion, or whether it was relief, that I was finally out of their hands, for a year at least. Whatever the motive was, it felt good.

Christy and I settled in quickly and made new friends both at the hostel and at college. I loved it, I felt so grown up not wearing a uniform, but civvies, and having the freedom that college allowed. There were lessons to attend, but it was so different to school, and we were taught by tutors, not mere teachers. During breaks, we had our own little coffee shop, and we gathered at the tables sipping coffee, and discussing the importance of our day, it was so sophisticated.

James called me at the hostel when he could, and we wrote often. I remember when he was on active duty, he filled an entire writing pad once, and I received this bulging envelope with a virtual book in it. James made no qualms about his feelings for me, he was deeply in love, and he was lovely enough to know that I might not feel quite the same then, perhaps not ever, but he considered it enough that I told him, I did love him, and just to give it time. He always said he had more than enough love for both of us.

During the first month, Christy and I travelled home over weekends. It was about a three hour drive, and if she drove, I 'rode shotgun' so to speak. We always had weapons in the car, which were loaded and ready to use if necessary. This was in the event of a possible ambush, and of course we had to observe the rule to avoid any object in the road, including cow dung, in case of mines. We also had to keep within the curfew, which meant we had to allow plenty of time for the journey to ensure we arrived at our destination before dark. If we were on the roads after dark, you ran as much risk being killed by our own forces as the rebels. God forbid you broke down, that was the biggest fear of all motorists, and of course there were no mobiles to call for assistance. Needless to say these trips were fraught with tension and fear, but we were young, and tension and fear translates into adventure when you're that age.

It was a couple of months into college, and Nigel, and Alex came to visit us and take us out for the evening. We had an absolute rave, and arrived back at the hostel just before our curfew of eleven. As we got out of the car, we heard screeching of brakes and then a terrible crash, and the sound of metal being dragged on the tarmac. We ran to where it came from, which was the road just adjacent to the one we were on, and were met by a scene of absolute carnage. The noise had attracted a lot of the girls from the hostel, and there were about fifteen of us who arrived on the scene at the same time. We could hear the screams and moans now, and the dual carriageway was literally littered with bodies. One of the large army vehicles, which was called a 'crocodile' was on it's side. It is a large long vehicle which has peculiar sides to defuse most of the blast of landmines, and it carried large numbers of troops. The only other vehicle we could see, was what was left of a mini. For seconds, although it seemed longer, we all just stood there, and then this 'coping thing' kicked in and I shouted to some of the girls to go back to the hospital and bring blankets, sheets whatever we could use to cover people with or stop bleeding with, and of course to call for ambulances. It was imperative that they told the emergency services they would need to send a lot of ambulances.

A couple of us started to walk through the men on the road. It looked as though they had all been thrown out of the crocodile. They were all in uniform, and then, on an island, between the two carriageways, I saw someone in civilian clothes, and assumed it was the driver of the mini. Some of the girls had got back with blankets, so I grabbed one and ran across. He was lying very awkwardly, and although I didn't know more about first aid, than what my dad had taught me, I knew to check for breath and a pulse. There was neither. I knew he didn't need a blanket for warmth or shock, but I did need to cover him, I couldn't bring myself to cover his face though. He looked about seventeen, my age, and it was my first experience of a dead body.

There were so many of them, where were the ambulances? There were only a few of us that seemed able to go to them, and somehow they were all looking to me for instructions, why? I just asked that everyone on the ground was to be covered with a blanket, I kept thinking of shock, keep them warm, and also nobody was to be moved at all. If they were conscious, spend a little time with them, and reassure them that help was on the way, and they would be alright. Don't react to any injuries you may see, don't show concern, try and be a calming influence regardless of how bad it may look. I was shaking and terrified inside, and I knew I was close to tears, but I managed to keep this calm exterior, and was seen to be cool as a cucumber in this crisis.

I was tested with my own advice, when I went to a young man who was moaning and crying. He'd already been covered with a blanket, so I couldn't see where he was hurt, but by the outline of his body, the angle of one leg looked horrible. He was hurt and he was frightened, and he asked me to hold his hand. He moved it out from under the blanket, and it was just a bloody lump with what looked like bits of bone sticking out. Shit, don't look shocked, and don't let on that he doesn't really have a hand to hold. I took him gently by the wrist, which seemed the most intact part, and just said 'I want you to keep warm, so keep your hand under the blanket, and how about I sit with you for a while', I sensed he wanted to be touched, so I sat and stroked his forehead, and I wasn't there long when I heard the sirens, and a convoy of ambulances arrived. There was a rush of mad activity then, and I thought it best, we just got out of the way. One of the paramedics came up to me, and asked where we had come from, and I told him how we had arrived on the scene seconds after the accident, and we stayed at the hostel just down the road. He thanked us and we went back.

It was only when I got back to my room that I started to cry, I know it was the shock, and also seeing that young man dead. It just seemed so ironic that these young men had probably just completed a tour and were congratulating themselves on getting back unscathed, and now this. I cried myself to sleep, still fully clothed. Two days later, a letter was hand delivered to the hostel. It was from some top major or something from the regiment that all those lads belonged to, and in it he thanked us profusely for what we had done that night. Only one of the army lads had died, and that was the driver of the vehicle, and of course one civilian fatality. I have never known where this amazingly capable calm part of me comes from, in a crisis, but I do thank God for it, because I've needed it.

I felt quite 'out of it all' for the next few days, and found comfort in writing it all down in a letter to James. I knew he was due to be in Salisbury soon, and I was looking forward to seeing him. We were walking back from the shops a couple of days later, and I knew James

111

was coming the following week, he was going home for a few days before coming to see me, and I remember it was tipping down with rain. We'd taken our shoes off, and were absolutely soaked. As Christy and I approached the entrance gates to the hostel, I saw two army guys walking out, and they were walking away from us. I knew that walk, not many people were that tall either, and the hair colour was right. It was James! I shouted his name, and he kept walking, I shouted again, and he turned. It was one of those moments you see in the movies, he started running, and I did, sort of that Cathy and Heathcliffe thing again, except we were sloshing through puddles, and could barely see with the rain. Fortunately we met, because it was possible under those conditions, running blind and all that for us to have missed each other completely and gone on past. I told you he was a big guy, and he picked me up and swung me round like a child. I just clung on for dear life, telling him to put me down. I was thrilled to see him, I really had missed him, and with what had been going on the last week, I really wanted some tlc (tender loving care). He was the right person for that. He sat in the communal lounge, whilst I went up to try and put myself together, work on a transformation from drowned rat, to femme fatale, which sort of worked, and then I was wined and dined as though I was breakable and fragile. Bless him, when he'd received my letter telling him all my trauma's and drama's he hadn't even gone home, he'd come straight to see me.

He stayed with a friend for a couple of days, and we saw each other every spare moment. James was a good listener, and he listened as I spoke about my feelings about leaving home, the good and the bad of it. They say you never appreciate things until you no longer have them, and I did miss the familiarity of home. I wasn't unhappy though, I was enjoying the experience and novelty of communal living, and I loved college. I was adjusting to a different life, different surroundings, and new and exciting challenges. One of my concerns was that Christy was desperately unhappy. She didn't like living at the hostel, and she was struggling with college. She was talking about leaving and going home and that rocked my comfort zone as she was all I had with me that was familiar. Anyway, I was able to talk it all through with James, and whilst nothing was really left resolved or decided, talking it out seemed to put it into perspective. I didn't want to go home, and I resolved to stay and see how things went.

James went home for the remainder of his leave, and during his absences the occasional phone call, and tons of letters continued. Christy did leave and go home, and I made other friends especially Barbara. Barbs was vivacious with a very big personality. She had been an exchange student, and spent a year in America, which left her with enormous confidence and ego to match, and a weird accent. We clicked immediately, and became close friends quickly. We also decided we wanted our independence, and although it took some months, we respectively persuaded our parents to allow us to move into a block of flats, into our own little bed sits. Mine was one room which contained my bedroom, kitchenette, and then a tiny bathroom. I also had the luxury of a postage stamp size balcony. Barbs was on the floor above me, so we were close enough for security and companionship, but we had our individual little flats, which gave us our independence, and this was the most exciting time for me. I really felt very grown up now. I did my own grocery shopping, and I could buy whatever I wanted. Of course to begin with it was all total junk food, eventually a few tomatoes, lettuce and odd vegetables found their way in, but the staples were things like rice, potatoes, and some meat. On my allowance, I had to budget less for food, and more for the essentials like, entertainment, booze and fags.

My brother and his friends often came to stay en route to their homes, and some nights there would be as many as three of them sleeping on my tiny floor. After they met Barbs, there were less on my floor and more on hers! James came to stay too, and we slept together in my single bed. I wasn't ready for a sexual relationship, I still felt like damaged goods, and although I knew the best person to do it with, would be James. I knew he would be gentle considerate and very loving, and that somehow made it more difficult for me to have sex with him. I didn't feel I deserved that, I felt that was too good for the likes of me. How could someone as good and kind as James love me the way he did, I couldn't get my head around the fact that the way I felt about myself, wasn't how he felt about me. He treated me like gold, and I couldn't shake this constant underlying feeling of being unworthy. It's hard to put into words, but I felt that if I had sex with him, it would obviously take our relationship to another level, and that somehow felt deceitful. I wanted to shake him and say 'look, I am not what you think I am, I allowed myself to be raped, and that is not good enough for you'. Take off the rose tinted glasses and see me and treat me for what I really am. Soiled and damaged goods, not worthy of this adoration. I didn't believe that I deserved this, and it was also new for me to be loved unconditionally, I didn't have to do or be anything other than who I was, this was the first time I didn't have to work for love, it was being freely given, and it made me suspicious. It was out of the norm for me, I had always had to give something of me, or do something to receive kindness, or attention, now I didn't' have to try, it was given freely, sadly however, I didn't know how to accept it without caution and uncertainty. I was unbalanced by it, and I kept feeling it couldn't last, it was going to end. Someday soon, I would be presented with the bill, and what would payment be. I couldn't trust that someone was giving this freely to me, no charge attached. These were thoughts and concerns I couldn't share with James, I was confused, and I was always waiting for that day, when somehow, in someway I would have to repay all his love and I didn't know that I would be able to meet the price tag.

He respected my feelings regarding having sex, as I said I wasn't ready yet, and I also now wanted to wait until I was married, and there were many nights when we slept spooned together, and I could feel his erection in my back. God he must have been so frustrated, but he never complained, he never tried to persuade me to change my mind, I think he must have just gone and done what single young men do when they are desperately horny, and I don't mean find someone else, James was so absolutely faithful.

On one of his leave passes, he asked me to go home with him and meet his family, and I did. It was obvious to me that he had told his parents how he felt about me, particularly one morning when his mum called me into her bedroom. There, spread out on the double bed, was a beautiful white dress, and it took a few seconds for me to register that it was a wedding dress. Oh shit, what now. She told me it was hers, and without coming right out and actually saying it, indicated that if I wanted to I could have it for my wedding, which would obviously be when I married her son. I was touched, and also overwhelmed, because it seemed that as more time passed, my debt to James was growing, and payback must be looming, especially if he was this serious. I was still waiting for the monster inside him to appear, my experience had taught me, that no matter how nice someone appeared to be, that monster would show itself, it always had in the past hadn't it. I didn't trust anyone, there was always an ulterior motive, there always had been before, why should it be different now.

We continued our relationship as before, and my year at college flew by. It was during this year that Mags and I went on our begging spree, and my brother turned twenty one. My parents held the party of the year for him, a twenty first to beat all twenty firsts, of course there was their reputation to be upheld here. The guests were, friends and family, all his army mates, school friends, and some of my friends. They spilled out of the house into the garden, and there was eating, drinking and dancing until the early hours. There were the traditional speeches, and the giving of the key, and the next morning there were a lot of very delicate and unwell young lads. Barbs and I had travelled through for the weekend, and Barbs had a brilliant time. She was the life and soul of the party, and spent most of the evening with my brother, which made him a very happy young man. I had my fair share of admirers and danced most of the evening, but my thoughts were of James, and I missed that he couldn't be there.

I graduated from college with good grades, not the best, but good enough. I'd had a brilliant year, and the graduation ceremony culminated in us putting on a modelling show for our families. This was part of the exclusivity of the course that we had the confidence to strut down a ramp, in clothes we had designed ourselves. I'd never have imagined I could do something like that a while back, but I did it, and I enjoyed it. My mum and dad were there, and I felt so proud of my achievements, both academic and personal. They were proud too, but disappointed that I wasn't one of the three chosen for best modelling and dress. I wasn't surprised really, for some bizarre reason I had decided to have my first perm ever, and my hair didn't take kindly to it. I ended up with a ball of frizz and fuzz framing my face. I do mean ball, it all stood out about a foot, and it was dry and brittle, no glossy locks for me. As for my 'designer' outfit, good God what planet was I on? It was a vivid red dress in this clingy fabric, and had a shredded style skirt. Bear in mind too, I didn't have the figure of a model, so there was this plump fuzz ball sashaying down the catwalk on twenty inch heels. You can't win them all I suppose, and I agreed with the judge's decision.

I'd spent a while trying to decide what to do after college, and I suppose because my confidence was the sort that faded rather quickly depending on where I was and whom I was with, I decided to go home and find a job in Umtali and back to familiarity.

16

With hindsight, I often wonder about the enormity of the decisions, which seem so simple and uncomplicated at the time that we make in life, and the subsequent outcomes. If I had stayed in Salisbury, and made a go of it in the big city, how very different my life might have been. There would have been people I might never have met, I might have just achieved happiness or at the least contentment. There again maybe not, I believe in destiny, and I believe we have our path to follow and our lessons to learn, and they would have caught up with me one way or another.

My dad had loads of contacts and he got me my first interview with an accounting firm. I was successful, and started as a 'junior everything'. I was to learn bookkeeping, and make use of my recently acquired 'executive secretarial skills', and that is where I met Sue. She was to train me in the complicated and loathsome world of figures, and I was a nightmare to teach. I had this mental block when it came to anything to do with sums, and no matter how high my IQ was, it just didn't fit for me. She persevered, and I struggled along, and in between, we became friends. Sue was older than I was, and had three children. Twin baby girls and a little boy, and she had her own home, and to me was the ultimate independent woman of our times. She was divorced, which then, was quite shocking, but for me it signified girl power, and in my absolute naivety I admired her enormously. She invited me to her home, and I became a frequent visitor. I was flattered that an older woman would consider me her friend and confidante, it was only much later I realised I flattered her ego, with my misguided admiration. The house was filthy, and smelt constantly of stale urine, due to the twins constantly walking about in wet nappies, and sleeping in them, which made their beds literally stink. It didn't seem to bother Sue much, but she was a very relaxed parent. I think the more appropriate term would be lazy, as the children were left pretty much to their own devices, even though they were so small, and they were sent to the room constantly, so that we could chat in peace. She shouted a lot too, but none of the above detracted from my admiration of her. What exactly I did admire, I'm not sure, I think it was to do with her sense of independence and the absolute brash confidence she emitted.

During our initial chats she confided she was in love with a man called George, strange that her son was named George too, but she said he had been a friend of her ex husbands, and that was why he'd been named after him. She was obsessed with this man, and by the way she talked about him, I believe he was part of, if not the main reason for her divorce. He lived just outside Salisbury, and travelled to see her occasionally, or she would take any opportunity to go to him. He had a younger brother who was in the police, and was based here in Umtali, and she suggested I should meet him. I told her about James, and she laughed it off, saying I was far too young to be thinking so seriously about any one man, and look at her, didn't she do just that, and where had she ended up. Divorced with three little ones, and knowing she'd married the wrong man. Shit I was so gullible, and so easily persuaded. We go back to the confidence thing, I didn't trust my own feelings and thoughts, and as usual, would do anything for anyone who liked me or showed me attention and interest. So, of course I agreed to meet the 'younger brother', another one of the decisions that you find out much later actually make or break your life.

George had come through for the weekend, and his younger brother and mates were at the house too when I arrived. I was shy and awkward, as they were all a bit older than me, and obviously knew each other, and I was the only stranger. Anyway, I had a couple of drinks and started to relax. I didn't think too much of Bruce, the younger brother, and he also seemed only interested in putting as much beer down his throat in as little time as possible. I stayed on the outskirts of the crowd, and then a call came into Bruce and the others for them to get to an incident, which was later described as a full on battle between the forces and rebels. I remember we heard the various weapons in the distance, and I decided to go home. I left feeling relieved, he obviously didn't fancy me, and I had gone a long with Sue's request to meet him, so I could retain my focus on James, and nobody was upset or let down. It was so important to me to not alienate anyone I liked or who liked me, I think I would have done almost anything to keep a friendship or relationship I enjoyed. I know that sounds contradictory as far as James goes, because I wouldn't have sex with him, but that was what was so special about James, I knew I didn't have to work at pleasing him or making him happy, he loved me anyway, and I trusted his love. Probably the first time I ever did trust in someone's love, and if I had known then that I was going to lose it, I would have treasured it so much more, kept it safe, and not defiled it.

I saw Bruce at Sue's more often when I visited, and I only found out later that he apparently was interested in me. I didn't have any feelings one way or the other at that point. Out of the blue one day he called me after he'd got my number from Sue, and invited me out for the day, with the rest of their crowd. We were all meeting at one of the hotels in the country, and would spend the day swimming, drinking, and generally having a good time. It sounded like fun, and Sue would be there, so I agreed to go. I took a long while getting ready, ages blow drying my normal hair, the perm had long since disappeared, and I wore a new skirt and top. Bruce came to fetch me in his car, which I had never seen before. I don't know much about cars, but what horrified me when I saw it, was that it was a convertible. Oh shit, there goes the hairdo, and everything with it. You didn't get waterproof mascara in those days, so with the wind whipping in, and my eyes streaming in response, along with a white knuckle drive, I arrived with a beehive for a hairdo, mascara streaked across my cheeks to my ears, and a terror inspired grimace stuck to my face. Very attractive! First stop of course was the loos, and I ducked in there before anyone else could see me. I ended up with more hair on the brush than on my head, when I'd finished trying to detangle it, and in trying to get the mascara whiskers off, I'd removed most of the painstakingly carefully applied make-up, so all that was left was lippie, and I'd left that at home. Well bare faced it was then, what a boost to the non existent confidence. What made it worse was Sue sitting at the side of the pool, in her skimpy bikini, and even after three kids, her figure was exceptional. I hadn't brought a costume because I had my period, and I had to wear about ten of those nappy things they called sanitary towels. Oh I felt lovely! It gets worse. Once the party got going and the drinks were flowing, Bruce decided in his misguided wisdom that I was missing out on all the fun by not swimming, so picked me up and threw me into the pool fully clothed. I wouldn't have minded so much, but visions of sanitary towels floating to the top of the crowded pool terrified me. I literally sprung right out of the water onto the side in one leap, and rushed to what was becoming a familiar haven, the loo. Thank god I'd brought extra sanitary towels at least I could patch that part of me up. The wet clothes would dry quickly in the sun, the hair and face now; well we'd just have to give up there.

When the suggestion that I go into the pool again arose, I took Sue to one side and asked her to dissuade them, as I had my period. Wrong move, she used it to her advantage, and whilst I thought she would be discreet, she said to all and sundry, that 'It's that time of month for Cheryl boys, so no more ideas of throwing her in the pool'. I could have died, but it was an eye opener for me. Sue craved attention, and didn't really care how she got it. She would use anyone for a moment in the spotlight, and that became more apparent as time passed. Stuck in my little world of mortification, I let the day pass me by, and soon it was time to leave. On the way home, Bruce said they were all meeting at the local disco, and would I like to go. Wow, after all was said and done, he still wanted my company, ok it might be fun, so I went home to change whilst he waited for me, and we went out. We danced and we kissed, and it was nice enough, and then he took me home. Well that was that then, but it wasn't. Bruce pursued me, and I missed James, so we went out a few times, but mostly met up at Sue's. I think she thought she was matchmaker of the year, and as she didn't appear to have any other friends, I think part of her motive in pushing us together was to keep my friendship, or heroine worship. She liked having someone about who didn't threaten her in any way, and looked up to her as a worldly wise woman, she liked having a young silly girl's admiration at her beck and call. I was happy to spend time at Sue's. I enjoyed the children, and it meant I didn't have to spend too much time at home.

I was doing it again, as if I hadn't learnt my lesson. I was juggling two relationships at once. I like to think this time it was different, but it wasn't really. James was very much like Eddie had been to me, dependable and trustworthy, and Bruce was the David, rebellious, loud, a hard drinking, fast living type, more exciting, and of course unreliable. No guarantees there, which I suppose added an element of uncertainty and challenge. I wasn't madly in love with him, but I thought he might be the right person for my experiment. Ever since the rape, I had concerns and visions of never being able to have normal sex again. I didn't know what it was like, as my distorted memory of what happened, didn't give me any idea at all, of the real thing. All my friends had 'done it', and they had varying views on it. Some thought it was great, others considered it a sacrifice all woman had to make, and I wanted to find out for myself.

Perhaps you're thinking, why not James then, he would be precisely the right person. Well not to my way of thinking. What if I ended up screaming and beating him off, James would be devastated and hurt, and it could have a major impact on our relationship. I couldn't expect him to stay with me out of some misguided sense of loyalty or pity, and he would do just that. That wouldn't be fair to either of us, so I felt I had to try it with someone who really wouldn't give a shit if it was all a complete disaster, and Bruce seemed to be just that sort of person. He knew about James, and he wasn't really concerned that I cared deeply for another man, which was a strong indicator that he didn't have any strong feelings for me. James had given me a St Christopher medallion, to keep me safe and I wore it always, and he knew that James was my confidante and also my best friend. I relied on him to always be there for me, and knew he would be. He would never need to know about Bruce anyway. Don't get me wrong, Bruce was nice enough, he was just incredibly self centred and self serving, and he was also arrogant enough to cope with the situation if it went bad, and not consider that he had anything to do with it, but that it would be my stuff. It absolutely would be, but James on the other hand, would take responsibility, and probably try even harder to ensure my happiness.

I thought this was logical, so I allowed things to progress naturally. I didn't plan a special evening, because it wasn't about it being special, it was just about seeing if I was normal. Bruce knew about the rape, and he said it didn't matter to him, I don't think it did, as long as it didn't impact on our relationship progressing to an intimate one. He was never too shy to talk about his sexual prowess, and he gave the impression that he had been with a lot of women, knew what he was doing, and I would be another notch on his chart. He was an open flirt, and often would make a play for one of my friends in front of me. We all took it lightly and in fun, none of us thought he was serious; surely he wouldn't belittle me like that so obviously. We were seen as a couple now, when we went out, so although there wasn't any commitment or talk of love, it was just the way it went, when you dated for a while.

My parents knew I was seeing Bruce, and I'd known from the beginning that they disliked him. They didn't feel he was good enough for me, and that's not in the emotional department. I suppose it was to do with his background. This is really where my family's snobbery comes in. It was his lack of manners at the dinner table, when we went out for dinner, and he didn't know which knife or fork to use, and to be fair, he was blatantly rude sometimes, burping and farting, and thinking it was hilarious. He never greeted them by name when he came over, would just ask 'Cheryl about?' and that really riled them, it was a combination of his behaviour and attitude; he was often drunk, and always really cocky. They weren't too concerned, as I was still very young, and although they also didn't think James was good enough for me, simply because he came from the wrong side of the tracks, they knew he was still in my life, so that meant I wasn't too serious about anyone right now. This somehow justified my motives.

The first time it happened, it was on the lawn in the garden, late at night, and it was awful. God it was horribly uncomfortable, and can't say I enjoyed it at all. I was heading for the 'sacrifice' verdict, but thought one more try and in more conducive surroundings, it might make a difference. At least, I hadn't behaved like a mad lunatic and tried to beat him off, that was positive, at least there was hope, I could be normal in that department.

During the rare calls I had from James, I wished I could tell him what I was doing with Bruce and why, but I knew I couldn't expect him to understand. I also knew it would hurt him deeply, and it was only my guilt that craved his understanding. Regardless of how I'd worked it out to suit me, I wasn't playing fair. We still wrote frequently,

122

and I hadn't seen him in a long while and I did miss him dreadfully. I think I believed that his return would be my solution and resolution.

Because we'd done it once, Bruce thought this could be his regular bit now, but as I wasn't prepared for another grass episode, and there were no ways it was happening under my parent's roof. Bruce suggested we go to one of the local hotels for the night, and I agreed it would be the best option. If this wasn't any better, then I would resign myself to a life as a woman making this sacrifice every now and then, and pretending it was good for me too, if I had to. My parents knew where I was going that night, my mum knew my relationship with Bruce had become intimate, I'd made sure to go on the pill, and she never missed a thing. We always made sure to leave contact numbers if we were away from home even for a short while, this was in case of a mortar attack, and we could remain in touch.

It was better that night, not good, but better. I felt that if I could see it through without panicking that was enough, and I did. I considered that was normal, I could have a normal life with a man, maybe not reach any great heights of passion, but at least I could move on knowing I wasn't going to suffer from any major paranoia about sex. I could never call it 'making love', that's not what it meant to me, that had been taken away, and I couldn't get that back.

I'd woken at the crack of dawn and snuck into the bathroom, to clean my teeth, transform the hedge back to hair, and put a touch of foundation on. Then I crept back into the bed, and pretended to be asleep. We took our time having tea and coffee before heading back to my house, and I was met at the door by my mother. She was furious, and I still wonder at that. She was ranting that she'd had to take a very difficult call on my behalf and had been embarrassed by me yet again. What was she on about? James's father had called late last night to speak to me, and again this morning. He'd called to tell me that James was dead. My mum repeated how awful she had felt, that she had received this call in my absence and I was doing God knows what with another man. Had I no shame! It was awful for her, knowing where I was and having to talk to James's father, and she went on and on and on. My father just looked at me, shook his head in contempt and left the room. My mother told me to at least have the decency to call James's dad back.

No, not again, please please not again, not my James. Not like this, not at all, please no. My legs wobbled, and I couldn't stand on my own, Bruce helped me into my parents room, I just wanted to use the phone, and call James's home and find out it was all a very bad mistake. I couldn't dial, my hands were shaking, and Bruce dialled the number for me. The phone rang, and a broken voice answered, and I knew it was true. I cried with James's dad, whilst he told me that it had been a vehicle accident. James had died instantly. He said he would call me to let me know about the funeral, I said 'I'm so sorry, so very sorry', and he replied that he was sorry too, for me, he knew how much James had loved me, and how I had loved him. James had told them how happy he was with me, and that he wanted to spend the rest of his life with me, and he thanked me for making his son so happy.

James, I know you understand now, what I was doing. You also know how I loved you, and how I missed you, and that I still think of you. I often wonder that if you hadn't left me, would the rest of my life have been completely different. You understand that I couldn't go to your funeral because I was consumed with guilt and self loathing. Whichever way, I tried to look at it and justify it, I still felt that I betrayed you, and for a very long while my mum reminded me of that. You also know that losing you rocked me as never before, and I clung to the only person I had left, which was the beginning of a very sad and painful journey for me. Retribution, who knows, I know that that you would only have wished me the very best, and great happiness. Thank you for being everything that you were to me, thank you that I had your memory to sustain me for many years, and thank you, that your memory reminded me, many years later of what being loved can be.

I tried to understand my mum's anger, and I could understand that she felt I was playing the game, and lost, so deal with the consequences, and that she wondered how I could be so upset about James, when I was sleeping with Bruce. She never once asked how I was feeling, and I never considered telling her. Her contempt for me grew, and my pain deepened, and it was time again for me to try even harder to make up to her for her disappointment in me.

Something changed in my relationship with Bruce that night. I saw a side of him I hadn't before, and in my grief, I clung to him like a limpet. He was softer more gentle and kinder than I'd known before, and I latched onto that part of him and ran with it. I expanded it, I imagined it to be much more than it was. I normally focused on the good in people, but now I ignored the familiar flirting and drinking, and the frequent negative comments he made about me. All I chose to see were the scraps of kindness he threw to me and made so much more of them than I should have. He responded accordingly, and he had a willing slave now, someone he could treat however he chose to, who didn't appear to be going anywhere and that is very seductive to a bully. They feed on what they perceive as weakness, it flatters their ego, and sadly they push the boundaries ever further. I was the perfect candidate too, because I was very accustomed to, and familiar with the role of the victim. I also felt desperate not to lose anyone else, and the guilt that consumed me was a major factor in our relationship. I thought I could make it right. This time, no playing the field, remain faithful to one person, surely that would put it to rights.

17

I had been sacked, in the nicest way possible, but there was no doubt, and I was asked to leave. The manager didn't feel this was the right role for me, and my potential as a bookkeeper was sadly unrecognised and non existent, so I was job hunting. I did some voluntary work during this time at nights, and worked in an underground, and I mean that literally, not figuratively, call centre. It was high security, and basically we patched radio calls from troops and commanders, to the relevant headquarters. There was nothing sophisticated about it, and if there was an emergency or a report of injured or killed soldiers, there was a red light that flashed, and it was the absolute priority, to pick up this call, and transfer it. One night, the young woman sitting next to me, got to the emergency line before I did, and I knew it was notification of a soldier killed in action, because of the notepad she selected. We had to have a record of all the calls, and their content. She started to write the details, and then just passed out, her head hitting the desk with a loud thud. I had a dilemma in trying to revive her, and getting her headphones on, so that I could continue with the message. A twenty two year old infantryman had been killed in a contact, and my role then was to pass his dog tag details across to his base, for them to notify the next of kin. In the meantime, one of the other woman, had got to her, and she was slowly coming to. She was hysterical when she regained consciousness, the young soldier whose name she was given, was her fiancé. Out of all the call centres, and

126

the personnel working them, she had taken that terrible, tragic call.

This epitomized how we lived during this time. We all waited for that call and we all dreaded instead, the personal visit from a stranger in uniform because we all had someone we loved out there fighting. We lived with fear and dread, and the constant fear of experiencing that dread. Every time the phone rang, there was that instant of panic, that 'what if', and then the overwhelming relief when it was a familiar voice. As we replaced the receiver on the cradle it was with a sense of relief and victory, thank God it wasn't 'that call'. For that person answering the hot line, it had been 'that call', and it should have been 'that visit'. Now it would be left to her to make that visit to his parents and deliver the worst message possible whilst suffering her own anguish and grief. Perhaps for his parents that would be kinder, than having a stranger at their door, cap in hand, offering commiserations, trying to respond to the grief and always the question 'how did he die, did he suffer?' He would give the perfunctory response that it had been quick, and of course their son had died for his country, the bravest of the brave. All the while he knows he has more of these visits to make, and tries to depart as quickly as he can, without appearing callous.

News travels fast in Umtali, and I had a call from my past. Jane, my best friend at school called to say she had heard I was looking for work, and the place she was at had a vacancy for a secretary, would I be interested. Absolutely I was, and she arranged for an interview. I got the job, and Jane and I became close friends again in a short while. We started going out for drinks after work, and soon, it was as though all the years in between were inconsequential and the childhood bond we'd shared was resuscitated. We laughed about the silly childishness which caused the rift in the first place, we were young adults now, and we could acknowledge how young and foolish we were then. I don't think either of us ever established exactly what had happened, it just appeared to be the bitchiness of our mutual friend Diane, which had become disproportionate, hence the bust up.

She was still absolutely beautiful, and had finally settled on one young man, who she was in a very serious relationship with. She was hoping a proposal wouldn't be too far away. I told her about James and Bruce, and was pleased I had someone too, although I did exaggerate his good points. They met eventually, and Bruce literally fell over himself trying to impress Jane, he flirted blatantly with her to the point of embarrassment, and I just sat there and watched it happen. Jane spoke to me about it, and suggested he wasn't the right person for me, but I wasn't having any of that, he was all I had, and he was what I deserved. I ignored another warning at around the same time, when Sue called me to one side one day, and although she voiced concern at upsetting me with what she was going to tell me, she felt it was only right that she did. I must admit there was certainly no concern mirrored in her face or her voice, she spoke with relish as she told me Bruce had tried to persuade her to have sex with him the night before. She was flattered! I challenged him about it, and of course he denied it. There were to be many of those denials, and many times I would believe him because it was easier for me to do that.

Jane and I had a brilliant time at work and at play. My relationship with Bruce continued, and my parents were planning a trip to South Africa, so I decided to join them there for a holiday. The trip they were planning was dual purpose. It was for a holiday, but it was also to try and get anything valuable out of the country. The war had intensified, and we had been totally ostracised by the rest of the world, and our numbers were far less than the rebels, so we were now literally fighting a losing battle. Everyone was beginning to accept that it was the beginning of the end. We didn't know how it would end and when, but it would, we would lose our country, and then it was whether we could survive the change. My dad was a coin collector, and over the years had established a valuable collection, which as a potential investment, it was essential to get it out of Rhodesia. People my parents age, had invested everything into their homes, pensions, and savings, and the anxiety about the financial structure of Rhodesia and the implications of a takeover could be devastating. If you didn't have money invested outside of the country, you became a financial prisoner. Some people went to extremes to get money out, and some lost everything in their attempts. You couldn't take anything through the airports, so the only solution was via the border between Rhodesia and South Africa, and because of the worsening situation in Rhodesia, the customs officials were alerted to the illegal trafficking and it was common practice for them to randomly select a vehicle, and pull it to pieces, literally. They would strip it down to a shell, and it was sheer bad luck if it was yours, because they were under no obligation to put

128

it back together again.

One of the stories was that someone had bought a large fire screen, opened it up and stashed thousands of dollars in it. They then returned it to the shop and asked that it could be sent to a relative in South Africa as a gift. The shop offered this service, and honoured the request. The recipient in South Africa however, opened the fire screen to find it empty. When the desperate sender made enquiries, they had indeed sent the screen, but not the one he had so carefully prepared, they had selected a pre-packaged one from their store and sent that. To this day, there may be a very valuable fine screen somewhere. Another person filled their car tyres with thousands of dollars, obviously carefully packaged in plastic bags. He crossed the border safely, and at the earliest opportunity, went to retrieve his money out of the tyres. Sadly all that remained, after the friction of a long journey and the heat, was dust. There were many similar tales, and hundreds of people lost fortunes in their attempts to make a new life.

This trip however was to confirm where to leave the coin collection if they managed to get it out, so there was no risk attached this time. They were going out a week ahead of me, and I would fly out and meet them there. Jane and I were staying alone in the house, until I left, and then she would go back to her flat. Bruce was in Salisbury with his father at this time, and our relationship was stagnant.

That night we had more excitement than either of us had bargained for. I was feeling unwell and had decided to go to bed quite early, and was already in my pyjamas, when there was a knock on the door. Jane went to answer it, and there was a ghost from my past. It was David, the Frenchman, whose main ambition in life had been to deflower me. He had been studying watch making in Switzerland for a number of years, and we hadn't kept in contact, so he was the last person I expected to see. Jane called me, and I felt like an absolute idiot going to greet him dressed for bed. Knowing him, even the flannelette pj's would be a 'come and get it'. I was polite and asked how he'd been, what had he been up to, and made other small talk. Jane was hanging about in the background at my frantic eye signals, and then David asked if he could have a moment alone. Well I was a big girl wasn't I, and it was highly unlikely he would be assertive with someone else there, so I agreed, and Jane went to the kitchen to make tea. David pulled this box out, a long flat one, and said he'd brought me a gift.

That was nice, totally unexpected, but what girl doesn't like gifts, especially ones that looked like it could be jewellery. I opened it, and there was the most exquisite watch I had ever seen. It had what looked like diamonds and rubies around the face, and it was gold. It really took my breath away. 'I made it for you', David said. 'It's beautiful', I replied, and it really was. 'I don't think I can accept this though', I went on, 'it looks awfully expensive, and we haven't even been in contact for ages'. And, then the clanger! 'Well, I thought you could give me something I've always wanted in return', David said. I think I knew what it was he wanted, before I asked, but I actually could not believe this obsession of his. Why in god's name was it so important to him to have sex with me? I still asked though, just in case I was wrong, and then no harm done, and I could keep this lovely watch, maybe he just wanted a cup of tea, or a dinner date. 'What's that?' I asked. 'Let me make love to you', he replied in his best smarmy French accent. Oh sod this, I thought, what a bloody insult, now I'm being paid for my services. I was furious, and it was mixed with disappointment, but anger was the overriding emotion. I smiled back at him, and saw the expression of victory and lust on his face, and that infuriated me even more. I'd taken the watch out of the box, and had been holding it in my hand, and I continued to smile at him whilst I slammed the watch onto the floor, and then stomped hard on it with my heel. Shit I only had slippers on, so some of the effect was lost, but enough damage was done, as I felt it crunch under my foot. 'That's what I think of your watch', I shouted, picked up the bits off the floor, threw them at him and shouted at him to get out. He was furious to say the least. Jane had come through at the noise, and all that was left for him to do, was gather the shards, stuff them into his pocket and leave. There was nothing more to say.

Jane was in hysterics when I told her what had happened, and I managed to see the funny side of it. It was insulting though, but I have never understood his total obsession with me, I am sure there were a lot of other girls out there who would have been willing and able, and perhaps that was just it, he wasn't used to refusal. Anyway, I never saw David again, I heard he'd gone back to Switzerland, and remained there.

Our night wasn't over yet though. After all the hysterics died down, I was feeling shocking, so we decided to call it a night and go to bed. We were sleeping in my room, and my bed was right up against the wall and window which led onto the driveway. Jane was in the other bed across the room. We both woke hearing the same noise; it was the sound of people walking cautiously down the driveway. Oh shit, we were on our own in this massive house, and break-ins were becoming more frequent. It was also common knowledge that the rebels mixed with the locals, and were known to be in the suburbs. 'Jane are you awake', I whispered. 'I am, can you hear that?' she replied. 'Fuck, what are we going to do?' she continued. We didn't have much time to do anything; the footsteps were approaching my open window. I had opened it earlier, because it was so hot, not giving a thought to safety. 'Get on the floor, and crawl to the phone', I said, 'and call the police', I added. I had a loaded pistol beside my bed, and I dropped off the bed onto the floor, pistol in hand, as the footsteps and muffled voices got to the window. I didn't know how many there were of them, and whether they were around the back of the house too, had someone got in? The last thing I wanted was for them to realise that there were two young women on their own in the house. I knew the police would never get there in time.

I couldn't hear Jane on the phone, and I turned and saw her lying on the passage floor frozen with fear. There was no time; it was all happening so quickly. The whispered voices were at the window, and I saw my curtain move, then I saw a hand come through the window. Jane had her hands over her mouth to stop herself from crying out. 'Stop right there or I will shoot you'. I said, shit, I hoped it didn't sound like the pathetic terrified squeak it felt like. The hand stopped moving, and I said 'I will shoot you, if you don't move your hand, and leave, the police are on their way', I lied. Please for god's sake move your hand, my finger was starting to squeeze the trigger, and I knew once I fired, I would hit him somewhere, perhaps kill him. I was just going to fire in the general direction of the hand, and I knew I couldn't miss the rest of him. 'We are the police', came the reply, 'who are you?' Why the hell was he asking me who I was? This was my home, I lived here, and they were the intruders. 'I live here,' I said, 'what the hell are you doing here?' 'This house is supposed to be vacant at the moment, the owners notified us, they were going away, and this address is on our patrol list', was the response.

This was common practice during the war, if you went away, you paid a fee for a nightly patrol, but that should only have been tomorrow. 'Show me some identification', I asked, sounds like in the movies. A BSAP badge was shown through the window, and they asked if I would come to the door. Jane was beside herself, 'how do we know they are really the police, what if they aren't?' She said. 'Don't worry, I've still got the pistol', I replied. Talk about false bravado, my legs were shaking so much I could barely walk to the door, let alone protect us. We got to the front door clinging together, and I opened the door. There were two African policemen standing there, and Jane and I nearly wept with relief. Apparently there had been a mix up with the dates, and they thought they were due to patrol that night. When they saw an open window, they assumed someone had broken in, and came to investigate it. Well, by now, I really needed my holiday.

I flew to South Africa the following day, and met my parents in Durban. It was a week of sun, sea, sand and shopping, and I had a single, wonderful evening with my mum. We had gone to a seafood restaurant, where you could eat as many prawns as possible for a set price. We loved prawns, and at last count we had both eaten over one hundred. We had also consumed a lot of wine, and on the return to the hotel, we both giggled and behaved like school girls. It was the first and only time I saw my mum let her guard down, she was funny, relaxed and happy, and it didn't take long to understand why this had never happened before nor would it again. My dad was furious. He wouldn't even sit near us on the bus, because we were an embarrassment, and the tension at the breakfast table the following day was tangible. During that week, I made one of the biggest decisions of my life, and it was one time I wish I'd listened to my parents, and followed their advice.

Bruce obviously knew I was on holiday, and about half way through, he called me at the hotel one night. It was quite late, and I could hear he was very drunk. During the conversation, he proposed, it just came out in the middle of another sentence, and without thinking I said yes. We ended the call with 'I love you's', and at that time I thought I did. Now, I wouldn't ever have to be alone, I would have someone to love forever, and all my friends were in serious relationships, and some were married, and I wouldn't end up a lonely spinster. I was so grateful, he wanted to marry me; I thought that was all over when I lost James. I ran to my parent's room to tell them, I was excited and happy, and when I burst in with the good news, my mum looked as though she was going to drop dead with horror. 'No you will not!' she shouted. 'I absolutely forbid it'. Ok, so no congratulations there then, my dad did his normal thing, and stayed out of it, until my mum had had her rant, I think this was the time he always used, to rehearse one of his lectures, and it came. I was too young, too foolish, Bruce wasn't good enough for me, and here I went again, hurting them with my selfishness, breaking my mother's heart yet again, what had they done to deserve this, where had they gone so horribly wrong with me, and of course, I couldn't be a part of my mother because she was an angel, and I certainly wasn't part of my father, as he always considered others feelings before his own, and on, and on it went. This fuelled my rebellion, and I was more determined than ever to go ahead and get engaged. The rest of the week was really unpleasant, and I couldn't wait to get back. I did think that Bruce may not remember the proposal, or retract it, because he was so drunk when he made it.

I was anxious and excited on the flight back, but most of my time was taken up on focusing on actually getting back. A commercial flight had been shot down by the rebels, killing all passengers and crew, and the pilots had developed a strategy to hopefully prevent this happening again. The Limpopo River bordered South Africa and Rhodesia, and it was once you flew over this that it became dangerous, because the anti aircraft guns were on the Rhodesian side. We were flying at night and that made it scarier, but it was also something we joked about. Remember that live for the moment rule we all lived by, over the years and so many deaths later, we had developed a sort of immunity to fear of dying. It was something that happened every day, to anyone at anytime, mostly the young during the war, so you just never knew when it was your time, and nothing would change it if it was.

The gin and tonics flowed, and we could still smoke on airplanes at that time, so we all drank and smoked as much as we could. As we approached the Limpopo, the captain came on to advise us that all lights would be extinguished and window blinds drawn down. We would make a steep and sudden descent and then level out. On approach to the airport, the landing would be equally steep and sudden. These were all tactics to hopefully, avoid being shot down. The joke of the time, was to cross your legs, because if we went down, it was easier to screw your body out of the ground like a corkscrew. I imagined I would probably just pop out like a champagne cork. During the moments tense silence, someone inevitably cracked a joke, which got the passengers going, and then everybody laughed too loudly and too long, but it was an outlet for the intensity and potential danger of the situation. The only time it became really quiet, was when we knew we had crossed the river, and went into a steep whistling sudden dive, and we all shared the same prayer, that the plane would come out of the dive and level. When it did, there was whooping and clapping, a standing ovation for the pilots and another chance at life for us.

We landed safely, and as I cleared customs, I looked for Bruce. He was there, and I felt awkward and shy, our relationship had taken a major step forward, and I wasn't sure how to respond. I didn't mention the proposal, but Bruce did, and asked if I was sure. I said 'I am, are you?' 'Of course', he replied, tomorrow we'll go out and look for a ring. I was so excited, this is what all little girls dream of, looking for your engagement ring, wearing it, saying to the world, 'look someone loves me enough to want to marry me'. We chose the ring, and suddenly I became left handed, and with every word I spoke, my left hand developed a flamboyant life of its own, and waved and flapped around. My parents had returned on a later flight, and were staying at my aunts, my dad's sister, Aunty Pat, who I adored, and she had always made me feel special. We were due there for tea, and I had told Bruce about my parent's very strong objections to me getting married, and that they wouldn't acknowledge it or accept it in any way. So double rebellion kicked in, and we went for tea, me sporting my new ring on my finger Nothing subtle about my greeting either, as soon as I saw my aunt, I extended my left hand and said 'look', she responded appropriately with oohs and aahs and big warm hugs and kisses of congratulation. We went into the lounge where my mum and dad were, and Uncle John, I really was pushing it when I went up to my mum with my left arm extended. She glanced at my hand briefly, and then said, 'I see you have blatantly gone against our wishes'. 'Mum, please just be happy for me', I asked. She turned her back on me and walked away. Aunty Pat diffused the situation in her lovely brash way, and said that any engagement should be celebrated with champagne, and didn't she always keep some in the fridge. I know my mum and dad didn't want to lose face with Aunty Pat and Uncle John, they didn't want to be seen as the bad guys in all this, so they went along with the small celebration, albeit with fixed smiles and very little to say. Eventually however, my mum conceded to acknowledging it, but it would be kept very quiet, that is, I was not to tell another living soul, and we were to be engaged for a couple of years at least. The time frame would have been sensible, but I was too young and excited and desperate to be sensible, and as for keeping it quiet, that would be impossible. The first thing I wanted to do when we got home was go and flaunt my ring, and tell all my friends, and I did.

My mum was furious, when one of her colleagues, congratulated her on my engagement. I told you news travels fast in that town. This did serve a purpose however, because she couldn't allow it to be known how angry and unhappy she was about her only daughter getting married, so she very grudgingly accepted to make it public, and our engagement announcement was put in the local paper. I know how deliberate and manipulative we were, in bringing it into the open, I felt that, this was supposed to be one of the happiest occasions of my life, and it was being hidden which made it feel tainted, and unacceptable, and I so desperately wanted the dream. The vision of engagement parties, lots of congratulations cards, and everyone being wonderfully happy for me was not going to happen, but I was prepared and happy to accept any sort of acknowledgement. Right or wrong, it should have been different, but it wasn't, so I took what I could, from it.

18

Bruce had moved in with us, and had my granny's old room. I totally accepted that we wouldn't openly sleep together in my parent's home, and respected their rule on this. I'm sure they heard us tiptoeing through to each other some nights, but we were as quiet and discreet as we could be, and became increasingly desperate to live together. It wasn't the done thing in those days though, especially in my family.

In the very early hours of one morning, there was another mortar and rocket attack. After the first mortars landed, my mum and Bruce collided in the passage outside my bedroom door, on their respective ways to rouse us all and get to the bomb shelter. I awoke at about the time they met, and I think all three of us realised at the same time, that Bruce was stark naked, all his bits swinging about. My mum screamed and covered her eyes with her hands, and discovered she couldn't go anywhere, because she had to get past him to the bomb shelter. Bruce, looking equally horrified at his future mother in law being this up close and personal, tried to cover himself with his hands, and I could see him trying to decide what the priority was here, get to me, or go and get something on. My dad had by now come rushing out of the bedroom and collided with them too. Isn't it funny how the eyes travel to things they don't really want to see? We don't normally glance immediately at one another's crotches, but somehow if a body is part naked, we have to check whether the remainder is, and as with my mum, his eyes went immediately to Bruce's semi concealed bits. Then they all tried to pretend there was nothing abnormal about it all, and became exaggeratedly polite towards one another. In the seconds all this happened, I couldn't go anywhere, because not only were they all blocking my doorway, I was hysterical. They all looked so funny.

Bruce was the first to move, and bare assed, shot down the passage to his room, with my mum, dad and I hot on his heels as we had to pass his room to get to the outside door and into the garden to the bomb shelter. The mortars were literally raining down now, and there was the constant sound of the whistle as they passed over, and the deep boom, as they landed close by. We were all in the shelter, when my mum realised the dogs were still in the house, and with that Bruce ran to get them. Oh god I wasn't going to lose him too, so I ran with him, we got to the door and found the dogs, they were obviously terrified, and so was I. We were totally exposed, and could hear and feel hits close by, but we made it back to the shelter with them, and that must have been the most frightening few minutes of my life. It also revealed to me that I was prepared to risk my life to retain his love.

We had another miracle in Umtali that night, no fatalities. We suffered very little damage apart from lack of sleep, but I was worried about my dad. He was warden of our suburb, and had involved himself totally in the role. He took it very seriously indeed, and felt an enormous responsibility for his people. This attack had really shaken him and as he radioed around to assess damage and casualties, he was clearly unsettled and anxious. He never seemed able to relax anymore. I think this war impacted on him more than us, because he'd already fought through and survived the Second World War, and now a second one in his lifetime.

Bruce had left the police force and was working for a tyre company, and he had to travel into potentially very dangerous places, visiting the farms, and I agonised over every trip he made. I was beside myself until he arrived home safely, I was paranoid I was going to lose him, as I'd lost Eddie and James. I even went on some of the trips with him, I thought if he is ambushed or hit's a landmine, it was better that I was with him and we died together.

I was on leave from work one day, and my dad had an extremely rare appointment with the doctor. He'd been suffering from indigestion, and the night before had been particularly bad. I went to meet him when he returned home, and he didn't look well at all. He said the doctor had instructed him to come home pack a small bag and go to the hospital. When I asked what they thought was wrong, I was absolutely shocked when he replied the doctor suspected a coronary. Why was he here then, surely he should have been taken to hospital straight away by ambulance. I made him sit while I packed for him, and called my mum to tell her to meet us at the hospital. I told her dad had to go in for some tests, as I didn't want her panicking whilst she was driving. I got my dad into the car and to the hospital, and once there hung about the corridors and waiting room with my mum whilst the doctors were busy with him. We were eventually told to go home, as they had called in the heart specialist, and would contact us later, but for now he was stable and comfortable.

We went home, and later that night the call came from the heart specialist. My dad had suffered a massive coronary, and he was critical. My brother was at university in South Africa, and my mum asked whether she should bring him home. The reply was yes, not to hesitate in getting him home, the specialist emphasised my dad was critical, and for us to prepare for the worst. I was distraught and confused. Why had he been sent home when he was so unwell, and why had he declined so rapidly. I understood that he had worsened when we got to the hospital, perhaps he'd had another coronary attack there, all we did know for certain though was that he was close to death. That coping thing came into play again, and I contacted my aunt and her husband, to come over. I got in touch with Andrew at University, my mum spoke to him for a while, whilst I made tea and whatever else she needed, and then I booked his flight home for the next day. We had to travel to Salisbury to collect him from the airport, and Jeffrey, my aunts husband said he would drive there with me, because we would be struggling to remain within the curfew due to the arrival time of the plane. I made the arrangements, no tears, no drama, and just cool calm and collected, whilst my aunt and Jeffrey comforted my mum.

My mum was in a terrible state, understandably, and Bruce was on one of his trips, so Jeffrey and I set off for Salisbury to fetch. On the way to the airport, Jeffrey said I was quite something. It was the tone he used, that indicated to me he wasn't complimenting me. 'What do you mean?' I asked. 'Well to put it bluntly, you are a cold-hearted little bitch' he said. I was totally shocked and upset by his reply. 'Why, what do you mean?' I asked. 'Look at you', he said, 'not a tear, nothing, you don't care about anyone else but yourself, do you?' he continued. Oh, why should I even try and explain that inside I was torn apart with fear and pain, but my mum couldn't cope alone, and I thought this was the best way to help. To try and support her, and not weep and wail at a time, when she needed comfort most. I didn't want her to have to worry about me too at a time like this. I didn't say anything, and the rest of the journey was in silence. At least I would see my brother soon, and that was a comforting thought. He could take over, and I could lean on him. He'd be grateful and pleased that I'd taken control and sorted things out for Mum.

We saw him come through the arrivals, and as soon as he saw us, I saw the tears spring in his eyes, that was all I needed, and I started to cry too. I ran to hug him, and he stopped me, and then he sent a knife through my heart. 'This is all because of you', he said, 'you have done nothing but give mum and dad trouble, and if dad dies, as far as I'm concerned, you killed him'.

I don't know if there are words to describe how I felt. I felt as though I had been thumped hard in the stomach and chest, it was actually a physical pain. I couldn't breathe for a moment, and I felt dizzy. I was absolutely devastated, gutted, shocked, and so very hurt. I must have looked like I'd been punched, but Andrew just looked at me with absolute hatred, tears spilling down his cheeks, and Jeffrey put his arm around Andrew, took his bag, and led him to the car. I followed behind on very unsteady legs, playing what Andrew had said over and over again in my mind. Andrew sat in the front with Jeffrey and neither of them spoke to me all the way back. Andrew didn't direct any of his questions to me, they were all to Jeffrey, and I sat there quietly weeping for the three hour journey back. I didn't want to upset my mum anymore, but by the time we arrived home, I was literally hysterical inside with sadness and hurt, and after she hugged Andrew, and they wept together, I said to her 'Andrew told me Dad's coronary was caused by me, that if he dies, I'm responsible.' and I waited for her to reprimand him severely, and take me in her arms and tell me that wasn't it at all. She just looked at me, and said 'Andrew's upset, he probably didn't mean it'. That was it, no denial, no anger, nothing. I went to my room, and sobbed. I didn't go with them to the hospital that night, if that was the general consensus it would be better if I stayed away. I knew I'd be called cold and uncaring by not visiting my dad, but what the hell, that was becoming standard feedback. Bruce called and he would be back the following day, and I didn't tell him what had happened, I was worried he might come back there and then, and he would risk breaking the curfew.

My dad was critical for a couple of days, and then, started to make a very slow but steady recovery. Bruce and I went to visit him as often as we could, and I made of point of being cheerful and try to lift his spirits at each visit. I was terrified he could die, and then I would have killed him.

Bruce was disinterested, and suggested they were upset and probably just lashing out! Didn't he understand they meant it, and believed it, and when I tried to explain this to him, he told me I was being paranoid? Was I? I went over and over in my mind, was I that bad, had I been that awful that I had caused this, what had I done? I did mental re-runs of my life, trying to latch onto what had caused this. I added up my childish pranks, my teenage tantrums, everything and anything. I eventually came to the conclusion that it wasn't any particular thing or even a collection of incidents, it wasn't about action, it was about who I was, and what I was. I hoped there would come a time, when I could perhaps talk to them about how they felt, perhaps then I could understand this terrible evil part of me that they clearly perceived, and I could try and change it. I didn't know how my dad felt about it, but I was to find out soon enough.

When my dad was discharged, and came home, he was different. That was understandable. He was a doctor and knew exactly how ill he had been, and he also knew the risks of another coronary. He became paranoid about walking too far, climbing stairs, in fact exertion of any kind. He retired as a chiropractor as it required a lot of physical exertion, which put the burden of financial responsibility onto my mum, and we were all at his beck and call, especially me, I couldn't let him die.

It was a difficult time, and they needed a scapegoat more than ever before, to vent their respective anxieties and fears. I tried to talk to them, and asked them to help me understand why I was so bad, 'it's just the way you are', was the answer, and the discussion, if it could be called that, ended. Bruce didn't want to talk about it or get involved in a family dispute, and I felt this was confirmation that he felt the same way; otherwise surely he would have supported or defended me. Life changed for me, if I made more noise than I should have, or, if I came home and was louder than I should have been, spoke in the wrong tone of voice, in fact if I did anything at all that my dad found irritating, my Dad would say 'haven't you done enough damage already', or 'are you trying to kill me?', or 'you are going to be the death of me, my girl', and the most hurtful was, 'one day you will kill me, and that's what you want, then you will be happy'. I lived in fear that he would die, and the worst of it was, I still didn't even know why I was responsible, I had had my teenage moments, perhaps more drama than most, but those had been my losses and I didn't think it had impacted on my parents too much. Sure, there'd been the evenings when I'd come home too drunk, or too late, but on the whole I didn't think I deserved this cross to bear. What seemed to be of no consequence was the stress of the war, the mortar attacks, the responsibilities of being a warden, my brother being shot. What about the times my dad had told me that he became too involved with his patients, and worried about them too much, and what about the time my mum let slip, that the day of his coronary, he had been fitting an aerial to the roof, and said he'd overdone things, and thought he'd strained himself. My brother returned to university, and I still loved him, and forgave him, he'd been upset, it's never been spoken about, but after he'd left, I certainly bore the brunt of my father's fears, and the ripple effect his fear had on my mum. The lectures were more frequent, and crueller, and all I wanted now was to get out. I eventually suggested to Bruce that we rent a place of our own and move out.

When I mentioned that to my mum, she went berserk, and of course I was going to kill my father this time. Living in sin was absolutely not going to happen, not her daughter, why, what would everyone say, it was just impossible. I gave her an alternative then, I insisted, Bruce and I should get married.

I couldn't get married without their permission anyway, I was nineteen years old. She relented only after many bitter arguments, and hated me for the gauntlet I had thrown down, but this time I was determined, I couldn't continue living in a home with people who regarded me as a potential murderer. With the wisdom of hindsight, I have wondered why I didn't just leave and go and make a life of my own elsewhere, become independent and do what I wanted. I know that I wasn't capable, I was too shy, too passive and too afraid, I was nothing. Besides, I had someone who loved me.

19

Once she got used to the idea of a wedding, my mum was in her element, and although I was able to design my own wedding dress for our dressmaker, my original design changed to what my mum thought would look nice. This was probably a good thing, after the designer dress for college disaster.

The date was set, to accommodate my brother's vacation from university, the decorations were chosen by my mum, as was the chapel, the service, the hall, the food, the bridesmaid's outfits, the flowers, the car. Don't get me wrong, she always asked me what I wanted, but it always seemed somehow to end up with what she wanted. It was going to be the wedding of the year, like none seen, since hers, in Umtali. We had a few of our friends there, plus Bruce's family, but the rest of the two hundred guests were made up of my mums friends, extended family, and work colleagues. Everyone and anyone who was someone were invited. The table sittings were arranged, according to their personal status with my mum, close to the main table, they were the important guests, and those that would be tucked at the back of the hall, our friends. My going away outfit was chosen by my mum and I, and the order of speeches, toasts and everything else, was to be done precisely and formally. My mum made and iced my wedding cake, which was indeed beautiful, and she spent many hours on it. I was constantly reminded of how very lucky I was how much she was doing for me. I began to hate that cake, and everything went with it. Every time something went wrong with the icing, or decorating, I was called in. She didn't know why she was spending all this time and effort on it, after my attitude, and I would be the death of her too. Wouldn't that be the 'icing on the cake', forgive the pun, then I wouldn't have a mother or father to worry about, and then I could be happy. Shit, where did this all come from, it was never ending, and how the fuck could they tell me their death's would make me happy. I told her to leave the cake, we could get someone else to do it, but she was determined it was going to be the finest wedding cake. Her father had iced her cake, and there were a lot of guests at my wedding, that had been at hers. This wasn't about doing it for me, she was competing with her father. Even so, I was still left feeling guilty and undeserving.

I met Bruce's mum and sisters a couple of days before the wedding, and it didn't go well. We were all very different, and there didn't seem to be common ground anywhere. I had met his dad a number of times, and he was a very cold hard man. His response to Bruce when told we were going to get married was 'You need to think with your head son, not your prick'. Well, it appeared neither of our families were particularly enamoured with this relationship, and I became more determined than ever to go ahead with it.

The day was everything little girls dream of. It was the big white wedding with all the trimmings, and we enjoyed it, along with everyone else. I took my vows very seriously, and as it had been ingrained in me since my earliest memory, marriage was for life, I was fully prepared for that. 'For better, for worse', and of course 'to love, honour and obey!' I now had someone to look after me, cherish me, love me, for the rest of my life, and I really believed that was how it would be. My bubble started to burst the first day of the honeymoon. We had arranged to stay in a wonderful hotel in the country for a few days, we couldn't afford much more. When we reported to reception, I understood that Bruce had specified a particular room, and I thought that was really sweet of him. We got to the room, and he told me why it had to be this one. The last time he'd been in this room was when he was going out with one of the receptionists, and this was where they'd last had sex, in this room, on this bed, and it was the best sex of his life. To say I was upset would be an understatement, and I decided to go for a walk, and cry away from him. I didn't want him to know how gutted I felt. He followed me, and told me to stop being pathetic, he'd married me hadn't he, and wasn't I the lucky girl.

There was the good and the bad in the very early stages. The good for me was that I had left home, and had a little home of my own. We entertained our friends and partied non stop, we drank too much, and whenever Bruce was drunk, he became verbally abusive and constantly told me he'd made a mistake marrying me, he could do much better. I was too fat, I wasn't pretty enough, I was stupid, and I suffocated him. The flirting continued and intensified, to the point where I would leave parties we were at, to try and preserve some of my dignity. I drank too, and I became mushy and clingy, and then weepy after one of his verbal sessions. Most nights, after he'd satisfied himself, it was my duty as a wife after all, I would vow and declare I was leaving him, but I also knew it was all empty threats, after all this was for life, and no way would I admit my mistake to my parents. Bruce just continued where my parents had left off, they couldn't all be wrong about me could they, I was clearly rubbish in this role too, and besides no one else would have me, would they? I withdrew to my safe place, that part of me that could block feeling, block pain, and I added to my brick wall, it was survival.

The war had come to an end, and nobody really knew what the future held. We had been married for 6 months, when we decided to make new lives for ourselves and emigrate to South Africa. This wasn't going to be easy, because neither of our qualifications met the criteria for acceptance into South Africa. They had become rigid in their rules for accepting immigrants, as Rhodesians had been entering their country in their droves, and this angered the South Africans enormously. They believed we were stealing their jobs, and changing their culture, and they became quite antagonistic towards us. The only way we could do it, would be to go across on 'holiday', and stay there. Try to find work and emigrate officially from that side. We sold what we could of all our brand new furniture and wedding gifts. Our little home had been fully furnished with lovely new stuff, but we were young and positive, and looked forward to a wonderful new future.

We bought my mums car, and bought a trailer, and all we took was two of everything. If we were searched at the boarder we had to look as though we were only going on a two week camping holiday, all I took of value was my jewellery. My dad had often exchanged coins for valuable jewellery, and most of my birthday gifts were these valuable trinkets. I had precious stones, gold, jade, a veritable treasure chest. My granny had also collected jewellery for me, and this was particularly precious to me. If we really hit hard times, much as I would hate to, I could sell some of it, but it all had enormous sentimental value for me, and it was all I had of my past life that I could take. I had turned twenty a month after the wedding, and as I wouldn't be home for my twenty first, my parents had given me a ruby and diamond ring, which I wore, along with my wedding and engagement ring, and a gold cross my grandfather had left for me. I couldn't wear much more without it looking obvious, so the rest I hid under my car seat, and I don't know how we got through customs so easily. We were lying about our intentions for the trip, and I wasn't a comfortable liar, and if they'd strip searched the car they would find my jewellery. I was petrified and must have looked like a criminal, I certainly felt like one.

We made it, and we travelled to the small town of Messina for the night. I carefully tucked my jewellery box under my bed, so grateful I had it with me, a lot of memories were in that box. We celebrated our victory, and had no idea how premature that was, neither of us had any idea that night of the enormous challenges that lay ahead. Thank god we didn't, I think we might have turned and headed right back home. Better the devil you knew. Sue and George, had been married a few years earlier and were settled in South Africa, and we stayed overnight with them en route to Stellenbosch where Bruce's mum lived. That was to be our starting point, and she had agreed we could stay a while with her, until we found our feet. My brother was still at university in Cape Town a short distance away, so I had to believe I had 'family' fairly close by.

I will try and describe how it was for me then. I had left everything familiar and secure, and now was thousands of miles away from anyone and everyone I knew apart from Bruce. I was living in a home that was very unwelcoming, his family clearly thought he'd made a mistake, and the first evening, his mum reminded him of an ex girl-friend that they had obviously decided was the right person for him. Surprise surprise, the phone rang and guess who, the ex girlfriend. I sat in the lounge whilst Bruce laughed, chatted and flirted with her and his mum and sisters regaled me with stories of their happy love filled past relationship, and the good old days.

146

I was so homesick, there was a language barrier too, as Stellenbosch was predominantly Afrikaans, and they particularly didn't take kindly to Englishmen. I had done the language for 'O' level, but was ridiculously bad at it, and knew only the absolute basics. Although this was our neighbouring country, it could have been the other side of the world as it felt so completely alien in every way to my previous life. The people were different, the food was different, the language was different, and I was a refugee. It was also very racist, and I was uncomfortable with that. There were no choices about going back either, because if I did that, I wouldn't have the opportunity to leave again, and I knew Bruce wouldn't go back. He was with his family, and his mum and three sisters and they had a common attitude towards the men in their family. They were gods.

The general idea was for me to find permanent work first, because there was always a need for secretaries, and Bruce would also look for something in the meantime. We had decided to allow ourselves a couple of week's holiday, to settle in, and find accommodation of our own. We were living in one room, with all our suitcases, and were clearly in the way, so it was a priority to find somewhere else. At least we had a car, and could get about for interviews and the such like. We also started the immigration process, and travelled into Cape Town frequently to deal with the paperwork. The worst of it was though, was that you needed a work permit, and in order to get a work permit, you needed a job, and you couldn't however get a job without a work permit. Talk about an impossible situation. Anyway, we were confident that I would get an office job soon enough, but then I started to feel really very unwell. I was so nauseous in the morning, and just felt different, not good at all. I thought it had to be some sort of virus, we didn't really do the stress thing in those days, and I thought I would feel better in a little while. I didn't, I got worse. I was vomiting a lot, particularly first thing in the morning, but then it would continue through the day, I knew I had to go to a doctor. I was so scared, I thought I was dying, I'd never felt like this before, and Bruce was impatient with me, because all I wanted to do, was sleep, I was so tired all the time. I had to get sorted out and get well in a hurry, because time and money were running out, and I needed to do some serious job hunting. It was at this time, that I remembered my jewellery, we at least had that to fall back on, but where was it, I didn't remember seeing it for a while. I turned the place upside down, and nothing, and then I knew what I'd done, I had left it under the bed, in the hotel we had stayed at when we crossed the boarder. It was all gone, and aside from the financial worth, the sentimental value was priceless, and I had lost it all. Bruce was furious, I was devastated, we had no life line now at all.

We made an appointment at the local surgery, and I prepared myself for the worst. They did a blood test, and a urine test, and it took a long while for the doctor to understand my symptoms because his English was non existent, and my Afrikaans was equally bad. Bruce did a bit of interpreting and then we made a follow up appointment, and that next week waiting to find out what terminal disease I had, was awful. I felt worse, Bruce and his family became more irritable at my obvious lethargy, and the increasing time I spent with my head down their toilet. I had called my mum to tell her I didn't feel well, and said I would let her know the results of the tests. The time came for the doctor's appointment, and I was petrified, what if I was dying, in this strange country, alone, well almost alone, I suppose. We went in, and in his very bad English the doctor said he had good news for me, thank god that probably meant I wasn't dying. His next words though, shocked me, frightened me and absolutely thrilled me. 'You are going to have a baby, you're pregnant.' 'Are you sure?' Bruce asked. 'Yes' the doctor replied, and then went onto to ask me about my last period, when it was, and the supplements I had to take, and that I could continue my life as before, just do what you have always done, your body will tell you when to stop. I sat there in a wonderful daze, I was going to have a baby, my own baby to love and care for, a little body was growing inside of me. I couldn't believe how blessed I was, that I could actually grow a person, me, useless, rubbish me, and I was creating the greatest miracle of all, a new life. I wanted to burst with the absolute joy I felt from the top of my head to the tips of my toes. None of the potential difficulties this could create entered my mind in those first moments of wonder, and instinctively my hands rested on my stomach. 'Hi baby' I whispered.

'What are we going to do now?' Bruce asked as we left the surgery. You won't be able to work, or not for long anyway, this really puts us up shit street'. We would find a way, I didn't care if I had to walk miles up 'shit street' if necessary, I was having a baby. I know we hadn't planned for this to happen now, and it was probably the wrong time, but this little life was inside me, and we would just have to make a plan.

Surely his mum would be thrilled; she was going to be a grandmother. Wrong again, she was horrified. 'I'm far too young to be a grandmother', was her response, and 'I will not be called granny', she added. Right, no joy there then, his sisters were equally unenthusiastic, but there was always my mum to share my joy with. I called her, and when she answered the phone, I blurted out 'Hi mum, I'm pregnant, you're going to be a granny', she wailed back at me 'oh no, Cheryl, you're not are you?' I started to cry. I thought this was supposed to be a time of great happiness, but everyone was totally dismayed with the news. I ended the conversation abruptly, and went to the quiet of my room to be with my baby.

One night, a drunk student crashed into our car, and it was a right off, because his father was a friend of my mother in laws, the police weren't called, we therefore weren't covered by insurance, and lost our only method of transport with no compensation. I was really sick, and there was no possibility of me looking for work, I wouldn't be any good to anyone, spending most of my time in the toilet, but we had one opportunity, and that was working on a commission only basis selling exterior wall paint. We had been able to rent the small house, two doors down from Bruce's mum, and he enjoyed this. I spent most of my time alone, whilst he spent most of his time at his mum's. He found my persistent nausea irritating, and often went to eat with them so he could vary his diet, as all we really ate was packet soup, bulked up with noodles. I was always invited, but once when I did go across, they were all sitting in the small garden, and when I walked in, the laughter and conversation stopped. The way it does when an unwelcome guest arrives, and the group are uncomfortable in their presence. There were all the artificial, totally insincere greetings, and then silence, and slowly, one by one, they made an excuse to go indoors, including Bruce, and I was left sitting outside on my own. I didn't go back, and nobody encouraged me to.

We had no furniture, only loaned cushions for the floor, a borrowed wardrobe and a home made bed. Fortunately the house came with an oven, so I could cook, but we had very little money left, and for the majority of my pregnancy I lived on a mix of instant soup mixed with noodles to bulk it up. Cravings, well I certainly had them, the main one was gherkins mixed with chocolate cake, but it was very seldom that I could satisfy them. My parents came to visit, and fortunately my mum had bought me preggie clothes, because we certainly couldn't afford them. She also brought over baby clothes, and bought us a combination pram and pushchair. I couldn't buy anything for my baby, and we were given a second hand cot. During the winter evenings we had to go out selling. Bruce insisted I went with him to help him measure, and it was winter, cold windy and very wet. On many occasions, Bruce had to pull over, so that I could open the door and vomit at the side of the road, and then I'd feel embarrassed about how I smelt and looked when we met prospective clients. I remember standing heavily pregnant, holding a tape measure in the biting wind, pouring rain, freezing cold, and then going into the client's home to quote them, and not even being offered a cup of tea. Once, we were actually forcibly removed, when they asked where we were from, and we told them Rhodesia.

I went to one ante natal class, but it was all in Afrikaans and I couldn't understand a word, so I didn't bother to go back. It wasn't only the language barrier; it was how I looked, and the fact that I was a foreigner. Stellenbosch was a very tight and affluent community, and I did look dirt poor in comparison to all the young coiffed beautifully made up, designer attired other young mums. I read as many books as I could on everything and anything about pregnancy, the birth and of course a newborn baby. The wonder of this still overwhelmed me, and I wore maternity clothes long before necessary, I would curve my back and jut my stomach out, and when I did have a bump, I would often stroke it, and loved having it. The first time I felt my baby move, my heart nearly stopped with excitement, and this baby moved a lot. In fact it did the most incredible somersaults, particularly when I was in the bath. I didn't want to know what sex it was, and things weren't as sophisticated then as they are now, so there was always an element of doubt anyway. I babysat my young sister in law after school, she was nine at the time, and she was my only friend.

I turned twenty-one during this time, and my gift was a washing machine. I was excited about it, as it meant I didn't have to hand wash everything in the bath, which killed my back. The washing machine scared me for a while, as had the vacuum cleaner and any other electrical appliance. Remember, I had come from a very privileged way of life, and up until now, I had never made a bed, cleaned anything, washed a dish or article of clothing. I had never been hungry before, and I'd always worn the latest fashions, I'd never been without money before, I had never had to want for anything material. In my childish romantic fantasies I always felt I would give it all up for love and happiness, well I'd certainly given it all up, but that's where the fantasy ended, love and happiness didn't come into it. This was certainly a 'riches to rags' story. I found it difficult to adapt initially, but it didn't take long for me to understand that, however strange and different this felt, it was possibly one of the most valuable lessons I would learn in life. It was a time for me to learn basic skills, to adjust to a completely different way of life, and to know that I could do it. To lose the privileged lifestyle took me into the real world, and I surprised myself that I entered this new phase with anxiety, but I was determined to adjust, after all I was soon to become a mother. There was no great party or celebration, and we didn't have any money to go out on my twenty -first, but I was allowed to buy a chocolate cake.

My mother in law continued to try and deny the fact that she was going to be a granny, so I wasn't able to talk to her about how it felt when you gave birth, what was it like and so on, and my mum was hundreds of miles away. They were in the process of immigrating to South Africa, and were hoping to get there before the birth. Fortunately, my mum was now showing a lot of enthusiasm for the impending birth.

Our paperwork was progressing rapidly, and hopefully we would be living here legally soon. We were expecting our permanent residence permit any day now, and it would be an enormous relief, but there was a shocking delay, which we were subsequently informed of. I say shocking, because I was horrified at the implied racism this involved. We were told we would not be issued our permanent residence until the baby had been born, and the colour of the child identified. Even though we were both white, the immigration laws necessitated that the child was white too, or we would be deported. I couldn't believe that if we had a mixed race child or non white child, they would kick us out.

20

We had to invest in another car, as public transport is virtually non existent. Bruce had also been offered a job as a security guard at the local sawmill, and the bonus was that we lived on site. We saw it as a bonus initially, but it turned out to be hell on earth. We were moved in just before the baby was due, and as we didn't have much of anything to move, it wasn't any trouble. We had bits and pieces of second and third hand furniture, and could make do. Unfortunately, because we were on the grounds of the sawmill, I couldn't open the windows because of the ash and dust, and it was like living in an oven. My baby was due the first week of February, and that is one of the hottest months in South Africa, and as it drew closer, I couldn't wait for the birth.

I was in my ninth month of pregnancy, and I know you're not supposed to have cravings at that stage, maybe it was because I'd been denied so many of them, I still had this thing for chocolate cake. There was a shop which sold home baked cake, and the very rare times I was able to have a piece we got it from there, it was heaven. We were wandering past the shop, and I thought I could have a treat, so we went in. I went to choose a slice, but Bruce said no, we couldn't afford it. We couldn't afford one slice of chocolate cake. I got angry and insisted we could, and he stormed out of the shop. Everyone had turned to stare at us, so I followed feeling embarrassed. Bruce was storming ahead, and I was trying to catch up, the pavements are cobbled and uneven, and before I could help myself, I tripped and landed directly on my stomach. I cried out as I fell, and Bruce turned and looked at me lying on the floor, and then continued to walk away. Oh god it hurt, and my first thought was my baby, had I damaged my baby. A passer by helped me up, and it was only then, that Bruce with a look of impatience on his face came back to help me to the car. I insisted we go straight to the doctor, and I was enormously relieved when he assured me all was well. Bruce sat there, the picture of concern and care, and when we left, I didn't really pay much attention to the lecture that ensued. Part of it was that I had behaved like a child having a temper tantrum, and I'd got what I deserved.

My due date came and went, and there was no indication at all of labour. Everything was ready, the baby's head was engaged, it was now just a matter of waiting. I was scared, as I didn't know what to expect, but I had read enough about the birth to know that this was going to be the most special moment of my life. I had daydreamt for months about seeing my baby born, and holding it to my breast. I wanted it to be as natural as possible, because holding that tiny precious new life once it emerged from my body was a moment I lived for. Bruce had taken the pregnancy in his stride. He didn't show much emotion one way or the other really, and I wondered how he would feel once he met his child.

I was two weeks overdue, and the doctor organised a scan to confirm my dates, and whether I would have to be induced. I did have to be induced as it turned out and I went to the hospital the night before. It was a very old hospital, and very basic and I was in a large ward with seven other woman, all of whom had had their babies, and nobody spoke English. They had their babies beside them, and the night was constantly interrupted with their small cries. I was going to have mine next to me the following night. I was very lonely and anxious that night, but I also knew that tomorrow was going to be the day; I met my baby, and hold it in my arms. I was going to be a mum! My parents hadn't been able to make it in time, and were expecting to arrive within the next few days, but my brother and his girlfriend were coming through in the morning, so they could celebrate with us after the birth. Bruce was going to be with me throughout, and he arrived very early the next morning. I didn't know what to expect, but very early I was brought two small pills, and told to let them dissolve under my tongue. Nothing happened. I was given two more, and then another two. Bruce arrived and I went through to the waiting room with him so that I could walk about.

I felt something strange happening and said I needed to get back to the ward, and on the way go to the loo. My waters broke in the toilet, and virtually immediately the pain swept through my stomach and lower back. It took my breath away. It was about eight o'clock in the morning. I got back to my bed, and thought I was going to die. The pain came in waves, or contractions, and from the first one, there was virtually no time in between them. I had never experienced such absolute mind numbing pain before, and I struggled to keep from crying out with it. I couldn't do that, all the other women were in the ward, and I felt sure they'd been brave. A nurse came, and checked the baby's heartbeat, no sophisticated instruments, just one of those tubular things with a wide circle at one end. She left with a frown, and unbeknown to me at the time, she had gone to call my doctor. The pain just kept coming, I could barely catch my breath between them, and I didn't know what to do with myself. It racked through my body, my back, my front, oh god please take it away. I asked for some pain relief, and was told I couldn't have any because of the induction. The doctor came and listened as the nurse had done, he didn't look particularly concerned until he checked me for dilation. I wasn't dilating. He said not to worry as it was a first birth, and to give it a couple more hours. Dear god, a couple more hours in this agony, how would I survive it? The seconds I had between contractions, I braced myself for the next onslaught, and I didn't want anyone to touch me. It felt as though molten liquid was coursing through me, whilst my belly and back was locked in a vice of agony. At one point Bruce tried to massage my back, and instinctively I lashed out at him. Don't touch me, I tried to shout, but all I could do was grunt. The same nurse returned and checked the baby's heart beat again. This time she was definitely frowning, and then my doctor appeared again. He checked for dilation, and then he put both his hands inside me, palms facing outward, and literally tried to pull me apart. I didn't feel a thing; there was just too much pain everywhere else.

I don't know how much time had passed, before the nurse came a third time, and this time she ran out of the ward. There was my doctor again, he listened this time, and then all hell broke loose. I was pushed across to the other side of the ward, and because I'd had the curtains drawn around my bed up until then, it was the first time, I saw the other woman, and they all looked very frightened for me. Something was going horribly wrong, and mixed with this all consuming agony, a horrible fear kicked in. Oh god something was happening to my baby. My bed was surrounded with nurses, one was putting a drip up, one was shaving me, and another was putting an oxygen mask over my mouth. Bruce came and told me that the baby's heartbeat was causing concern, and I hadn't dilated enough, they were going to perform an emergency caesarean. Noooo, I tried to shout, but it just came out as a moan. Oh no, I wanted to see my baby born, this was the moment I had dreamt of and waited for, please no. I was being rushed down passages, there were nurses running alongside the trolley, Bruce was running with the drip stand, and as we passed the waiting room, I saw my brother.

I was pushed into the theatre and transferred to the table. Oh dear God, the pain wouldn't stop, but there was a new very strong feeling inside. I wanted to push, everything in me was urging me to bear down and push. The nurse who had kept checking the baby's heartbeat was with me whilst everyone else appeared to be rushing around in the theatre. I told her I desperately needed to push, and then she told me the truth. My baby was in distress, it wasn't getting enough oxygen, and they believed the cord was around its neck. If I pushed I could kill my baby, and suffer a fatal haemorrhage myself. Oh sweet Jesus, don't let my baby die. Why weren't they putting me out, just give me the anaesthetic, I couldn't manage to hold off pushing much longer. 'Why aren't you operating yet?' I managed to ask. There was a big round white clock on the wall directly in front of me, and if this was such an emergency, why had I been lying on that table for twenty minutes. Her reply terrified me, 'the instruments for the operation are being sterilised, we weren't prepared for this emergency', she said. I didn't think about dying, I couldn't, I had to keep my baby alive. I saw my doctor leave the theatre, he was gone for a few minutes, and then came back in, and looked at me with immense sadness in his eyes. Why? Then all there was, was blissful nothing.

Someone was calling my name, it was Bruce. I was alive but what about my baby. 'My baby?' I asked. 'It's a girl and she's fine', he replied. The tears flowed, 'I want to see her, I want to hold her now'. I wasn't allowed to, she was in an incubator, and they were going to keep her there overnight, and I wasn't allowed out of bed. I couldn't even see my daughter. Bruce had held her and seen her, my brother had seen her in her little incubator, and I couldn't see her until the following morning. Bruce left to go and 'wet the baby's head', and promised he'd be back later. I didn't care really, all I wanted was my baby girl. Fortunately what was left of the anaesthetic and pain killers knocked me out again, and I was woken by a very drunk husband. He had brought me some cheap earrings to celebrate the birth, and he decided to cut the umbilical cord in his own way. When I had seen the doctor leave the surgery, he had gone to speak to Bruce. The situation with the baby and I was critical, and he told Bruce they might have to make a choice between whose life to save, mine or the baby's. He was very sorry that he had to ask Bruce, but if that time came, it would have to be an instant decision, and therefore he needed to know from Bruce which it was to be. Bruce told him to save the baby's life, not mine. He told me that at least I'd had a life, and he felt that the baby deserved a chance at one.

How did I feel? I knew that I would have gladly died trying to save my baby's life, but that was my choice, I had borne this child, and only I could bring it into this world, if it meant me dying in the process, that was my sacrifice. My husband had chosen to sacrifice the mother of his child in an instant, before that child was born, and his motive was that because at twenty one I'd had a life. He hadn't been that involved in the pregnancy, he'd never spoken about how wonderful it would be to be a father, and the only time he'd felt his child inside of me, were the times, I insisted he feel her kicking or moving about. He'd never shown me any consideration whilst I was carrying, so where had this sudden enormous bond for an unborn child come from. He didn't even consider a future with me.

How did this make me feel about my baby daughter, she was innocent to all this, but it made me feel excluded from their lives. It was as though, Bruce had laid claim to her, he'd ensured her survival at the possible expense of mine, and that made me feel as though my life was truly unimportant, and useless. I had been lucky enough to survive, but clearly, it wouldn't have mattered much if I hadn't. I got out of bed that night, against instructions, and I leant on my drip stand as I shuffled to the nursery. She was pointed out to me. She was so tiny, and so beautiful. I literally did physically ache to hold her, and my breasts hurt, but that was as far as they would let me go.

We named her Emma, after my mum, and I held Emma the next morning, but as soon as she was put in my arms, she cried, and when I tried to put her to my breast, she wouldn't suck. It was as though she was confirming I was useless even as a mother. My own baby was rejecting me too.

The ward was empty now, and Emma was kept in the nursery. I went to the toilet during the morning, and when I came back to the ward, the doors were closed. They were open when I'd gone out. I pushed the door open, and there were my parents and Bruce. Oh I needed my mum, and they seemed happy to see me. I clung to them both, I just desperately needed some sort of confirmation that they were happy I'd survived. A nurse came in carrying Emma, and I warned my mum she would probably cry. My mum took her in her arms, and she looked down at my baby girl with such absolute love it took my breath away. My dad joined them, but it was my mum I couldn't take my eyes off. She looked as though she was holding a priceless treasure in her arms, and so she was, but this was my treasure. Emma lay contentedly in her arms, and I think it was at that moment, I knew I'd lost my child to my mother.

I was allowed home after ten days, and couldn't wait to start my life with my baby. I was anxious, as she cried a lot, and apparently she had colic, but I didn't have a clue what that was but found out soon enough. She didn't take the breast easily, so I had to combine her feeds with the bottle, but I wanted to persist. She was so tiny too, and I had that first time mum thing, that she might break. My mum and dad were living with us, until they could find a place of their own, and my mum offered to have Emma with them alternate nights, to help me out. I was grateful for the help because I still felt very tired, and was still recovering from the surgery. I loved and hated that wound with a passion. I loved it, because my baby had survived because of it, and hated it, because it had denied me the opportunity to give birth naturally.

Life changed radically, sleep was a thing of the past, and the days were filled with Emma's screams. She didn't feed easily because of the colic, and there were days, when the four hours between feeds just blended together. It was baking hot, and I couldn't open the windows, or take her outside, because of the soot and dust, and there was no such luxury as disposable nappies. We had the cloth ones, which I couldn't hang out to dry, but had to dry them over a heater inside. It felt like we were living in an oven.

The worst of it was that I had to share my baby, and she seemed to prefer my mum's and her dad's company. She always relaxed and calmed down when either of them held her, with me, her little body became stiff and rigid, and she howled. My mum gave Emma her first bath, because we only had a large tub, which we put on the bed, and I couldn't bend easily for any length of time. I did try, but I couldn't stay in that position for as long as it took to bath her. I tried sitting on the bed, but that unbalanced the tub, so I just had to bide my time, until I healed more. So, bath times were my mothers, with me watching. One morning, after a particularly bad night, I was woken with my mum storming into our room, Bruce had gone to work, and she was shouting 'what kind of mother are you', that poor little thing has been crying for ages now. She took Emma out of her pram beside my bed, and marched out with her. I hadn't heard her, I was exhausted. I was a bad mother too; I didn't even wake to my baby's cries. My confidence as a parent was non existent, I couldn't feed her, I couldn't bathe her, and I left her to cry. My mum took over more and more, and the harder I fought it, the more insistent she was, that Emma relaxed with her more, and didn't I want what was best for Emma. Of course I did, so I withdrew.

There came the time that they found their own place, and I really thought this was my chance to re-establish my relationship with my child. She screamed and screamed, and nothing I did helped her, her nappy was dry, she wasn't hot or cold, or hungry, and I didn't know what to do for her. I was rubbish, I couldn't even stop my child crying, I so badly wanted to be able to do this on my own, and I couldn't. I remember picking her up, one day, and I wanted to shake her, to stop her crying, I didn't shake her, I put her down gently on the bed, and did the last thing on earth I wanted to do, I called my mother. She was there in an instant, and of course, true to form, as soon as she picked Emma up, she relaxed, and her screams quieted to a normal cry.

Life moved around the unbearable heat, feeding, winding, rocking, holding and still the constant screaming. We tried everything on the market for her colic, but there were no quick fixes forthcoming. The long days, with just me and Emma, my mum was working now, the long walks to try and help her to sleep, the nights filled with waking and feeding, and burping, and the miles and miles I walked, back and forth with my baby at my shoulder, trying to ease her discomfort. There were the evenings when Bruce came home from work, and Emma was still screaming, 'what kind of mother are you?' became the mantra. There were no health visitors, just visits to the clinic, and all they would say, was that she was gaining weight well, she was a healthy baby, she just had colic. 'Just colic', was causing my child persistent discomfort, but I was assured it would end after about six weeks, and this was my hope and salvation.

The weeks became months, and the colic continued, I didn't know it then, but there were many more months of it to come, she eventually outgrew it at ten months. To this day, I can distinguish a colic cry from any other, and my body tenses. My poor little baby screamed for eighteen hours a day for nearly a year. During this time I didn't have any other young mums to discuss all those things that young mums talk about. I didn't have anyone other than Bruce and my mother to refer to, or share anything with, and I desperately fought against needing them so much. I so badly wanted to be able to cope. It was the most important thing in the world for me to prove I was a good mother, and I prayed for my baby to stop crying, especially when I held her. She didn't though, she couldn't, and the harder I tried to convince everyone that I was doing my best, the more it appeared that I couldn't even comfort my own baby. I lost a lot of weight; I was the thinnest I had ever been. I used to admire my ribs and jutting hip bones in the mirror. Surely Bruce would love me more now that I was thin. Sadly, although I didn't recognise it, I looked gaunt, and far older than my twenty one years. I had huge black bags under my eyes, my skin was bad, because of the poor diet, we spent most of our grocery money on the right food for Emma, and of course there were all the 'miracle cures' for colic which we tried. On pay day, my one luxury was a bag of disposable nappies, and I loved the day or so, that I could just take the nappy off and bin it.

Bruce had been offered a job in Port Elizabeth, via a contact my aunts husband had. This was a long way from Stellenbosch, and although I had never felt at home here, it had become familiar, and gave me some sense of security, but he was determined this new job had better prospects. He had been offered it via a contact of my aunts husband Jeffrey. They had been living there for some time now, so it was time to pack up and move on. My mum was devastated; I was taking her baby away from her.

Emma was six months old when we left, I wasn't sad to be saying goodbye to his family, I still hardly knew them, and I really didn't feel there was anything to miss there. We started our new life in a flat on the beachfront in Port Elizabeth. Different surroundings, but nothing else changed. Bruce went to work, I sat in our tiny flat, took Emma for walks, and there was still the colic and the screaming. The only people I had to talk to were my mum on the phone occasionally, and I was able to visit my aunt. She wasn't particularly partial to visits constantly interrupted by a crying baby though, so they were few and far between. I had no transport of my own, and as I mentioned earlier, public transport is virtually non existent in Africa. When Bruce came home, the arguments started because 'I was no fun to be with', as he said, all I did was moan, so the evenings were spent arguing or not talking at all. The latter I found worst, because I craved company, and I would go along with whatever Bruce said, apologise if necessary, just to have someone to talk to.

My parents relocated to Port Elizabeth to be close to us, I know the truth of it was to be close to Emma, but I was grateful for small mercies. I had some comfort in having them there. I had taken Emma to a top Paediatric specialist in Cape Town prior to leaving in a desperate attempt to help her colic, and confirm that was what it was. I remember after all the tests, when he spoke to me, he said there was nothing physically wrong with her, it was only colic, and she would have to out grow it, and he was sorry but there was absolutely nothing he could for her. Then he asked me 'what can I do for you, you must be at the end of the line', The tears flowed, that was the first time anyone had even acknowledged how desperate I was in total, but there was nothing he could do for me, what could I say to him. Please write a prescription for another chance at this life, I have cocked up so monumentally, that the only good thing in it for me is my baby, and even she doesn't love me.

21

Bruce lost his job. He told me he'd been made redundant, but this didn't make sense. We'd relocated for this job only a few months back, surely the company wouldn't take on new employees if it was in financial difficulties. He refused to discuss it further, and decided on a completely new career. Whilst we were still in Stellenbosch, Bruce had taken an aptitude test in computer programming, which he had received top marks for. He hadn't pursued it then as he wanted to come to Port Elizabeth and accept the job offer here. After enquiries we discovered that he could do a six week intensive course, and qualify as a computer programmer. Computers were definitely the way forward, so this seemed sensible. My parents funded the course, and covered all my living costs for that period of time, on the promise that when Bruce started work again, the money would be paid back. I was now on my own twenty four hours a day for six weeks. Emma became even more fractious, and I knew she understood her father wasn't there, and I spent those weeks in a haze of feeding her, changing her, walking her, and eventually just crying with her.

Absence does make the heart grow fonder, and the phone calls and letters Bruce and I shared during this time, were filled with affection. I actually thought our relationship was much better when kept at a distance, because no sooner had he come home, than it went back to normal. He eventually found a job, and we looked forward to new beginnings.

A few weeks later, his new company were holding a corporate bar-beque one Sunday, and it certainly became a day to remember. My parents were baby sitting Emma, and it was the first time I was out socialising since she'd been born. I was looking forward to it with some trepidation however, because I had lost touch completely with the outside world. I had become very shy, and withdrawn, and my self confidence was at zero, gone was the popular brash teenager; I'd for-gotten how to socialise. I agonised over what to wear, I hadn't bought clothes in years, and eventually decided on jeans and t-shirt, always a reliable combination, but I was very anxious, and did consider find-ing a reason not to go. I tried to explain how I felt to Bruce, and he told me to stop being pathetic. How did I think I was going to make friends or meet people when I shut myself away like a hermit? He was right in that respect; it might be an opportunity to make new friends.

I enjoyed being out, and the company of other adults. I hung back a lot whilst Bruce was the life and soul as normal, but just having a few glasses of wine, and being out in the sunshine was good enough. Bruce was drinking heavily, and I offered to drive home. It was quite a long drive on the motorway, but he got angry and refused. I decided to keep the conversation light, if I talked at all because I recognised his mood, and it was ugly, exacerbated by the alcohol. A short while into the trip home, he suddenly said 'I love Emma much more than I love you, and I love her more than you do'. I was stunned, at the total unexpectedness of the remark, and the content. I didn't think to keep my cool, I was livid, how dare he suggest he loved my child more than I did. 'How can you possibly say you love Emma more than I do', I shouted, 'you have no idea how much I love her', I continued. I couldn't believe the insanity of this conversation anyway, what in gods name had prompted it. 'You make me sick,' he yelled. 'You're an embarrassment to me; you couldn't even join in today. Hanging about me, hardly speaking, you are totally pathetic, and I'm sick of you', he ranted. 'You're own child doesn't love you, and neither do your parents', he said, 'neither do I for that matter. You can't even be a good mother, all Emma does is cry, and you know why?' he screamed. 'Because we all hate you, you're fucked up and a useless piece of shit' he concluded. We were on the motorway, and it is isolated out there, apart from the traffic. It was also dusk. Bruce brought the car to a sudden screeching halt on the hard shoulder. He got out and came around to my side, opened the door, and said 'get out'. 'What do you mean get out, we're miles from home and its getting dark', I replied. I was scared now, very scared. He dragged me out of the car, locked the passenger door, and went and got back into the drivers seat. I was terrified, but I thought he's only trying to scare me, he'll drive a short way down the road and make me beg to get back in. I was reeling from the unexpectedness and viciousness of his verbal attack, but I would beg if I had to, I didn't want to be left in the middle of nowhere at this time of day, nor any other time to be honest. Bruce drove away, and kept driving, I started to cry now, I couldn't believe it, he drove out of sight. I started to run down the hard shoulder, and then a white surfing van pulled up alongside me. I was petrified. Rape and murder were frequent and regular occurrences, especially a white woman. Dear God, this was it then, I was going to die, and what would happen to my baby? A white man got out of the van, and said 'come on, get in we saw what happened, and we'll give you a lift home'. It was quite reasonable they had seen the incident, because the motorways are long strips of road, which go in a straight line, with nothing but scrub either side, for as far as the eye can see.

He could see I didn't know what the hell to do. Take my chances that Bruce would come back, or get into a van with strangers. 'It's ok,' he said and opened the sliding door of the van, to show me there were others in the back including two women. Oh shit, I thought, it's probably safer than assuming Bruce would come back, it was getting dark anyway. I climbed in the back, and the van took off and gathered speed quickly. They were really going very fast, and before I could say anything, the chap who had offered me the lift, said 'we are just trying to catch up with the other car, who is the driver?' 'My husband', I replied, and I caught the shocked expressions on all their faces. I saw his car ahead, and we quickly caught up with him, and travelled behind him. I was sick with anger, fear and hurt. He was driving home, he had no intention of coming back for me, and he had no idea I was in the vehicle behind him. He had actually intended to leave me out there. They followed him to our block of flats, and when he started to enter the underground garage, they hooted. He stopped and got out, and both the driver and the other man, were out in a flash and had him flat on the boot of his car. They were holding him down, and the driver shouted at him. 'You bastard', he yelled in Bruce's face. 'How the fuck do you leave your wife like that, knowing it's likely to get her killed. What kind of man are you?' he went on. 'He's no man', said the other one, 'he's a fucking bully'. Bruce was quiet, and looked frightened, he didn't say anything, just stood there cowering.

They didn't hit him, just made it very clear, he was an absolute bastard, and then came the good bit. The driver then told Bruce they were off duty detectives, and they had noted his registration. They would highlight it to the police and retain it themselves, and if there was even a minor offence involving his vehicle they would turn it into a major one. I thanked them profusely for my safe journey home, and they told me to take care and then left. My angels had been with me that day.

Needless to say, when we got into the flat, Bruce was furious, and so was I, and it was the first and last time I ever slapped him. I hit him across his face, and he didn't hesitate in hitting me back. When my parents arrived with Emma, I was in tears, and of course my parents wanted to know what was going on. I didn't want to incur his wrath any further so I said 'We've had an argument', and Bruce added, 'why don't you tell them you hit me', but he didn't bother to go into any detail as to why. 'I hit Bruce, and then he hit me back', I said, and I didn't go into the rest of it. 'Well you hit him first my girl, what did you expect' my mother said. I just got up and went to the bedroom, and I heard my mother asking my dad and Bruce, 'what is wrong with that girl, what did I say wrong now?'

22

I remember Emma's first steps, every mother does. We were visiting my parents, and she pulled herself up onto the coffee table, and stood holding on, her little head turned, to look at my mum and I sitting on the sofa. 'Come to mummy', I said, 'come sweetheart', I held my arms out to her, and she turned and stood on her own. I knelt on the carpet, arms outstretched, 'come and give mummy a cuddle', I crooned, maybe this was it, and maybe those little feet would take those few steps. She did, she took a step, wobbled a little, and took another, and she started to walk towards me, and then my mum was there, next to me. 'Come on darling,' she said, and she was closer to Emma now, and Emma took another couple of steps into my mothers arms.

Bruce lost his job, but soon found another one, in sales. He was struggling to break into the computer world, and took this in between. That is how he met Dan, and I made my first friend, Dan's wife Pat. Bruce was out now all hours of the day and night, 'selling', and he and Dan thought it was a good idea that their wives met. Bruce was frustrated that I never got out and met people. All I did was stay in the flat. How he thought I was going to get anywhere, when he had the car, and where I was supposed to go, to meet these people I didn't know. Pat had two little ones, and it was lovely to have company for Emma, we got on well from the first, and as she had her own car, she would fetch Emma and I to go shopping, picnicking, swimming, all lovely outings and it was wonderful to have company and friendship. I understood she was having a hard time with Dan, he was out most nights, and came back very drunk. She also believed, he was with other women, and I felt sorry for her and counted my blessings. Bruce drank and was out a lot, but I was certain he hadn't been with other women.

In the meantime, we had found a small maisonette to rent, and we would have our own tiny little front garden. I was thrilled. There were ten in the block, five either side, face on to each other with a path down the centre of the two blocks. I loved it. There were lots of young couples living there, and other children, at last I would have the opportunity to meet more people.

Pat and I lived in each others pockets, and she taught me patchwork, and sewing. We decided to make enough to go and sell at the local park, where they had stalls for home industry, and I started to feel life was taking a turn for the better. I didn't feel so isolated anymore, and I had a sense of purpose. We didn't make much money from our work, but the days we spent on the stall, were great fun. The kids came and spent the day at the park with us, and Emma was thriving being in the company of other little ones. We all went out for days at the beach, with our husbands, and it became routine for Dan and Bruce to get absolutely paralytic, and Pat and I would drive them home. The early part of those days out, they would both play at being father of the year, for about an hour, and then the beer became the priority. I noticed that Dan belittled Pat very similarly to the way Bruce was with me, and she also, tried to hide her tears. She was as proficient as I was in diffusing the situation, when they became aggressive, and abusive, and would behave just like I did. Placating, sweet talking, and agreeable to whatever insult was passed, for the sake of the kids. Sometimes this didn't work either, and our placid acceptance of their abuse, annoyed them. They would get more vicious with every remark to try and provoke a reaction, and some of the things they called us were totally vile.

Bruce and Dan fed off each other, it was as though they competed in who could be the most abusive, and then they'd laugh and congratulate each other when they finally got the reaction they wanted. This could be tears, or taking a walk with the children down the beach. We very seldom reacted strongly, because this would only lead to a lot of shouting and swearing, and attract the attention of other people, and of course the children. The weekends were all about what they wanted to do, and it was mainly go to the beach, in all kinds of weather, and barbeque, which they never ate, because by the time it was cooked they were too drunk to eat anyway. Often, if it was windy, it was impossible to keep the sand out of the food, and the children were unhappy, and miserable, because they couldn't do much, other than sit close by for protection from the stinging sand. This meant nothing to Bruce and Dan, they were having a rave, and sod the rest. It was 'put up or shut up'.

Pat and I talked about our lives, and there were many similarities. I don't believe that either of us recognised that we were abused, but in retrospect, our behaviour patterns, were almost identical. They would change, this was a phase, it would be different one day, wouldn't it. We both held onto this ridiculous ideal. I clung to the 'morning after', apologies, and knew after a particularly bad session, Bruce would be remorseful for a day or so, depending on the severity, the extent of my emotional response, and what if anything, he could remember. There were so many times that I had to tell him what he had said or done when he was drunk, and I'm not sure that he didn't always remember, or that he hoped I didn't, and took his chances as to what I did recall. Sadly, for me, it was very seldom, that I didn't remember, every insult, every derogatory remark, every time I watched him come onto another woman. On the occasions that he actually felt he'd overstepped the mark with his behaviour, he would be nice the next day, and he could be very nice, when he chose to be. He would blame it all on the drink, and of course didn't I know he loved me, why did I take everything so much to heart, I needed to grow up, why was I so insecure, and why couldn't I even take a joke, why did I take everything so seriously. I would end up feeling stupid and over sensitive. Sometimes when he was more of a bastard than normal, I would let it be, knowing there would be one day at least, that would be reasonably pleasant, because the worse he was, the better the next day often was. I traded his maliciousness, and abuse for a day of peace.

During the many conversations Pat and I had, I learnt her life mirrored mine, this somehow made it more reasonable to assume, that our marriages were obviously more the norm than not. Thank God we had each other during that time. Bruce was out all the time now, and he frequently came home in the early hours of the morning. He drank constantly and heavily, and he often said he had to go out and drink, because I wouldn't be his drinking partner at home, and the company out there was a hell of lot more interesting, attractive and fun to be with. Why should he be expected to stay home with someone like me? I had nothing to offer anyway, all I had to talk about was kid stuff, and that was soooo boring. Another frequent favourite was that he worked hard all day to put food on the table and clothe us, and I sat at home all day in the lap of luxury, I was a spoilt and ungrateful bitch. There was that ever so familiar theme again, so I believed that my parents and Bruce couldn't be wrong about me, it had to be me, I was a total waste of space to anyone, and I was lucky he didn't just get rid of me.

Bruce eventually got a job in the computer field, and I hoped because he wasn't constantly in Dan's company, things might calm down a little. They did, and he seemed to settle down for a while, and then I had that familiar nausea. I was pregnant, and I was ecstatic. I hadn't wanted an only child, I'd wanted another baby, and sibling for Emma. I didn't expect much more than what life offered me at the moment, and whilst I wasn't particularly happy and content, it was familiar, and I didn't have any more dreams and fantasies of that little cottage, white picket fence, and a loving and secure marriage. Even though the term 'soul mate' wasn't bandied about as it is now, I still believed however, that there was a part of me that just one other person on this earth could connect with. When I imagined being with this someone, it was all my childish dreams in one, and I used this fantasy to sustain me. At the same time, it was clear to me that Bruce wasn't this person, and I was with him for the rest of my life, this meant that even if there was someone out there, as my gut, and soul indicated, it wasn't likely I could be with him, and where or when would I meet him, if ever. Hard as I tried to ignore it, the minuscule part of me, that persisted, that my soul mate walked this earth, lay dormant for many years, but never disappeared. I just accepted what I had, I'd made my bed, I had to lie on it. I also had the sad misconception that another baby might make things better for us. To be honest, I hoped this baby could be mine, I was going to be stronger this time, I was going to fight for this baby, I knew more about the enemy and their tactics now, and I knew how to fight back.

I went to Bruce's work to tell him the good news, and he appeared excited, I think that was for the benefit of his colleagues though. That night he didn't come home after work, and it was the early hours of the morning when I heard him come in. I met him in the kitchen and he was very drunk. 'Where have you been', I asked. 'out', he replied, 'nothing to do with you anyway', he went on. 'I thought you would be happy about the baby', I said. 'What's to be happy about, I don't really care one way or the other', he replied. 'God help me', I said, and he responded, 'Well he's about all who is going to help you, because I'm not'. I went up to bed, and strangely, I wasn't upset, I would make sure I was always there for my babies. 'Don't worry', I whispered to the tiny life inside me, 'mummy's here'. Pat and I saw each other less often now though, she was focusing most of her time and attention on trying to save or at least salvage her marriage, and was at Dan's constant beck and call.

We had met some of our neighbours, amongst them a young couple called Harry and Laura, and they had two children Ben and Kirsty. Kirsty was a year older than Emma, and Laura and I became the very best of friends. They lived two doors down from us, and we must have worn a path between the two homes. We did everything together from early morning to feeding and bathing all the kids together in the evening. Harry had been physically abusive to Laura in the past, but he was now a re-born Christian, and apparently he had turned his life around. He was now a loving, considerate husband, and a wonderful father, and I wondered what that must be like.

I talked often to Emma about the baby growing in mummy's tummy, and told her that one day soon she would have a little baby brother or sister. She was a happy child, she was enveloped in love. Her grandparents adored her, her father gave her his own obsessive sporadic love, and then there was me, always competing for her love. I don't think we give enough credit to how clever children are, and how perceptive. She sensed this competitiveness and used it to her advantage, what child wouldn't, no matter how young. She learnt very early on that if mummy wouldn't allow her to have something, daddy would, or granny. This slowly undermined the basic disciplines I tried to teach her, but I wasn't prepared to give up because I didn't want her to grow up believing that life was that simple. Sometimes she had to accept 'no', or that certain things could seriously harm her, like going out of the garden gate on her own, matches, sharp objects, hot tea. This initiated more abuse from Bruce and my parents. I was told, I was hard on my child, to leave her alone, to stop nagging, stop always saying no.

I believe 'no' is the most common word we use with very young children, I know today there are different techniques and attitudes, but back then it was how we taught them of the risks and dangers. This sadly caused enormous conflict, and Emma was also taught that mommy was always the one that didn't always allow her the sweeties she wanted, or that she couldn't always do what she wanted, and it was always mommy that made her eat those nasty vegetables, or there was no pudding. Daddy and granny weren't like that. Bruce left that part of it to me, he didn't like being seen as anything other than father of the year, and although he disciplined her, it was normally out of impatience during the rare times he was alone with her, and she irritated him.

Bruce became friendlier with Harry, and one evening nearly killed me with shock when he said he was going to a prayer meeting with him. What, I couldn't believe it, this man, who never spoke about religion, believed himself to be an atheist, was going to a prayer meeting. Miracles do happen. I'm not sure what prompted this, perhaps he was at a time in his life, where he was searching for something, and he found it in the church. The metamorphous happened overnight, it was radical and extreme, and our lives changed enormously, for better and for worse. Bruce became fanatical, he now went to prayer groups instead of pubs, which was absolutely wonderful, he gave up drinking and smoking overnight, and he read the bible as if his life depended on it. I think it did sometimes. The downside was I was expected to follow suit.

I had, and have my own spiritual beliefs and they didn't conform to any of the formal religions, but I retained my own philosophy. I do believe, that there is a supreme being, I believe in angels, and I believe we live after death, I believe Jesus, as a healer did walk this earth, and I have read and studied the bible, and I had no objection whatsoever in attending church. It wasn't that which I found difficult, it was that suddenly I couldn't take Emma to the doctor if she was unwell, the prayer group would lay hands on her and heal her. Perhaps my faith wasn't strong enough, but I wasn't comfortable with this. We weren't allowed to retain friends that were not of the same faith, and this included my parents, and Dan and Pat. We had to convert them, and lead them on the right path, or withdraw from them. Well, how would Emma understand that suddenly she couldn't see her granny and grandpa, because they didn't go to church. There were lots of things that I felt were extreme, and the arguments continued, it was only the subject matter that was different, and now Bruce looked at me as though I was infested with evil. So, yes, it was better that he wasn't drinking, and out until all hours, and he was more considerate, but it was a strange time. Bruce also seemed to be worshipping the minister, more than God, and I tried to suggest this to him, but there were obviously those little devils in me, trying to turn him away from the light.

I went to church with him, but I wouldn't attend all the prayer groups and meetings, because Emma needed to sleep in her own bed, and not at a different house every night in a camper cot, until after the prayer meeting. I did parrot the God Bless you, to all and sundry, because this religious tide had washed over our little community, and everyone in the maisonettes had converted. We were all so nice to each other, and 'praise the lord', was the phrase that was used for everything and anything, it just felt so artificial. You know, when your neighbour comes to you and says 'praise the lord, brother, but would you mind being more thoughtful, and lower your tv volume', or 'Brother Bruce, you have blocked my parking space yet again, God bless you anyway'.

23

I had a wonderful pregnancy this time, very little morning sickness, and I bloomed. Somehow as my baby grew inside me, so did my sense of inner peace, and joy. I felt so different, calm and content. One morning Laura came over, and I wasn't feeling very well, apparently I looked shocking, so Laura bundled us all into her van, and took me to the doctor. He said my blood pressure was dangerously high, prescribed some medication, and told me to go home, rest, relax, and not to worry about anything. It was particularly important I didn't get upset. We got back in the car, and Emma was on my lap eating a small packet of peanuts. We were just about to drive off, when she pulled at me and was pointing at her nose, smiling. Oh shit, she had a peanut stuck up her nose. I didn't think it was anything much to worry about, but suggested to Laura that whilst we were there, I would check with the receptionist. I took Emma in, and I was embarrassed to tell them what had happened, I really thought they were just going to laugh it off, and tell me it would drop out in its own time or something. They became frantic, and the doctor was interrupted, and he had Emma brought in immediately. She had started to cry now, and I was panicking, what was so dangerous about a peanut up the nose. He put her on the table, and tried to ease it out with these tiny forceps, and he said to me it was crucial she didn't sniff it back. How do you tell a two year old not to sniff, when they're crying? In the meantime he was asking the receptionist to get his car ready, as he wouldn't waste time with an ambulance, if we had to get to the hospital. Shit, what was going on! Emma suddenly sneezed, bless her, and the peanut popped out. Apparently, if she had sniffed it back, it could enter the lung, which in turn created all sorts of complications. Anyway, so much for, go home, relax, and don't let anything upset you. Well that peanut had certainly upset me.

My pregnancy progressed safely, and I was longing for the birth of my baby. I had to have a caesarean, and the gynaecologist wanted to schedule a date. I had asked to have a natural birth as that was still so very important to me, but they wouldn't allow it. There was too much risk involved they said.

My birthday was two weeks prior to the due date, and I thought that would be the best birthday present ever, so I suggested this to him, and as the baby was absolutely fine, he agreed.

I was admitted the night before, and was in a big empty ward. I felt marvellous, and I was so excited, I was going to meet my baby tomorrow. I slept easily, and was woken at about four in the morning to go and have a bath. The caesarean was scheduled for eight o'clock, and Bruce was coming up at about seven. I got into the bath, and then felt the gush between my legs, and the first contraction. I was in labour. It felt so different from the time before, it was painful certainly, but not as intense, and there was time in between. I called the nurse, and she examined me once I was back on the bed. Then all hell broke loose again. Suddenly there were nurses everywhere, and I was being rushed down a passage again. I was having a drip put in, being shaved, the same routine, and the nurse said they had called the gynaecologist, anaesthetist and everyone else who was attending, and they would be here as soon as possible. 'What's happening, what's wrong', I asked, now I was terrified. It was happening all over again, my baby was in trouble, dear God no. My labour intensified very quickly, and I felt that familiar pushing sensation. It was close to six o'clock in the morning now. The nurse gave me an internal examination, and said we have to get her in now, and I was rushed into the theatre. The operating team, were rushing about, and before I knew it I was out.

I woke up, whilst they were taking me back to the ward, and Bruce said the baby was fine, and it was a boy. I closed my eyes and went back into the land of ether. Sometime later, I opened my eyes, and beside my bed was the incubator, and my baby boy. He was beautiful, my precious baby, thank God you are safe. I lay looking at him only for a few moments, and his little eyes opened, and he looked straight back at me. How do I describe that moment and how special, and wonderful it was. As our eyes met, I experienced a joy, a peace, a love so profound, so deep, so pure, that it is a feeling I will never forget, and one I am fortunate enough to have experienced again later in my life. It was as if he had reached out and touched my soul, and I knew in that moment, that this beautiful little being, would bring hope, and joy, and love, and so much more back into my life.

I reached through the opening in the incubator and stroked his soft perfect little body, and he knew my touch, he responded to my touch, he didn't cry. 'Hi darling boy', I said, 'I'm your mummy, and it's my birthday today too'. He was two weeks earlier than his due date, and regardless of the scheduled caesarean, my baby boy was determined to be born on my birthday, this was certainly very special and precious indeed.

My parents were allowed in to see me as it was my birthday, and I watched carefully when my mum held my baby boy. It was totally different. She did the customary 'oohs' and 'aaahs', but it was unexceptional, and nothing like the absolute adoration she'd shown Emma, the first time she held her. I was relieved to say the least; this wasn't going to be a battle then. We named him Jack.

The nurse who had been with me the morning of his birth was back on duty, and at the first opportunity I asked what the emergency had been, had Jack been in distress, because hadn't they even checked the heartbeat. 'Oh no, nothing like that', she said. 'The baby was ready to be born'. I wanted to scream, why they hadn't just let nature take its course. I so desperately wanted to give birth naturally, and it could have happened. Why in Gods name hadn't they just let it go ahead, I felt sick, another half hour to an hour, and my dream of giving birth, alert and awake, and holding that tiny little body, as it emerged from me, could have been realised. They had decided it was too risky, but they hadn't even considered asking me, whether I was prepared to take the risk, or given me any advice or choice in the matter at all. I had no intention of having another child, so I knew it was a dream I would never realise. I counted my blessings that I could have children, but after carrying that baby, growing it inside for all those months, feeling it move inside, I felt cheated. I'd been in labour, I'd got to the

174

very edge of pushing my babies out of me, and it had been snatched away, I felt robbed.

Over the next few months, life was simple and calm, and it was wonderful. Bruce still attended his church, and I was happy at home with my children. Jack was about six months old, he was a content and happy baby, and hadn't suffered with colic like Emma did. She was fascinated with her new baby brother, and took every opportunity to help me with him. I had taken care that she was made to feel very special when we brought him home, and this had obviously helped with the normal jealousy a child feels when suddenly they are faced with competition. It is difficult juggling the two, a baby requires a lot of attention, and it was important to me that she didn't feel deprived in any way. Fortunately her grandparents and father didn't appear to have the same intensity of feeling for Jack, and they showered her with as much, if not more affection and attention than normal.

One night I went to wake Jack for his feed. This had created a huge row, because Bruce thought I should leave him to sleep, and said I doted on that baby too much, and wouldn't it be nice if I gave him the same attention, and on and on, but I stood firm on this. Something didn't feel quite right somewhere deep inside me, and my instincts told me to go to Jack. When I picked his little body up, he was so hot, and it took me a little while to rouse him. He started to cough, and it was a terrible sound, it sounded like a dog barking, I was frightened now. I rushed down to Bruce and said I was calling the paediatrician, and he suggested I have faith, and he would lay hands on Jack, and heal him. Not a chance, with Bruce shouting at me of little faith, I made the call, described the symptoms and was told to meet the specialist at the hospital. Bruce was reluctant to go, and I told him, I would go alone if necessary, I wasn't hanging about whilst he berated me for my lack of faith. He came with me, and after Jack was examined, he was diagnosed with pleurisy. I didn't know much about it then, but he was a very sick little boy, and I was beside myself. They wouldn't let me stay with him either, it wasn't allowed in those days. I stayed as late as I could, and then went home, and had an exhausted couple of hours sleep. When I woke, I was so hot, and I was having difficulty breathing. Every breath I took caused an agonising pain in my lungs, I didn't know what was wrong with me, but I knew I was really ill. I had to get to see my baby. I called the hospital, and they said he'd had a good night, and then I called my doctor. He visited me, after I described my symptoms. I was diagnosed with pleurisy.

Pleurisy is not contagious, apparently as I was told; it can be caused by a prolonged underlying infection or sometimes by shock. My bond with my son was obviously very strong, as I believe it was my terrible fear that he might not get well, and the distress of our separation. What I found hardest of all, was that I couldn't visit him. I wasn't allowed into the hospital, I was confined to bed. I didn't see my baby for five days, and during that time, I felt as though my heart had been ripped apart, the separation was one of the most awful times of my life. I had never spent more than a few hours away from Emma, I couldn't imagine being apart from either of my children for any longer than that, and this was my tiny baby. I tortured myself during those days. Did he feel abandoned, he wouldn't understand why his mommy wasn't holding him, feeding him, loving him, and when he eventually did come home, I wouldn't let go of him for days, even whilst he slept. My anxieties centred on my own mortality. I believed that as long as I was there, I could prevent tragedy befalling my children. I didn't have the same faith in my own well-being however; and I felt that at sometime, I would be punished for being such a failure all my life. I had two little people that I adored, and I became convinced that I didn't deserve this blessing and my fear of dying and leaving them crept in slowly and insidiously. I also made it very clear to Bruce that if either child became unwell; they were going straight to the doctor without argument. If possible this really made me an ally of Satan as far as he was concerned.

Bruce became more and more obsessed with church. He often talked about the minister and how he admired him. The sermons were based largely on the unity of the family, and this was wonderful for us, Bruce really did start to become father and husband of the year. I felt strange with this, I didn't feel it could last, and although I never voiced my concerns to him, I waited for it to all fall apart. Don't get me wrong, I prayed it wouldn't. He still didn't drink at all, and I didn't have the nights wondering where he was, was he alright, who was he with, and what would happen when he came home. I was able to relax into a routine for the first time since we were married. It was good for the children too; there weren't the bitter angry arguments behind closed doors, and the tension that followed. Their father wasn't unpredictable and volatile, and although Jack hadn't experienced any of this and Emma was very young, I do believe it impacts on them.

It did go horribly wrong, suddenly. We had all gone to church that day, and it was the day the minister, who valued family unity above all else told his congregation that he was having an affair. Apparently it had come to the attention of the elders, and they had suggested he step down. Perhaps he felt that his confession would be his forgiveness, and for many it was. For Bruce however it was devastating, he had for far too long been worshipping the man, not God, and this man had now let him down. This man had gone against everything he preached about, and it blew Bruce away. As he had changed overnight, when converted, so did he change when he reverted? He went out after taking us home, and came home the following morning still very drunk and very dishevelled, and life went back to normal. This time however, if possible it was worse. It was as if a starving, deprived man had suddenly been offered a feast, and he was determined to gorge.

We moved home, a couple of blocks away from where we had been. The house was bigger, and it was very close to a playschool. I enrolled Emma, and took her there every morning. She loved the stimulation and company, and it freed me up a little for housework, shopping and everything that went with being a housewife. Bruce had his favourite sayings, some of them were, 'keep them barefoot and pregnant', and 'be mean, keep them keen', and his favourite, although I can't remember it exactly was that women should be chained to the kitchen sink, and only have the chain let out for them to bring you a beer. The friends I had, lived similarly to me, so I didn't know how totally wrong this was, and don't forget I was a nothing still, so I was lucky to have anyone at all.

Bruce was very seldom at home, and I became accustomed to the interrupted sleep, and I worried about him until he came home. How would I survive without him? I had no job, I had two very young children, and I had no self respect or confidence. I couldn't perceive of a life without him. The more disrespectfully he treated me, the more I disrespected myself, whatever self worth I had left, disappeared, and my dream of a soul mate disappeared into the recesses of my soul. I couldn't quite bring myself to believe he was with other woman, that would hurt too much, and then one night, even I couldn't deny he was.

177

He'd come home very late, very drunk, and he passed the bedroom door lurching his way to the bathroom. I followed him quietly, and he didn't go to the toilet as I'd expected, he went to the basin. He took his penis out, and washed himself, as carefully as he could, he could barely stand.

I crept back to bed, and cried. I couldn't go anywhere, and how did I tell my parents that I was giving up on my marriage. I call it a marriage; well I suppose it was one of convenience, convenient for Bruce. He had a cook, a cleaner, a carer for the children, and someone he could have sex with, as and when he so desired. I didn't know how to say no, that word seldom in any way manner or form fitted into my vocabulary. It was just that, sex, I suppose he hoped I enjoyed it, because it would boost his ego as a skilled lover, so I faked orgasms, anything to make him happy, and avoid confrontation.

Of course, I had considered leaving Bruce, in moments of total fantasy, or after a few glasses of wine, and the world becomes a much brighter, friendlier, and forgiving place, but that was all it was, fantasy. How would I support my children, work is scarce in Africa, and I hadn't used my secretarial skills for years. Any casual labour, jobs at supermarkets or in shops were taken, and fiercely defended, and I wouldn't be able to afford child care on that income, let alone basic living costs. There are no benefits, no support systems, nothing really, nowhere to turn. You needed money to survive as a single parent, and that I certainly didn't have. I was trapped.

24

Bruce continued to go out each night, and always came home in the early hours of the morning, stinking drunk, and the following morning there was only a brief time whilst he was home before work, to put up with his hangover. I would make sure he had his coffee the minute he woke up, so that he wouldn't be too angry, start shouting and upset the children. I would also try hard to keep him in a good mood to prevent this too, and I would do whatever it took really. The children didn't know about his nightly outings, because he went out after they went to bed, and if one of them woke for water or whatever reason, they were accustomed to me going through to them. He would brag about what a good time he'd had, and the women he'd flirted with, and what the hell had he done to deserve a miserable cow like me. 'Look at you, sitting there with a face like a lemon ,just because you don't know how to have a good time, no need to resent that I do.' Then the familiar, 'does nothing make you happy, why are you always so miserable, shit, I'm going to work'.

Basically, I didn't say much at all, because one way or another it would be misconstrued, and manipulated to allow him to start an argument, so 'least said, soonest mended' was the philosophy I adopted. Therefore, he interpreted my quietness as sullenness', and it would have been impossible for me to try to explain myself. We didn't talk about anything, other than how his day had been, how he was feeling, and how tired he was. My day was of no interest to him, as it consisted of feeding, bathing, and nappy changing, absolutely nothing he wanted to hear about.

I felt I should really make more of an effort to appreciate what I had. I had two lovely children, a roof over my head, good friends, I was lucky, and I was ungrateful. I should show more appreciation, and I did, I tried harder to be more pleasant when he came home, I made sure I had make-up on, and didn't smell of baby sick, and I was at his beck and call, this still didn't keep him home. I was boring company, and he spent as little time as possible at home in the evenings. During the short time he was home, he was normally father of the year. He spent about an hour playing with the children, making them laugh and giggle, he never disciplined them as aside from when he lost his temper, which was frequently, and then he just smacked or sent them to the room. They adopted my attitude over time, make sure daddy's happy when he's home.

I spent hours trying to cook imaginative meals on our very limited budget, he hardly ever ate anything as he was either hung-over by that time or in a hurry to leave. I knitted all our jumpers, and made a lot of the children's clothes, or gratefully accepted 'hand me down's' from friends. I baked all their birthday cakes and treats, and I never once questioned all the money he spent on going out. He earned it, didn't he, what right did I have to ask for more. I would be especially nice just prior to either of the children's birthdays or Christmas, so that I might get a little extra money to buy them their special gift. I would also cut down on the groceries one way or another for a few months and keep little bits aside for these priorities. Birthdays and Christmas were and are extremely important to me, days of celebration and fun, and I always begged Bruce on these days not to get too drunk, so that he could spend quality time with whichever child was celebrating their birthday. My birthday was only really acknowledged by my parents, as the focus was on Jack, and that is the way I wanted it. He had been my ultimate birthday present anyway, and I don't remember ever getting a birthday card from Bruce. I would remind him weeks in advance, still having my childish fantasy of a loving card and maybe even a gift.

Actually, to be honest, I did get 'birthday cards' from him. They were a few simple meaningless words, written on a piece of paper. Once, he didn't have any paper to hand, so he tore a corner off a cardboard box, and wrote on that. When he gave me these 'cards', he would always say, 'see, don't ever say I don't give you anything'. He also found this hilarious, and would fall about at his wittiness. His idea of a gift for me was to suggest putting a ribbon on his penis, and what a lucky girl I was to get that!

One of the most difficult things I experienced was the lack of sleep. I normally lay dozing until he came home, and when he came to bed he snored as only the very drunk can. The worst of it though was the bed wetting. He frequently wet the bed, and always said it went back to his childhood. Initially I sympathised with what must be a sign of distress, and god knows what trauma's he might have suffered as a child, he never spoke about his childhood. Eventually I came to realise there was nothing psychological about it, it only ever happened when he was drunk. After finally dropping off into a deep sleep, I would awake to a warm wetness spreading through the sheets, and I had to get up, strip the bed with him still in it, as he was close to comatose, and then pack towels down, another sheet, and wait until morning, when I could soap the mattress down, and clean and change all the bedding. This became virtually a nightly routine. I always panicked that the children would come and jump on the bed in the morning, and notice it was wet. A couple of times they did, and I explained that one of us had spilt water during the night.

There were also times that we were out at friends, and he reached that point of inebriation that he would pass out in their chair or on their sofa, and I would dread seeing the stain spread across his crotch. To begin with, I always had a jacket or cardigan to cover him with; eventually I had to be honest as friends were ending up with stained and stinking furniture. I was absolutely mortified about it, Bruce found it funny and enjoyed my embarrassment, and played the sympathy card childhood trauma thing, with our friends.

I was no paragon of virtue, there were times when I would over indulge in the wine, and with the Dutch courage, and carefree attitude it gave me, I was much more assertive to the point of aggressive with Bruce and his comments. This was when I answered him back, and gave as good as I got, but I soon learnt that it didn't do me any favours, in fact it worked against me. If we were in the company of friends when I chose to 'get into one of my moods', Bruce used this as justification for his behaviour. There were many times when he would encourage me to have another glass of wine, goad me into an argument, and then, when I went into one, shrug his shoulders with a look of a long suffering badly treated man, shake his head, and say something like 'what else can I do, but look for peace, quiet and a good time away from home, when I have this to contend with.' He was so clever, and I was so gullible.

It got worse, much worse, and it is after much deliberation, and anguish that I have decided to include this in my book. I consider it one of my most shameful secrets; however I do believe that all of the story should be told. This retrospectively is indicative of the extent of my complete immersion in the role of the abused, and consequently a victim.

I find this next part very hard to write about, as for me it signified total betrayal in the worst possible way. I started to experience discomfort in my nether regions. Constant itching and I eventually went to my doctor. He checked me over, looking up at me with sympathy and even sadness in his eyes, and told me to get dressed and take a seat. His diagnosis devastated, and shocked me. He used the medical terminology, which I didn't understand and then he translated it in a few words. 'You have genital crabs, Cheryl.' My immediate reply was, 'I must have got them from a toilet seat'. 'That's a myth and not possible', he replied, and added, 'You can only get this from very close contact, for example intercourse'. That was impossible, the only person I'd had sex with was my husband, he must be mistaken, not even Bruce would stoop that low would he. What kind of person had he been with, that had this kind of vile, dirty infection. I wept whilst my doctor prescribed a shampoo and powder, and said it was imperative that Bruce used it too, on all parts of his body with hair. I went home in a horrible daze, this had to be the final straw, but how did I explain to family and friends that I was leaving Bruce because he had given me crabs. I couldn't tell another living soul about this shameful thing, and apart from Bruce, I haven't, until now.

I waited for him to come home, and I was angry, very angry, this was inexcusable. Initially he tried to tell me the doctor had been wrong, I had picked this up somewhere, he knew he couldn't accuse me of sleeping around, because I never left the house without the children and friends, and eventually he resorted to the now familiar tears. He and Dan had been out, and got very drunk when they'd been approached by prostitutes. Needless to say they had taken advantage

182

of the situation, hence this horrible outcome. Dear God that meant he could have infected me with anything, and I was terrified that this might be the least of it. As time went by I was fortunate enough to know that this was the worst of it, thank you my angels, but it set off a new line of abuse from Bruce. He told me that if I ever told anyone about this, he would tell them that I had lost the plot completely, and he would leave me, and take the children. He managed to convince me that I wouldn't have a leg to stand on if I fought him for the children, because I had no money, no job, and without him, no roof over my head. I would not be seen as financially capable of keeping them, and at the very worst, if I did get to keep them, he would make sure to kidnap them if necessary, and take them out of the country, and I would never see them again. I believed him, every word, and I knew that he would carry out his sick plans, not out of love for his children, but to hurt me. I couldn't bear the thought of being without them, or leaving them in his care, so I never said a word, and went back to being the dutiful and obedient wife. He threatened me often with this in the future, and I took the threat very seriously indeed.

25

I'd been having very painful and heavy periods for some months, and I visited my doctor. I had endometriosis, and it was severe. I was referred to my gynaecologist, and after further tests, he confirmed the diagnosis, and the spread and severity of the endometriosis. He suggested a hysterectomy. I wasn't planning to have any more children, and didn't think there would ever come a time that my life would change so dramatically that I would consider another child. Anyway, if I didn't have the operation, it wouldn't go away and it wouldn't get any better. My periods were debilitating and irregular and it was impacting on my life. I couldn't be unwell and take care of my children properly, so I agreed to the hysterectomy. Things happen very quickly in South Africa, there was no free health care service, and because you paid for your medical care, there were no delays. Within days I was booked into the hospital.

It was a state of the art private hospital in Port Elizabeth, and I knew I would be in for about ten days. It was very hard saying goodbye to my children, but my mum had offered to help take care of them, and stay over if necessary. I had asked Bruce to commit to staying at home at night during that time, and I had to believe he would. The operation was scheduled for the following morning, and I was in a ward with three other women who were undergoing the same surgery. I felt reassured that this time, I was in good hands. I knew my GP, would be in the theatre, and I trusted him. I should possibly not have made so much of what I considered the 'bad omens' the night before. There were certain preparations essential prior to surgery, and we were told that keys for cupboards which housed the antiseptic douche, had been misplaced, so it would all have to be done the following morning. I took a sleeping pill, and although I was nervous, I slept.

I awoke the following morning to the crippling fear that I was going to die that day, I didn't know what exactly had caused it, because I wasn't particularly anxious about surgery, and I was looking forward to the relief this operation would offer. I hadn't really given much and not nearly enough serious thought about the enormity of this decision to have a hysterectomy, all I really knew was that there was really no alternative, to the pain, and extreme discomfort. The pre surgery stuff was done in a hurry, and was quite uncomfortable; they hadn't had time to warm the douche to body temperature, so it was inserted cold. Fortunately I had company in my discomfort, and we all complained. I was the last of the women to go into surgery, but I was looking forward to the pre-med to calm these irrational fears that I'd woken with. Bruce came to the hospital, and as the morning went on, my fear increased. I believed I was going to die in that theatre. I tried to tell him that something was going to go wrong, and how terrified I felt, and he put it down to pre surgery nerves. I also tried to rationalise that this is what it was. In the rush to meet theatre deadlines, my premed didn't arrive, and by the time I was wheeled down, I was hysterical with fear. I truly thought that something was going to go wrong, and I was going to die. It was that extreme, that as they took me down, I told Bruce I had an overwhelming urge to get off that trolley, and go home, in fact I tried to get off once or twice. He told me to stop being so silly, it was just a bad case of nerves. I was a big girl for goodness sake, grow up. I was twenty six years old.

I had said my goodbyes to Bruce, and asked him to hug and kiss the children for me, and tell them mommy loved them. I have often wondered why I didn't follow my gut instinct, and go home, perhaps rescheduled the inevitable surgery, maybe then it would have all been different, maybe then I wouldn't have suffered the way I did for all the years that followed. I have learnt since, to take these deep sometimes irrational feelings very seriously, no matter how foolish they may make me look.

I was wheeled to just outside the theatre, and my GP came out

185

to calm me, and explain there was a slight delay; I would be in soon enough. I suppose I would have found this somewhat comforting, if his gown, mask and glasses hadn't been spattered in blood. I lay there for what seemed hours, and the terror increased, I was in a terrible state of anxiety by the time they took me in and put me on the theatre table. There was that large round white clock again, the one they always seem to have in a theatre. 'Please just put me under quickly', I begged, I thought if they didn't, my heart would burst with its terror filled pounding. The anaesthetist told me to mentally count back from ten, and I remember eight, and then I was gone, thank you God.

I was awake; my mind was clear as a bell, and I felt relief wash over me, it was over, and it felt as though I'd only been under for a short time. Nobody was calling me awake though, and there were strange sounds and I recognised the voices. I heard my GP's voice, and my Gynaecologist's. Oh God, what was happening, why were they with me in the ward, what had gone wrong in the theatre. I couldn't open my eyes, why couldn't I open my eyes, had I gone blind? Speak, tell them you're awake, the words shrieked in my mind, but I couldn't make a sound. My throat felt blocked, and unnatural. Sheer terror swept over me, had I suffered a stroke, what had happened. I felt as though I was suffocating in panic. Move your fingers, move anything my brain screamed, I willed myself to make any movement, but my body would not and could not respond. What were those sounds, there were all sorts of beeps and bleeps, thank god one of my senses was working, and at least I could hear. Then the terrifying, horrifying, truth came to my alert wide awake mind, I was still in the theatre. Oh dear God, I was awake and they were still operating. There was no pain, in fact I couldn't feel or move anything, I was totally paralysed, and I was wide awake, I couldn't indicate to them I was awake. I didn't want to hear them say that my uterus was one of the worst they'd seen, and hear it plopping into a vessel of some sort to be taken to the laboratory. I didn't want to hear them discussing what they were going to have for lunch, and I didn't want to hear them say they would hurry up now, they'd had a busy morning, 'so let's get her done, and get of here'. I did hear all of that though, and whilst I was hearing it, no matter how hard my brain screamed to any part of my body to just move, no matter how small the movement, my body would not respond. I couldn't tell them I was awake. I heard a metal pipe in my mouth and throat, I heard it knocking against my teeth, and I heard a sucking sound, I couldn't feel anything. I felt a tugging and pulling sensation on my lower abdomen, and realised they might be stitching me up. How much longer, my petrified mind screamed, please please, someone stop this, I don't care what you do, what happens, please take me away from this. I felt as though I had been buried alive, I was alive and awake, and I was trapped in total paralysis. I had no control, I was helpless, and as alert as my mind was, and my body was equally inept. I don't know what part of my petrified body eventually indicated absolute distress, but from behind my right hand shoulder, I heard the voice of the anaesthetist, say 'Oh Fuck, she's come out of it', and then the voice of my GP, 'Shit, put her under, put her under', and then nothing, wonderful, peaceful, nothing.

My name was being called, and I woke slowly, I was fuzzy, groggy, and very tired. 'It's all over now, and you're in the ward', a voice said, and I was swept back into the land of nothing. It took me a long while to come out of the anaesthetic; I don't remember much of the night that followed nor the following morning. I remember them checking my drip, catheter, and my blood pressure. Apparently there was a problem there, my blood pressure had soared, and they had to notify the doctor. I believe that there can be problems with blood pressure after surgery, but mine was abnormally high, and I was given medication to bring it down. At the first opportunity, I told the nurses what had happened in the theatre. They called my GP in, who denied everything, but when I told him that he had mentioned he was going to have 'one of those corned beef sandwiches on Black, that were so good', for lunch, we both knew he was lying. The system in South Africa, is similar to that of America, it is easier to sue the medical profession. Even the Gynae and Anaesthetist paid unscheduled visits to me, to confirm that I had imagined it all, they backed each other up, and did their very best to convince me I hadn't woken up at all. In each of their faces, I saw the lie and the anxiety, and it was only some-time later, when they felt comfortable I wasn't going to take it any further, that my GP admitted to my unfortunate experience, off the record of course. I believe he felt obligated to at that time, because of the terrible impact this 'unfortunate experience', had on me, and my life. At the time, I just wanted to get out of the hospital, and go home. Everything in this awful place terrified me, the smells, the sounds, everything. In that theatre I had felt like I had been buried alive, that is about the closest I can come to describe the terror, fear and absolute helplessness of those moments, and the hospital was my tomb.

The first day I was home, I was thrilled to be alive and out of the hospital. My mum was there to help with the children, and the first few days I was to stay in bed. I had only been home a matter of hours, when I needed to go to the toilet. When I wiped myself, I felt a wave of sheer terror sweep over me, and I thought my heart was going to stop in absolute fear. I was bleeding. I screamed for my mum, and I was completely hysterical. 'I won't go back to hospital', I screamed, 'I would rather bleed to death here', I added hysterically. My mum was making frantic calls to Bruce, who subsequently contacted my specialist. He phoned me, and I was virtually incoherent in my absolute panic about the possibility of having to be re-admitted to hospital. After I had managed to describe the colour of the blood and the extent of it, he informed me that this was perfectly normal after the surgery I had undergone, to continue with bed rest and contact him if the bleeding persisted or worsened. I never did call him back, and remained in bed, until the bleeding stopped. I was determined that I would not under any circumstances go back to hospital. This experience sadly triggered one of the most distressing and challenging periods of my life. I have over many years managed to control my fear to a certain extent, however my body has never recovered completely.

Shortly afterwards, I developed pneumonia in both lungs, and even the visit to my GP set my heart pounding and my pulse racing. Whilst in the waiting room, I felt an anxiety I had never experienced before, which grew to an overwhelming and uncontrollable terror, and it was only Bruce, telling me what an absolute pathetic idiot I was being, and the embarrassment I was causing him, that made me stay. Obviously my GP strongly advised that I go to hospital for treatment, I refused. I would go home and get better, or not, but I would not be going into hospital. I became even more unwell at home, apparently the fluid in my lungs was solidifying, my apologies to medical experts, but that was how it was described to me, and I was told that if I didn't go into hospital, it was quite possible I could die. My fear of hospital was that overwhelming, that I chose to stay at home, and I believe it was sheer will that made me better. Of course I didn't want to die, I had two small children, and my family thought I was irresponsible, and quite mad really not to receive professional treatment. Perhaps I was a bit mad at that time, all I knew was this fear that consumed me, and I could not be logical or sensible about it, and I could not control it.

A few months later, we moved house. We had a small semi with our previous neighbours from the maisonettes next door to us, and the house was smaller, cosier and close to everything familiar. The doctor's surgery was diagonally across the road, as were a number of shops. I'd not felt the same since my operation, and had this constant undercurrent of anxiety which plagued me. I couldn't quell it or dismiss it, and the best I could do was try to ignore it. If I thought about it too much, my heart started pounding, and I became afraid. This phantom fear, was unpredictable, it happened randomly which made it even more frightening. I was unpacking, and hanging clothes in our bedroom wardrobe with my mum helping and Bruce working in the room. I was chatting about where to put stuff, and then it happened, just like that. My right arm went numb; the words in my brain weren't the words coming from my mouth. I couldn't talk properly, I couldn't make sense. I knew what I wanted to say, but I couldn't get the words out, and then I lost the sight in my right eye. It happened so quickly, so unexpectedly so terrifyingly. I couldn't breathe, and I was desperately trying to draw air into my lungs, and began to breathe rapidly, I felt dizzy and more and more light headed, most of all I was absolutely petrified, I didn't know what was happening to me, I believed I was having a stroke, and fortunately Bruce and my mum were frightened enough to take action. Between them, they carried me across the road to our doctor's surgery, and I was seen immediately.

He checked all my vital signs, my breathing, and then sat beside me, talking to me, gently persuading me that I was going to be alright. I was there with him, I was safe, and I wasn't dying. I hadn't had a stroke; I was having a panic attack. What the hell was a panic attack, I hadn't been doing anything to cause this, I had just been unpacking clothing for gods sake.

I did eventually start to relax, and my GP spoke to me at length. I trusted him implicitly, and this had the desired effect. I believed him, and I believed in him, and if he said I was going to be ok, then I was. His only concern was that my blood pressure was too high, and as it hadn't really gone anywhere near normal since my hysterectomy, he prescribed medication. I was fortunate that he was into alternative therapies, and quite innovative for that time. This was 1986, and not many people had ever heard of panic attacks. He explained that they could happen at any time, and the symptoms were often similar to those of a heart attack or stroke. They were very frightening, but if I understood what was happening to me, it would help me to come out of it. The main thing was to experience it for what it was, and not what it may appear to be. That was probably the most useless advice I was given, fine if its not happening to you. For those of you reading this, who may have experienced panic attacks, in whichever form they take, you will certainly understand me.

This was my experience. You know that feeling you get, when you are taking an exam, or going for a job interview, or taking your driving test, that feeling of anxiety that settles in your stomach. It may not be severe; it's just that nervous feeling of the unknown. Will I pass that exam, will I get the job, will I past my test. That feeling was with me always, but there was no forthcoming challenge, no event to incur this, it was just there, twenty four seven. Even when I managed to sleep, I would often awake, in the throes of panic, heart pounding, gasping for air, dry mouth, and when we are faced with fear, it triggers a fight or flight reaction. The devastating thing about a panic attack is that there really is nothing tangible to fight, and you can't run away or escape from it. it was relentless, it never let go. Then the paranoia set in, everything and anything scared me. I became paranoid about eating, I imagined I had difficulty swallowing, what if I choked. I worried about my medication, even down to every day pain killers. What if I suddenly developed an allergic reaction?

What if they are all wrong, what if the next time, it isn't just a panic attack, what if it's the real thing, heart attack, stroke, asphyxiation, what then. What happens if I have one when I am out shopping, what if I collapse, they won't know what's happening to me, they won't know how to help me, they will send for an ambulance, and I will be taken to hospital. Thoughts spiral and ripple, and every day situations become sinister and threatening, fear is everywhere, and anywhere, fear is everything. I was too afraid to drive, what if it happened whilst driving. When I went in the car, to perhaps visit my parents or friends, I suddenly had this overwhelming, inexplicable sensation that I couldn't breathe, I became claustrophobic. I had to tell Bruce to stop the car, so that I could just get out, try and get under control, and confirm that I could breathe. I developed an irrational but overwhelming fear of dying, and leaving my children. I gave up my social drinking, and I desperately wanted to give up smoking, but I couldn't because I felt it calmed me down, but, I would argue with myself, I am risking all sorts of diseases by smoking, and the mental dialogue would become torturous, self persecuting, guilt ridden, and sweep me into an attack.

I am so afraid, and the worst thing about all of this, is that I knew my fears were irrational, I knew my behaviour was extreme, I knew how strong I could be, I knew I was a survivor. I knew all this, but it meant nothing in face of the fear, and I began to believe I was going insane, I was losing my mind, and that was the biggest fear of all. I can't stop this, I can't control this, and how could I continue to live like this

You spend all your time trying to persuade yourself that you are going to be ok, you are not going to have an attack today, and whilst your mind tries so hard to convince you its ok, you literally talk yourself into a panic by trying not to. It truly feels like a desperate, hopeless situation, and it is one of the most despairing, difficult and sad times of my life. I couldn't focus on my family, my home, I couldn't focus on anything. I spent all my time trying not to have a panic attack, and this was perceived as neurosis, selfishness, self -centeredness and extreme hypochondria. My family and friends became impatient, frustrated, exasperated, and eventually angry with me.

Now there was nowhere to turn and no one to turn to apart from my doctor, and I should have just pitched a tent at the surgery I was there so often. In those days, the vast amounts of drugs that are prescribed now for people suffering this way, were either non existent or just not widely and automatically prescribed. I am, in a perverse way grateful for this, because I was never given any medication to subdue my symptoms, and although I know that at the time, I would have taken poison if it had taken these feelings away, I am now hugely thankful that hard as it was, I had no option but to work through this without medication. I sank deeper and deeper into a pit of fear and hopelessness, and eventually I didn't go out of my home much at all. I couldn't, as I was too afraid.

Walking Emma to her playschool, with Jack in his pushchair took every bit of mental energy I could muster each day. My body shook all the way there and back, I was petrified something would happen during the short walk, and my two babies would be left abandoned and helpless, whilst their mommy had collapsed. I had a mantra, 'just to the school and back, just to the school and back, and then you are safe, then you are safe'. I couldn't concentrate on their childish sweet little chatter; I had to keep saying my mantra. For a long while I couldn't even go to the corner shop, I had also become paranoid about people. I felt they were all looking at me as though I was the local nutter. Complete strangers, people I had never seen before, let alone met, I felt were whispering and talking about me.

During this time, which was about a year, I withdrew from life, and just tried to survive each day. It was one of the times in my life that I felt as though I was living in hell. It was an endless struggle, and the hardest thing was I couldn't see an end to it, I didn't know how, or if I was ever going to be free of this crippling, debilitating, nightmare. That is probably the best way to describe this time in my life. I'm sure you have all at one time or another had a really bad nightmare, the kind of one, that you wake up from, still afraid, and then that overwhelming relief when you realise it was all just a nightmare, and it takes a little while for you to settle your heart, calm yourself, slow your breathing. Eventually you can snuggle back down, perhaps have a little self conscious laugh about how silly you were feeling so afraid, and with the covers close around you, feel extra safe, because you know it wasn't real, thank God. Imagine if it was, imagine if, the terror in your sleep was real, you are awake and its there, enveloping you, consuming you, and you can't get away from it, you can't wake up. That's what a panic attack feels like.

My husband one day said to me, in an artificially kind and sympathetic voice. *'I know how you can get better; put your left hand on your right shoulder, and your right hand on your left shoulder, and fucking pull yourself together'.*

I continued to visit my GP, and my blood pressure eventually levelled out, but I had to continue with the medication, to control my blood pressure, and still take it now, all these years later. He told me I had developed 'white coat syndrome', which is a fear or phobia of doctors, hospitals and anything to do with them. He also agreed that this along with my blood pressure was due to my experience in theatre, and there was no quick cure, or really any cure at all. I had to learn to live with it, if not; my quality of life would continue to be as non existent as it was now. I knew I didn't want to continue like this, and worked out a strategy for myself to get better. I started a sort of self therapy, and on a daily basis, over many months reminded myself of who I had been, what I truly had been, and was, capable of withstanding, and that I chose not to live in this prison of fear. When I became afraid, which to begin with might have been walking a little further than I normally did, I forced myself to remember who and what I had been, before now. I latched onto the most difficult times in my life, and remembered that I had come through those, and persuaded myself that this could be overcome too. I would fight this, one hour at a time. Every hour I was able to subdue the feelings of panic became a victory, and then do another hour and then maybe another. I started taking slightly longer walks each week; I couldn't do it each day; that was too difficult. Every time I went that little bit further it was scary, but when I made it back home, I felt triumphant. This feeling built on itself, and gave me strength and courage to continue, and I got angry. I suppose I was fortunate that I had always turned my anger inwards, I was good at self blame, and in this instance it helped me.

Remember I had said earlier that these panic attacks weren't easy to fight because it was a feeling, there's nothing tangible to fight or flee from, well I now visualised it as a disease, unseen, but present, in its insidious guise, a disease that was drawing at my strength, depriving me of life, destroying me, slowly sucking me into its dark depths. The only treatment I had available to me was anger, my energy reserves were low, most of my other feelings and emotions had been beaten into submission by this disease, but I wasn't going to let it eat into my anger, and I fuelled that anger with every panic attack I had. When those feelings of panic began, I had a different mantra 'I will not let you in, you bastard, I will not allow you to take over'. I would chant, this over and over, personalising the panic, giving it an identity, it was easier to fight it that way.

This took many months, most of a year in fact and there were times I felt like giving in, and giving up, and then I would conjure up that anger. It was useless for me to project the anger outside, I could have easily named and blamed all sorts for my panic attacks, but none of them would have been an adversary easily beaten, if I fought myself in this, there was only one victor or loser, me, and I had to win. I had to beat this, and eventually I did. Years later those panic attacks would rear their ugly heads again, and I once again relied on my methodology, and it worked. I discovered they could be beaten, as can most things if we don't lose sight of how strong we actually are. In our weakest and most vulnerable moments we forget how powerful the mind is, and however powerful it can be in a negative way, it can be equally powerful if not more so, when we learn how to use it to our advantage. Anger is one of our most powerful energies, use it constructively, and use it to your advantage. Get angry, be angry at this intrusion. Make a choice, and if it is to get out of that fear filled place, fight it, and keep fighting, don't give up. There is an end to it, it can stop, and although there may be times, when you feel you are losing the battle, understand that is when the enemy is becoming weak, and that is when it is most important not to give up.

26

I continued however, to be completely gullible, although to be fair, I had always looked upon doctors as very powerful people. Well, they are the people we rely on to make us well when we are ill, and I had always put them on a pedestal. Making an appointment was a massive issue for me, and actually keeping it, even more so. Fortunately the health system was such that appointments were available virtually as and when you requested them, and I made a point of having as little time as possible, prior to the appointment, for me to wind myself up in. I was petrified sitting in the waiting room, and basically had a permanent panic attack, and by the time I got to see the doctor, I was always in a terrible state of anxiety. This was and is all part of this terrible fear of anything connected with my experience in the hospital, even down to the smells. This anxiety and subsequent avoidance, I believe very sadly, contributed to the most difficult decision and ensuing circumstances that I have and continue to, endure. Bruce now always took the children to the doctor if they were unwell, and I didn't take into account that because he was drinking so much, this might fog his memory, which, god forgive me it did, to the enormous detriment of my beloved son. I will come to that soon however.

When I went for a blood pressure check, he always insisted I remove my bra, and he cupped my left breast. This he said was to check for any enlargement of the heart! I believed him. If I arrived in a state of panic which was really inevitable, just making the appointment gave me palpitations; he would lie me down on his examining table, and then gently stroke parts of my body. This started with my arms, but over time, bearing in mind I was a frequent visitor, it extended to my legs, and once to my inner thighs. His fingers started to travel higher than I felt comfortable with, and I stopped his hand with mine. 'I'm only using relaxing techniques Cheryl', he said angrily, and I felt embarrassed and stupid. It was some years later that I read about him in the newspapers whilst he was facing several charges of sexual abuse. At this time, I was pleased, and hoped he'd suffer greatly, not for what he did to me, but for what he failed to do for my son. That comes a little later on though.

As I grew stronger, I'd made friends with one of the women who worked at the play centre that Emma attended. We socialised together, spending most weekends in each others company. Bruce had found another drinking partner in her husband; therefore they were best of friends. Kathy and Peter, had a daughter Megan, and Emma and Megan were soon good friends. Megan had enormous challenges however, as she had been born with a heart defect, and had open heart surgery annually. She was constantly breathless, and had to be monitored carefully against infections of any kind, but the two little girls spent endless hours playing with their dolls and with the simplicity of a young child, Emma became her carer and protector. I confided in Kathy more than my other friends, and as she had similar concerns about Peter, although he drank frequently and heavily, she didn't experience the abuse I did, but still found his drinking difficult to deal with. She hated alcohol, and didn't even have the rare outlet that I did in getting horribly drunk herself. Kathy however didn't put up with Peter's behaviour easily though, and if he went out and didn't come home at the agreed time, Kathy had no qualms about locking him out, and leaving him to sleep in the garage or wherever. She stood her ground, and it was very seldom that Peter wasn't home on time. I tried this once, but it didn't quite work out the same way.

I double locked the front door one night, and knew there was no way, he could get in. I was wrong. Our front door had glass panels in it, and when he eventually arrived home, totally drunk and tried to get in, he became enraged. He was shouting and kicking at the door, and I was tempted to rush and open it to prevent our neighbours and the children being woken. Before I could there however, he smashed his

196

hand through a glass panel, and opened it from the inside. Then I was terrified, he was very drunk and very angry, and I managed to get into the children's room and lock the door. He ranted and banged on the door for only a brief while before passing out thank god, and I spent the rest of the night on the floor of their room. He awoke early and still drunk, and there was broken glass at the foot of the door and into the hallway, and he told me to clean it up. I really didn't want to, because that felt like I had defeated the object completely. The children were waking up though, and they could easily cut their feet, so I vacuumed it all up, and thought that was good enough. It wasn't, when he woke later, he said he would not be mending the broken pane, and that meant that anyone could break in. I had created the situation and I was therefore to remedy it, and with that he went into the bedroom to work, or sleep more likely, and slammed the door. I did fix it, because I was anxious that whilst he was out, anyone could break in, and the children and I were there alone. This had really backfired on me, and I never tried it again. It was also at this time that my brother Andrew was getting married to Jane, and the wedding was in Zimbabwe. They had asked me to be a bridesmaid, but I had to decline, as I could barely get by, day by day, let alone travelling to Zimbabwe. The thought of meeting and being with a lot of people I'd never met, absolutely terrified me, and as I would have to go alone, and leave the children with Bruce, I didn't attend the wedding at all.

I was asked to stand in for one of the teachers whilst they were away on sick leave, and I worked at the playschool for six weeks. It was ideal, as I could take both Emma and Jack with me, whilst I was there, which gave Jack the opportunity to interact with other children. This was my first experience of working, and being outside the home for years, and it helped me enormously. It gave me a sense of purpose, and increased my confidence, even though I was doing little other than feeding and supervising a few children. My responsibilities were limited due to my lack of experience, and there were always other members of staff close by, but I enjoyed the time I was there, and apparently I did the job well, as they were sad to see me go. The owner of the playschool praised me quite highly, and I began to believe that I wasn't as useless and helpless as Bruce and the rest would have me believe. This proved to be quite a turning point in my life, it gave me the desire to try and get back into the real world.

It was also at this time in my life, that I believe I was blessed in being given the opportunity to save two young lives. They were both completely separate incidents, time wise and their locations. The first happened late one night, whilst we were still awake. I was awake because I was struggling with panicky feelings, and couldn't quite relax enough to sleep. Bruce was awake and working on the computer, and it was then that the night was interrupted with screams of panic and terror, the sound of running feet, and then pounding on the front door. A hysterical woman in her night gown was screaming for help, there was a fire. I ran with her, Bruce close behind, and two or three houses down on the corner was this woman's home, which was clearly on fire. Everyone in the street had been woken, or alerted to the situation by now, and someone was shouting they had called for the fire brigade. Standing outside the house was another elderly woman and a man, both appeared to be dazed which was understandable; I was to discover later however that they were all quite drunk. There were two very young children with them. The woman, who had come to our front door, was screaming that there was a child still in the house, and Bruce and other neighbours had gone to try and get what water or hoses they could, to try and subdue the flames, which were clearly now beginning to engulf the house. It all happened so quickly, the woman screaming about her child inside, no men about, only onlookers with that expression of morbid curiosity, and the worst kind, that had come hoping for tragedy and some sort of sick thrill that seems to provide. There were also those with a smug expression, thanking their lucky stars it wasn't their home going up in flames, and those that had sensed the hysterical occupants were inebriated, and they stood there with their saintly expressions of contempt and condemnation. Nobody in this sea of faces appeared to be responding to this woman's hysterical screams about the child inside, and I didn't think to question why she hadn't attempted to go in. In those few seconds, I didn't debate the situation, I didn't consider the danger, and I, probably thoughtlessly, didn't take into account that I could potentially be depriving my children of their mother, I just thought about a little person, trapped in that burning place, and I ran into the house. The smoke was dense and the heat was intense, and both hit me like a brick wall as I went in. I remembered hearing or reading somewhere that you need to get low, so I dropped to the floor and started to crawl, screaming over the noise of the crackle for the child. I didn't know it's name or sex, I just kept screaming 'where are you, I have come for you'. My eyes were burning, and I knew I was in the front hall, and I heard a cry, it was to my right, and when I stretched my hand out, I felt a little body, I grabbed for it, and didn't know what limbs I was pulling at because I couldn't see anything, but no matter, as long as I could get hold of the child and get out. I realised I was pulling a leg, so my hands travelled up to the arms and I grabbed both, stood, turned, and hanging on to the little body, ran for our lives. I stumbled and bumped into the door frame, and then I was out, and I fell to my knees, still holding the child, both of us gasping for air. Someone ran towards us, shouting, and I couldn't understand the fear in their voice, and then there were hands everywhere, dragging and pulling us over the lawn. It was seconds later that the windows of the house exploded. The mother of the child came and took her, I realised it was a little girl then, and she sobbed as she thanked me. I got up and walked home. My neighbour and friend were there, and a few moments later we heard the wail of the fire engine siren, and Bruce returned. He had been with the other men, trying to get water to the house, and had heard about some crazy woman who had run into the burning house to save one of the children. 'What an idiot thing to do', he said. 'They were too bloody drunk to save their own kid, so why does some stupid woman play the hero'. Then he looked at me, and I was black and shaking, and he said 'it was you, wasn't it, you fucking stupid cow, you risk your life to save a strange child?', and he went on and on about my lack of sense, my stupidity, and what had I been thinking of. I could understand a little of what he was feeling, but it didn't come from care and concern for my well being, it was more his anxiety about losing his live in house-keeper, child carer, and available bonk. I never saw the people from that night again. In the morning there was absolutely nothing left of the house. There was just a charred mass of rubble on a plot of land.

The next time it happened, the only similarity was my lack of fore-thought of potential danger or risk to me, which was contradictory to my continuing fear of dying. It was some months later, and we had gone to our favourite beach. It is called Van Staadens, and there are miles of beautiful beach, and an enormous lagoon, which was fed by sea. About eighty feet of the lagoon was only ankle deep in water, and then there was a steep drop into the deeper water. It was a favourite of families with young children, because they had a vast area, they could paddle in quite safely, as long as they didn't go too far inland, to where the deeper water was. We had set up our little camp on the edge of the lagoon, and Emma and Jack were playing with their buckets and spades in the shallow water. It was always crowded, but there was a particularly boisterous group on the bank above the lagoon. They looked like they were having a really good party, and it was obvious the drinks were flowing. Bruce had gone looking for mussels to cook on the Barbie, and I was enjoying the relaxation and sunshine. I watched a little girl come down the steps to the beach alongside the lagoon. She was a pretty little girl, in her little costume, sandals, and she had a little flower petal hat on. She couldn't have been more than about four years old, and she was approaching the shallow water. I turned to look down the beach, and saw Bruce approaching, and I checked on my two, who were coming to have something to drink. They sat on their towels, and I gave them their drink, I could still see the little girl in her bright little hat from the corner of my eye. As I looked up after sorting my two out, I saw the little hat, but not the little girl, her hat was floating on top of the water at the edge where it became very deep very suddenly. Dear God, she had gone over the edge, I was up and running, shouting to Emma to call her dad to come and help me. 'Watch where mommy goes, I shouted, and get daddy to come quickly'. I went into the water where the hat was, and felt her little body immediately. I pushed her up to get her head out of the water, but mine was still beneath the surface. I wedged my feet into the steep bank, intending to use my legs to get me up and above the water. The bank was soft and slimy, and my feet just slid over its surface, I couldn't get a grip of any sort with my feet, they just slid straight back down. My arms were stretched above my head, to keep the child above water, and I knew at that time, that if I used my arms I would have to let go of her, and it would be highly unlikely I would easily find her again in the murky water. It had been churned up with my attempts to get out. This was all happening very quickly, but I was acutely aware, that I would need to take breath very soon, and in those moments, I prayed that Bruce was on his way. She was starting to struggle in my grip now, and I thanked God that she was obviously alright, but it made it increasingly difficult for me to keep her above the water. I couldn't let her go; because I knew she would just go straight under again. I was becoming desperate for air, and panic was starting to set in, when I felt her weight lifted, and I was able to get to the surface. I was literally like a fish out of water for a while and flopped onto the bank in the shallow water, gasping for air. Seconds after Bruce got to me, so did a number of other people, apparently some people had seen my sprint across the shallow part and this crazy dive into the water, and then a small child being held up, and they had respectively tried to reach me. Amongst them was one of the party group. He wasn't the parent of the child; the parents were waiting on the beach. He thanked me profusely, but when we reached the parents who had made no effort to come to their child, they were blasé, and reprimanded the child for wandering off. Neither of them even said 'thank you'. They were clearly drunk, and the man who had met me in the water, explained that they were all on a company outing, he was absolutely furious at their negligence, and more at their lack of appreciation, and he said that he found his employees attitude deplorable, and would take action the following day. He asked for my name and address, which I gave him, and a few days later I received a letter of thanks from him on behalf of his company, and he informed me that the father of the child had been sacked, after being told he should consider his and his wife's responsibility to their child.

27

We moved house yet again. Bruce was working independently, and had employed a young woman called Mandy. She was a competent computer programmer, but she was also very attractive, and he was in his element. He was working on a computer programme for optometrists, and he made another friend who he brought home to meet me, her name was Jackie. Jackie worked for one of the optometrists, and was going on holiday, she suggested I stand in for her during this time, and I was more than happy to have the opportunity to work again. I worked for the two weeks and thoroughly enjoyed it, and a number of things happened during the next few months that encouraged me to eventually make a decision that I should have made a long while back. It was to be a life changing decision, and although once made, that part of it was easy, the rest was going to be so challenging, that perhaps if I'd had the opportunity to look into a crystal ball, I might have hesitated.

It was at about this time that Emma and Jack had to have their tonsils out, about a year apart, and this was my worst nightmare. I had come so far with my phobias, but I didn't think I could cope with going into a hospital, and I had a recurrence of the panic attacks. They were less frequent, but equally distressing and frightening. On both occasions the smell of the hospital was enough to send my heart racing, and make me feel dizzy and disorientated. I tried to have a routine of coping strategies, but the only realistic one, was going outside as often as possible for a fag, and try to focus on my child's need. What I hadn't expected, and which was nearly the complete undoing of all my preparation, was that a parent could take the child into the theatre, and stay with them whilst they were put under. Emma wanted her father with her, and that felt like a door slammed in my face. I watched Bruce walk with her, and he turned and gave me a long gloating, self satisfied, smug look. All I could do was pray all would be well, and cry quietly for my little girl who believed her daddy loved her best. How would I ever explain to her that this wasn't a competition? When she came out of theatre, and woke up, she howled with the pain and that was Bruce's cue to leave. He had also volunteered me to spend the night with her, and whilst I was happy to be with her, it was a terror filled night. I couldn't sleep in a hospital, I could barely stand being there, and it was only her interruptions for water or comfort that got me through.

When Jack had to have the same surgery, my little boy wanted me, and I wasn't going to deny him this comfort. I just knew that my strength had to be my love, and I couldn't let him see that I was more afraid than he was. I remember carrying his frightened little body into the theatre, and laying him on the table, stroking his forehead, and holding his little hand, whilst they put the mask on his mouth. His eyes were wide with fear, and I promised him, he was going to have a sleep, and mommy would be right there when he woke up. 'Nothing to be afraid of ', I crooned. Liar my mind shrieked, 'just close your eyes, and everything will be alright', I went on. Please God keep him safe, don't let him wake up, afraid, not knowing what was happening, please don't let him wake up under anaesthetic'. And then panicking, as paranoia set in, 'I mean he must wake up, just at the right time and in the right place, not here, not too early,' and then I was taken out, he was asleep, and whilst I waited, I cried with fear, I made obsessive compulsive promises. If I say something over and over again, and say it the right way, he will be fine. Maybe God thought I didn't want him to wake up at all, but that wasn't what I'd meant at all, I had to make sure he didn't misunderstand. I stayed the night with Jack, and nothing had changed, nothing was better, it was another night of fear and panic, and unwelcome memories, provoked by the sounds and smells. Would I ever get this over this?

Bruce's nocturnal outings continued, and got worse, if that was possible. There were occasions when I would contact Peter to check

Bruce's local haunts when he hadn't come home, and there were many times, that Peter found him at one or the other places, passed out in his car. The few times he did come home in the early hours, he was verbally abusive and aggressive until he passed out, and he wet the bed nightly. How he managed to get up in the mornings and work, I don't know, but I think Mandy was his incentive. When he was relatively sober, I tried to talk to him about why he was behaving this way, and the response was always the same, it was because of me. I made him drink, I made him go out, and he now often told me how he regretted marrying me, wished he was free, and didn't love me anymore. Then, he would apologise, say he hadn't meant it, he was just going through a bad time in his life, and he needed me to be there for him. He wanted me to accept the drinking, the womanising, the abuse, anything and everything in fact, because he promised he would change, it would get better, and he did love me. It was like a roller coaster ride. I still felt I should stick it out for the sake of the children, he was their father after all, and they didn't see or know about the really bad parts. I realised they sensed the atmosphere in the home, and knew it wasn't good for them, but I didn't want to take responsibility for removing their father from their lives. Emma adored her father, and his manipulation of her was horrible to see. He constantly played her against me, telling her mommy didn't love her, as much as he did, mommy loved Jack more. This had gone on since her birth, and when Jack was born, he was always included in Bruce's little talks with Emma. Whenever I tried to discipline Emma, Bruce would tell me not to be so hard on her, to stop always picking on her, and it was always in front of Emma.

If I ended this marriage, God knows what she would be told, and there was my greatest fear, that he would take her from me, and I knew that given the choice she would choose to go with her father. I couldn't blame her for that, it would be an easy choice for her to make. I couldn't bear to lose her though, so I stuck with it, for a while longer anyway, as long as I could really. The confusing thing was that while Bruce kept telling me how unhappy I made him, when I suggested we split up, he went berserk. I'd been married for nine years, and there were a series of events that eventually led me to decide to try and change my life. In the grand scheme of things I suppose these seem insignificant, but for me they were clear indicators that nothing was going to change. I have, as we all have, had to make choices, and I always view them as crossroads in my path of life. If I continue on the path I am currently on, I have a reasonable idea of where that is leading, taking into account all the challenges and obstacles that life often surprises us with. Then there is the other path, the unknown, unfamiliar and altogether scary one, and when it came to the point that that one was preferable, I realised that I was prepared to take my chances with the unknown. I think one of the major factors in this, was that I had begun to lose hope. I had lost hope that he might change, that things might be different, that it could get better. I started to realise that even those very brief and rare occasions when he was a nice kind person, were not enough to sustain this marriage. I started to realise that I couldn't help him, and I started to learn to live with the self inflicted guilt, that I somehow was responsible for his anger, disrespect and cruelty. My vision of a better future might have been naïve, but it had to be better than the life I knew now. I started indicating to Bruce that I wasn't prepared to continue this way, and slowly began to make it clear to him, that I meant what I said. The fight in me was growing, and he sensed that in the not too distant future, I might just take action, instead of only talking about it, or making empty threats as he called it. It started I suppose with standing in for Jackie whilst she went away, the confidence boost that had given me, and that combined with his open flirting with Mandy day in and day out, and the nightly disturbances and general irregularity of life was wearing me down. One night I had a very late phone call from one of Bruce's clients and friends, Brian. They had become good mates, and we had visited Brian and his wife a number of times. Brian owned a chain of photographic shops and was extremely wealthy, but I also had the impression that behind the wide smile, and friendly manner was a self serving man, with little respect for women. Probably why they got on so well, they recognised certain things about each other, they obviously had in common. It was only later that I learnt that Brian had often treated Bruce to 'special massages', at an exclusive club, that he himself attended frequently. Anyway, back to the phone call. It was Brian, and apparently, he'd been out with Bruce, from the early afternoon, and Bruce had got totally paralytic as normal, perhaps more so that time. Bruce had started weeping and wailing about me leaving him, and that he wanted to change, because he couldn't bear life without me. Even Brian had become concerned about Bruce's physical and mental state, as he was virtually comatose with the amount of booze he'd drunk, during the afternoon and evening. When Brian couldn't rouse him, he took him to A&E. Apparently he had been admitted to the alcoholics ward, and Social Services and the alcohol team would be coming in that morning, and would want to meet with me. I got the children to playschool and school, and arranged a lift to the hospital. The team were waiting to speak to me before I saw Bruce. He had obviously told them, he had drunk so much, because the wife he adored, was considering leaving him, and I had a cold reception. They indicated that I was probably responsible for his drinking habits, because he loved me so much and hadn't been able to bear the thought that I might leave him, therefore he drank. I didn't even bother to try and explain that that was so far from the truth, it was actually laughable, he had convinced them, and I don't think anything I said would have changed their attitude. They asked me to have some compassion, and as he had made the very brave decision to dry out, I should at least give him the benefit of the doubt, and stay with him. What kind of person was I, that I would turn my back on this loving husband, in his time of need, and of course, didn't I have to consider my role in this. I was after all contributory to his emotional upheaval. I had just started to regain and rediscover my own strengths, and now I was to put it all aside because of his needs. Needs that I believed were based on utter deception, and selfishness. Then, they hit me where it hurt most, they found my Achilles heel. How would I explain to the children, that their Daddy was unwell, and Mommy had left him, and taken them away from him during this difficult time for him? Shit, I was cornered. Brian knew the children, and they liked Uncle Brian, and he made it clear to me, that he would let them know that their Daddy was trying to get better, and needed Mummy there to help him. Bastard!

I visited Bruce, and he held my hand and wept. He told me how sorry he was for everything, he begged me not to leave him, he promised me he would get better, he promised me it would all change. He told me he'd realised how badly he'd treated me, what a monster he'd been, and that it would never happen again, and I felt a spark of hope, I thought it might all work out, eventually what I'd been hoping for all these years, might actually happen. We could be a family, in the little cottage with the white picket fence, I could have a loving husband, and the children could have a devoted father. Hope stirred,

I believed him, I was still such a fool! He spent ten days in the hospital, and it was the first ten days in many years that he hadn't been drinking. He was on medication for that time, and he was instructed to attend AA meetings on his release from the hospital. He agreed with it all, and he came home. The first AA meeting was just a few days after he was home, and I agreed to go with him to support him. We arrived and after about a half hour, he got up to leave, on the way home, he said he wasn't an alcoholic like that bunch of fuck ups in there, and he didn't belong there. On the way home, he stopped off at the local liquor store, and bought enough beer to fill a pub, and we went home, where he sat and drank, telling me all the while that he had it all under control, until he passed out. He had been sober for just on two weeks. I felt like an emotional wreck, and it took a while to come down from the happy place I'd started to build mentally, but come down I did, and the straw that broke the camels back happened about two weeks later.

I'd taken the children to their friend's birthday party, and Bruce, who had no time for all that crap, had promised to come and fetch us at the time we'd agreed. He was going to carry on with some work. He was due to fetch us, as five that evening, and shortly afterwards when he hadn't arrived, I tried calling him at home. We didn't have any such thing as mobile phones; they were too expensive at this stage anyway. There was no reply, and I was starting to feel embarrassed as my friends wanted to tidy up, and settle their children into bed, it had been a long day for them. Emma and Jack were tired too, and becoming niggly. I tried to think where Bruce might be, and phoned a couple of friends to check whether he was there. At a loss to find him, I decided to try Jackie, and I desperately hoped I would get the same message, that he wasn't there. He was, and when he came to the phone he was furious. How dare I intrude on his time, he would be home when he was ready, and I could get spare keys from my parents, and he slammed the phone down. My friend offered me a lift home, and I phoned my parents and asked them to meet me at home with the spare house keys that they kept. I just said that Bruce had been delayed, and I needed to get the children home and ready for bed. It was about seven o'clock when we got home, and I was anxious waiting outside the house for my parents, as we lived opposite a pub, and there were often drunks coming out, who could be aggressive, and I had the children with me. Eventually I saw my parents' car, coming down the road, and directly behind them, Bruce. They all arrived at the same time. Bruce screeched to a halt, and as usual he was drunk, and he went off on one again. This was all taking place in the street, and attracting a lot of attention. I thanked my parents and asked them just to leave, and eventually got the keys to open the door and get myself and the children inside. Bruce came in after us, carrying what was left of a case of beer. I got the children into the bath, and then prepared to face the music, which I did. He was livid, that he had to interrupt his time with Jackie, he volunteered; he'd been that close to getting Jackie into the sack, when I'd phoned, and he was furious that I had destroyed the moment, and his opportunity, and with that, he stormed out, to go and try regaining his lost ground.

That was it really; something inside me died, and anything warm and fuzzy towards Bruce became ice cold. The following morning I called a solicitor I found in the telephone book and made an appointment to see him, to file for divorce. I still didn't have any money, I didn't have a job, and I didn't know how I was going to put a roof over my children's head, and feed and clothe them. There were still the awful feelings of guilt regarding the children and being responsible for what was certain to be upheaval and massive changes in their lives, but one thing I was certain of, and that was I was keeping my children, both of them, and I would fight him to the death if necessary to achieve this. I didn't have to fight him at all, he was only too happy to relinquish responsibility for the children, and quite happy to move out of the home and start a new life for himself. In fact, he was excited about it. Divorce in South Africa is conveniently or brutally fast, whichever way you choose to look at it, and uncontested it takes about six weeks from start to finish. During this time, Bruce moved to another town, got a job and settled down remarkably quickly. In this time, I had to find a job, and look for other accommodation. I had no working experience apart from the few weeks I'd helped out in the last nine years, and my secretarial skills were now well behind the times. I had learnt to type on a manual typewriter and now everything was electronic. I had lost my shorthand speed, and as for my book-keeping skills, well, past experience had shown they were non exist-ent. As I mentioned jobs are scarce, and there aren't opportunities to work behind the counter anywhere, I was very anxious about finding something, but equally determined not to go back to Bruce purely and simply because I couldn't find work. This, however put me in a critical position, because as I mentioned earlier the benefits system is non existent and all a divorcee with children can rely on is child support, but of course the father of the children needs to be prepared to support his children, which Bruce was very reluctant to do.

28

Via the extended family grapevine, my dad learnt that my cousin, who was my senior by about twenty years, was looking for someone to join his company. He owned a publicity company, and one of their projects was to produce a tourist guide for the South Eastern area, which was where I lived. It would entail meeting with Regional Representatives, over a vast area, and basically selling space in the guide. Apparently my dad had explained my situation, and I am sure it was a charitable gesture, when Alistair, my cousin, contacted me to suggest I take the job. I was more than terrified. The job I had envisioned was far less demanding and challenging, and I really believed this was totally out of my capabilities. I think Alistair thought so too, but he had always admired and adored my dad, and perhaps he thought this would make amends somehow. You see, Alistair was an alcoholic, and had had some dire moments after each of his many marriages failed, and he made and lost fortunes. He had won national and international awards for sales, and had literally made and lost millions, and whenever he hit a low, he always called my dad for support and advice. Alistair had been in and out of our lives since I was a young child, and we had visited him when we lived in Stellenbosch and he lived in Cape Town. It was during that time, that Bruce and I had received a number of these desperate calls, and once we had rushed through to Alistair, after he called and said he'd taken an overdose when his latest wife walked out on him. We'd spent the rest of the night with him, whilst he slept off the enormous quantity of booze he'd consumed, and once he had vomited up the few painkillers he'd swallowed, all he really had to recover from was a hangover and his wounded pride. When he went through one of his divorces or bankruptcies, he was very needy and emotionally demanding and I had spent many hours on the phone to him, whilst I was pregnant with Emma. Perhaps he remembered this and also considered this as payback for me. Alistair was a kind person, but he liked to talk about whatever favour he had done, and he ensured everyone knew about his charitable nature, but, whatever his motives, for the offer, and whilst I was scared out of my little mind, I was also incredibly grateful for the opportunity. It all happened very quickly, and I was flown to Cape Town, where the company was based, and given forty eight hours of intensive training, and then I went back to Port Elizabeth, and was told to get on with it. This was the first time I had been away from my children, they were with my parents, and I found that really hard. The most difficult part of it all though, was that I had to literally propel myself out of the little cocoon I had lived in for the last nine years, and overnight, project a confident, self-assured, and competent image to Alistair and his staff, because they had to believe I could do this. There were already snide remarks passed around the office, because of me being related to Alistair, which were justified really. They were marketing professionals, and suddenly little Cheryl from 'Hicksville', had been employed. The position I was filling was at management level, and would normally have accommodated an experienced member of staff, and I had no relevant experience at all. I don't know how or if Alistair justified my employment, he probably charmed them all into believing I was the right person for the role, and not just orphan Annie, being given a break. If nothing else, Alistair was an amazing charmer. He had managed to snare four wives, all of whom were exceptionally beautiful, and intelligent, and although his marriage was always on the edge, his current wife, Marguerite appeared to still be quite smitten with him, although impatient about his on, off drinking habits. Alistair was always trying to dry out, and had more detox's than most people have breakfasts. None of them were successful. He was a very good looking man and charisma on legs really. The family always said that Alistair could sell ice to Eskimo's. He used his skills on me, and at the end of the training, I believed I could too. I had

211

been extremely anxious about everything really, from the flight out, everything in between, and the return flight, and I'm not sure exactly what got me through it all quite admirably too. I think it was my sheer determination to change my life, the children's life and of course to be able to feed and clothe them and put a roof over their heads. I know, along with this executive team, I drank a lot of wine, it seemed to flow, morning, noon and night in this environment, and that obviously helped me blag my way through, but at the end of the day, I believe it came down to sheer will and determination to achieve a new life. Of course there was the strong encouragement from my parents, that they'd put their necks on the line for me, and it wouldn't be nice for me to let them down.

I arrived home, thrilled to see Emma and Jack again, although Emma was disappointed she was meeting me and not her dad at the airport, and from then on there was no turning back. The challenges came thick and fast and en masse. I now had a very demanding job to do, along with finding a new home, and the divorce to finalise. Bruce had left it all up to me, as far as he was concerned, he had allowed me to keep the furniture, and as we didn't own any property or have any other financial issues to resolve, he believed that because I had filed for the divorce, I was responsible for dealing with it.

I had the bonus of a company car, which was wonderful, office accommodation had been arranged for me, and I was given my targets, and deadlines, and told to get on with it. Selling advertising is particularly challenging as the client cannot actually see what they have bought until the finished product. Although they are provided with proofs, this can also encourage the client to constantly change their advertisements, and things always seem to be left to the absolute deadline for print. Cold calling, as any sales person will know can be time consuming and a thankless task, and I had a lot of people to persuade in a very short time. I had another major problem too, I wasn't bilingual. I still didn't speak Afrikaans apart from a few greetings and my vocabulary was very limited. As I was meeting with either the relevant Mayor and councillors, or the Town Clerks, and they were predominantly Afrikaans speaking, I wasn't sure quite how I was going to resolve this. It was difficult enough trying to arrange the appointments with my ridiculous lack of their language, eventually; I would rattle off a date and time, and hang up. I learnt one of the most useful phrases, basically greeting the people and explaining to them that I was useless at Afrikaans, and would it be alright to continue in English. Well that went down like a lead balloon, nine times out of ten, what was I thinking. I was a foreigner in their country, and not prepared to learn their language. I was a fast learner though, and agreed that the meeting would continue in Afrikaans, and then I would explain my role, speaking English, with Afrikaans words thrown in as and when I knew them, or not, I just carried on like a lunatic, and it worked every time. They would be in hysterics at this stupid young woman, who couldn't speak their language, and I either got the sympathy vote then, or the grudging admiration one. At least either way, I was prepared to behave like a total fool to accommodate their request. How any negotiations were made, or agreements reached I don't know, it certainly was on a wing and a prayer, because I left each meeting praying I had the photograph they had chosen, but in my ignorance, not really certain if it was the one they had most definitely declined.

Alistair and his assistant Christine did visit me regularly, and I knew they were shocked and impressed at the work I was sending back for processing. I was too actually. During these weeks and months, I drove thousands of miles, sometimes taking Jack with me, as Emma was in school now, and I always made a point of getting home each night, and not having to stay away. I felt their lives had been disrupted enough, and it was crucial for them to retain some sense of security. We were staying with Kathy and Peter for a couple of months, as my dad had managed to secure a ground floor flat for me in the block he supervised as caretaker. It was conveniently right next door to their flat, but it would only be vacant in six months. I was splitting my time between friends, and was ever so grateful for their support and kindness at this time. As the finalisation of the divorce loomed, Bruce communicated less and less, and it was clear that he thought I would withdraw from the proceedings at any time, and would never go through with it. I did, and I attended court as required. The divorce was granted on the grounds of 'irreconcilable differences', and as his solicitor was obliged to contact him to confirm this, I left it at that. Later that day, I received a call from his current colleague, Don, who told me I was a total bitch, amongst other things, in fact the way he went on, I was certainly spawn of the devil. He had found Bruce curled up on the floor of his office, weeping about the end of his marriage. How could I treat such a kind loving husband and father this way? Bruce had told him how much he loved me and the children, and how he'd always tried his best, but nothing he did was good enough for me. I had destroyed this gentle kind man. I didn't respond, what for, Don would believe what he chose to, and it wasn't up to me to tell him what Bruce really was like, he'd find out soon enough.

Soon after the divorce, Bruce left to join his mum and sisters who had moved to Italy, and we received the odd letter and tape messages from him. The tape messages were full of apologies, and regrets, and he begged for another chance. I felt guilty, and sorry for him, and it didn't occur to me that these messages were predominantly about him, his regrets, and full of self pity. I still apologised for him in my head, and made excuses for him. I also believed him.

Over the next six months, I achieved my targets, and virtually single handed I had covered the South Eastern Cape entirely. I think everyone was shocked to the core, I think I was too, I hadn't known I had it in me, but I believed I was a given an opportunity and I had to deal with it really. I had one final deal to close, and it wasn't about a difficult negotiation, it was just timing that had made it the last. It was with a casino chain, that was in a neighbouring 'country', there was a border post, which was never manned or patrolled, and it was really only there as a landmark. Casinos were illegal in South Africa at the time, so this was how they got around it, and it was a two hour journey through tribal land, on poor roads, that weren't maintained. When I had driven there in the past for meetings, I ensured it was during daylight. It was potentially quite a threatening part of the country, and it could be extremely dangerous to be stranded along the roadside at any time of day, let alone when it was dark. Alistair had come down to finalise the paperwork with me for the publication, and as he knew the manager of the casino, had suggested he come with me. I didn't and couldn't object really, and I was pleased things were coming to an end as he was going through one of his binge drinking periods, and was very unpredictable. I knew he was on medication to try and prevent him drinking, and that it would make him quite unwell, if he had alcohol whilst he was taking it. Anyway, I didn't know that it was up to me, or my responsibility to try and prevent him from having a drink if he decided on one.

We arrived at the casino later than I was happy with, and I mentioned to Alistair that I wanted to get back before dark, and suggested he stay the night there if the meeting went on. Once Alistair was in full flow, he could talk and entertain for hours. The manager was dealing with a staff crisis, when we arrived, and asked if we would relax, have a drink and he would be with us as soon as possible. Alistair said he was getting a drink, and I mentioned he might want to reconsider, if the pills were going to react and make him ill. He said he hadn't taken them that day. I knew then he was going to go at it like there was no tomorrow, and I wasn't wrong. I watched him go to the bar to order the drinks, and four glasses were put in front of him. Three with what I assumed was neat whisky, as I knew that was his drink of preference, and then a glass of white wine for me. He downed two before he returned to our table with a drink each. I didn't say anything and tried to draw him into conversation about the upcoming meeting, he did discuss it, but the booze he'd had, had already hit him hard, and he was already slurring. I'd taken a sip of my wine, and he was up getting the next round, and again at the bar, I saw him throw an extra one down his throat. I think he believed he was being quite clever in assuming I would think he'd only had what he brought back to our table. Anyway, in a very short time he was getting quite drunk, and I was getting pissed off. I needed to get on the road, if I was to get back before dark, and although I would have had Alistair as support or company in the car, I didn't think this was going to happen now. One of the staff came and told us, the manager would be with us in about another hour, and apologised for the delay, and then offered us complimentary drinks. Shit, Alistair was ordering two whiskies in an instant. I decided to suggest that he continue with the meeting alone, and perhaps arrange a lift back the following day, but he wasn't having any of that, and in very strong terms reminded me of who my employer was, and who paid my salary, and my company car. This turned into a bit of a rant, and then he suddenly said he was going to reception and would be back shortly. He came back and said he'd resolved the problem of the delay. 'What do you mean?', I asked. 'Well I've booked us in for the night', he replied. I was furious, 'Alistair, I've told you, I don't stay away from my kids for the night, I have to get back.' I said. 'Well, I am the boss, and I have booked a double room, and I thought you could express your gratitude to me tonight. I could also teach you a thing or two', he leered. You sick stupid drunk old bastard, I thought furiously. I was absolutely appalled at his suggestion, and basically fuck the opportunity he had given me, I had worked damn hard, and achieved all the required results, so I had nothing to thank him for, and besides, how dare he assume I would agree to this.

Even the opportunity he'd given me had been to serve his purposes, because I think he thought I would fall flat on my face at the start, but at least he could then tell my dad, at least he'd tried to help me. I'd proved them all wrong, and now he expected me to spend the night with him, and, we were related, and he was old enough to be my father, and he was married, and it was just totally disgusting. I was livid in those seconds this flashed through my mind, and I stood, picking up my briefcase, and said as calmly as I could, 'I'm going back to my children, you can either come back to Port Elizabeth with me, or stay', and I walked away. He followed in full rant all the way to the car park. 'You can't abandon me here, and let me remind you that is a company car, you can't take it', and on and on. By the time we reached the car, I was shaking with anger. Then came the clanger, 'if you leave now, you are fired', he said. That was it, you absolute drunk bastard, I opened the boot, and threw his things onto the ground, closed the boot, opened my door, and said 'Fuck you're job, and fuck you'. I got in the car and drove away.

Overriding my anger and anxiety about just losing my job, was the total fear of the journey home, cars were often stoned, and there was the added concern of goats, and other animals on the road. Driving through the populated areas at night was equally worrying, as it was pitch black, and difficult to identify bicycles and people until you were virtually on top of them, and very little regard was taken to the proximity of the road. It was dark now, and I was on my own, and I was terrified. I drove fast and furious, praying all the way, and arrived safe and sound. The hysteria of the day could set in now that I was home, and whilst I was telling Kathy and Peter what had happened, there was a call for me, and it was my mother. Alistair had phoned them in an awful state, and what did I think I was doing, how dare I tell Alistair to 'fuck off', and chuck my job in, just because he'd asked me to work a little later than normal. How did this make them look, they had vouched for me, and I had let them down enormously, why was I always so ungrateful, how could I do this to them, how could I embarrass them like this. Oh, and the really good part, Alistair's wife had phoned them, and was furious that I had encouraged Alistair to drink, when I knew he was on medication. Alistair had phoned and told her, I had insisted he have a drink, to be sociable, and didn't I know it could have killed him. I couldn't get a word in during this tirade, so I just waited for her to run out of steam and then said, 'Alistair chose to drink, and then arranged to spend the night with me, so I could thank him very personally for what he'd done for me, so I told him to fuck off', and I put the phone down. It was only later, I realised that in all this, and there had been no mention of me having to travel alone, in the dark, because of circumstances beyond my control and comprehension.

Funnily enough, the next morning, I received a call from Alistair asking me to meet him, later that day. I did, and he looked shocking. He referred very briefly to our 'disagreement' of the day before, said it had been an unfortunate misunderstanding, then he launched straight into work related issues. I obviously wasn't sacked then, and for now I would continue in the job, with little or no further contact with him, until I could find something else.

29

I went to stay with other friends for the last three months until my flat became available, and it certainly wasn't without its dramas. Lynne and Roger had come to South Africa from the UK, because of better job prospects and life in the sunshine. Roger loved the lifestyle, Lynne hated it. They had a little girl called Tanya, and they doted on her, and spoilt her accordingly. She was a very spoilt little girl, and I had difficulty maintaining any form of discipline with my two, when they saw Tanya get away with anything and everything. Lynne was a very large woman, both in size and personality. She was loud, and hot tempered, and kept a very tight reign on Roger. Roger was tall, and walking bones, he was so skinny, and together they looked completely mismatched, and it was evident who wore the trousers. Lynne and Roger were heavy and regular drinkers, as in all fairness most of the population are, and I certainly did my fair share. To begin with, all went relatively well, and as I was at work all day, it was only the evenings that I had to involve myself in their lives. I tried to allow them as much privacy and personal space that I could by spending a lot of time in my room with the children, but inevitably they insisted I join them. Roger, looked like a tall skinny ferret, and he insisted on wearing his hair longish, which always needed a wash. Each unto their own, and aside from the fact he was married to my friend, he really wasn't my type, but he fancied himself as some sort of don Juan. Lynne was obsessively jealous of Roger, and watched him like a hawk at all times, wherever they went, I think he played on this a bit, and went out of his way to flirt with other women. Lynne could be super scary if she thought another woman was after her Roger, which was doubtful really, because all the women were terrified of big Lynne anyway. I had discovered that there is this bizarre perception amongst a lot of men that divorcees are gagging for sex. They seem to think that we are bereft and lost without that part of our lives, and desperate for someone to oblige. Sure, when I settled down a little more, I was going to enjoy myself and possibly date, but that would be as and when I felt ready to. It really was quite funny, if I was out and introduced to a man, the normal small talk would ensue, and when it came to the part of marriage and children, as soon as I mentioned I was divorced, this glint would appear in his eye. Why? I mean what part of being divorced meant that I had dropped all my standards and ideals for a bonk. Anyway, I'm digressing, but it is relative to the next part of my story. It was one weekend, and I had met someone who I rather fancied, and we had ended up having that bonk. Earlier that day, we'd had a barbeque with Lynne and Roger, and everyone had a good quota of wine and beer, and later we'd gone to my room, leaving Lynne and Roger still drinking up a storm. I knew there would be a shouting match later on, because they both got quite aggressive when they were very drunk, but they had their own little ritual of a huge argument and then making up with goodness knows what kind of sex, I'd been unable not to hear the goings on in the past, because it sounded very physical, very loud, very long, and if the howls were to be believed, very satisfying for them both.

Cliff, was a golf pro with the local golf club, and nice enough for a bit of a fling, which we both knew was all it was and would be, and I suppose with maturity and age, there was little shyness and embarrassment leading up to knowing that we would have sex that night. It was in the little innuendo's and gestures, the touching becoming that little bit more intimate, so it felt quite natural and uncomplicated when we went to my room together. It was pleasant enough, not earth shatteringly wonderful, but probably a lot of that for me, was to do with it being my first time, in many years with another man. We'd both fallen asleep, and I awoke to a hand between my legs. I thought Cliff was obviously thinking about another session, and turned to look at him. God forbid, he was the other end of the bed, with his back to me, how the hell was his hand where it was, when I could make out two hands on his pillow. I then realised that the arm attached to the hand was coming from my side of the bed, and it must therefore be connected to a body lying on the floor beside my bed. In an instant I grabbed the hand and flung it so hard, it cracked against the wall and a howl of pain came from the floor. A head came up, and it was a very drunk Roger. What the hell was he doing there, and more to the point, what the hell was his hand doing on me. I'd screamed as I threw the hand off me, and Cliff awoke as Roger was trying to crawl out of the bedroom. Roger got to the door at the same time as Cliff did, and all hell broke loose. I was screaming at Roger, that he was a sick little man, Cliff was threatening to smash his face in, forgetting he was stark naked, and Roger was trying to squirm his way out of the room. I threw a t shirt and nicks on, and told Cliff to let Roger go, and get something on, and then I did panic, because the opposite bedroom door opened and big Lynne came out. Good God, she was a sight to terrify the bravest. Her hair was standing out on all ends, she was in a tent sized nightdress which did nothing to cover her massive swinging boobs, and she came out with the stomp and stance of a wrestler walking into the ring. She'd heard her Roger cry out, and woe betide anyone hurting him. Cliff had his hand around Roger's throat, and we all stopped mid flow as she appeared. I tried to tell Cliff not to say anything, and we would sort it all out in the morning when everyone was more level headed, but he said 'take your husband, and keep him in his own room, and tell him never to bother Cheryl again'. Well out of that sentence all Lynne chose to hear was 'husband and Cheryl', and she launched at me, lifting me off my feet, and up against the wall in an instant. 'What the fuck are you doing with my husband', she shouted. It was like being threatened by the Incredible Hulk, and because she had her hand around my throat, I couldn't answer her, but I did think this was one hell of a way to die. Cliff and Roger had watched this with their mouths open, and Cliff's hand was still resting around Roger's throat. I thought, 'say something, one of you, tell her it wasn't me, and hurry up'. Here I'm having the life choked out of me, and these two morons are standing watching it. I think what did it for all of us, well, what certainly crossed my mind as she came at me, was, how did someone of that size, stomping her way out of the room, suddenly transform into a butterfly that literally swept across the space between us, as if on air.

Cliff eventually opened his mouth, and said, 'let Cheryl go, you stupid woman', (oh shit Cliff, diplomacy would be good right now, not name calling) 'it's you're bloody husband you should have up against that wall'. Lynne's face turned towards them, which was a blessing, really, because it had been about five millimetres from mine, and that had been particularly unpleasant. Stale booze breath, and angry spittle, was not nice. 'What', Lynne boomed, and now all I could think about, was her letting me go, it was starting to get very uncomfortable up against the wall. 'He was in our room, feeling Cheryl up', Cliff replied, and I thought 'that's it then, it's going to be a massacre'.

Lynne let go, and it was so unexpected, that I landed in a heap. Roger had tried to shrink, and slink away, but she did that butterfly thing again, and as I crawled to Cliff and the possibility of safety, she had Roger up against the wall, only this time she was banging his head against it, whilst screaming at him to confirm what Cliff had said. Well how did she expect Roger to answer, the man had her hand around his throat, banging his head against the wall, and then the occasional slap, when he didn't reply. 'Let's talk about it in the morning Lynne', I said, and with that she glared at me, and dragged Roger into the bedroom by his hair. The kids had woken, not surprisingly, and wanted to know what had happened, and I said we thought that someone had been at the front door and for them to go back to bed, and this gave me the opportunity to gather my wits.

They knew I was lying, because the sounds coming from Roger and Lynne's bedroom left little to the imagination, and they didn't sound like Roger was having much fun. Cliff and I went back to my room, and he started to dress, and explained he had to get home. I couldn't blame him, I would have liked to leave this mad house too. Whilst he was dressing, I started to giggle, and then I couldn't stop laughing. It must have looked so funny.

I realised that it would be impossible for me to continue to stay there after that, so we were on the move again, and as I was running out of options, we had to stay with my parents in their two bed roomed flat. I was grateful for them putting us up, but it was a very difficult time, as during the month we were there, my mum was in her element with her granddaughter. My authority went down the toilet, and after a week of constant arguments about me trying to keep the children under control and maintain some sense of discipline, I gave up, until I was able to move into our own place.

30

My parent's favouritism for their granddaughter was actually disturbing and sad at the same time. My heart ached for my little boy when he tried so hard to get their attention, and when he had it fleetingly, to try and hang onto it for as long as he could. I compensated for this, as I had done from the day he was born, and spent most of my free time with him. Emma didn't really want to be with us anyway, and I couldn't blame her, she had two people falling over themselves to keep her happy, and of course, every time mummy told her to pick up her toys, or do her homework, she knew that one or other of her grandparents would step in, and let her do fun stuff instead. What child wouldn't enjoy the constant attention, adoration and defence system they provided. I tried to talk to them and explain that they were undermining me. It was hard enough trying to maintain basic obedience standards without their father around, and now whatever effort I had put into that, it was being destroyed. I wasn't a strict mum, in fact I was too much of a soft touch really, but I did believe in teaching them respect for others, especially their elders, good manners in all things and towards everyone, and basically to listen to me, and when it was no, it was no. I was longing for our own space, but I was becoming progressively concerned about how close, we were going to be to my parents. I thought I would be able to control the situation once I was in my own flat.

Eventually the time came when we could take occupancy, and

it brought the constant moving and upheaval to an end. I'd tried to make it an adventure for the children, but it had been too long, and I knew they needed to know that they were going to stay in the same place for longer than a couple of months. I felt it was critical now, that they were able to resurrect a sense of security, and routine, and, although we didn't have much, we had enough to keep us comfortable and make a little home for ourselves.

My main concern at this time was that I needed to look for another job, and quickly. The guide was in print, and there was nothing significant left for me to do. If I'd chosen to, I could have kept my job, maintaining a low profile and shuffling papers, but the relationship with Alistair was non existent really, and when we did talk, out of necessity, it was strained and awkward. I knew he wouldn't ask me to leave, because he was paranoid that I would tell Marguerite about his proposition, and whilst he could easily deny it, the seed of doubt would be planted, and anyway she had enough experience of his womanising to consider that I was telling the truth. I had no reason to do this, as I didn't want to be responsible for trouble in their marriage, and at the end of the day, no real harm had been done. I'd felt insulted, and my position abused, but there wasn't anything unusual about those feelings for me.

I've gone on as if everything was matter of fact and easy. It wasn't. I was really scared about such a lot of things. I was the only single person in my circle of friends, and remember when I mentioned that strange perception men have about divorcees, well woman have another one. They all seem to think we are out to steal their husbands. I tried not seeing the expressions on my friend's faces, when I laughed and chatted with their husbands. They were my friends too, and what was considered quite acceptable and normal when I was married, suddenly became threatening. I stopped visiting as much, so as not to create difficulties, and it was hard to make new friends, because they were men and women with the same perceptions and anxieties. I was scared of being a single parent, the responsibility felt enormous. I had no-one as back up or support in any decision I made for the children, and I had to learn just to rely on my instincts. I was anxious I could be too protective, and smother them in cotton wool, shielding them from too much, or I could try too hard to instil independence and confidence in them, and allow too much freedom and exposure. It was difficult for me to deny them much of anything I could provide, because I felt responsible for the lack of their father in their lives. It wasn't up to me to explain why I'd done what I had, and that I had then, and still did, believe it was the lesser of two evils that as they grew older they would be more exposed to the actualities of their father's and my relationship. That didn't help all those times that Emma became angry and defiant with me, because I'd sent her dad away. I was scared one of them would get hurt or sick, and I was even more scared that I might get ill or die, leaving them alone. I missed having someone in my life, and I started to make more and more excuses for Bruce's behaviour, and focus on what very few good times there had been. I did the pigeon hole thing, and started to file the bad memories away. I began to blame myself for the problems, and started to convince myself that I had a lot to do with his behaviour, the drinking the womanising, the abuse. I began to follow my old pattern, and I started to turn it all around, and take much more responsibility than I could ever have realistically been accountable for. I was afraid of all the change that had and was taking place in my life, and I craved familiarity. I also never believed I would meet someone who would love me, and in these reproachful thoughts, I began to believe that I should have perhaps been more patient and given Bruce more time. I also began to believe I missed him, and maybe I loved him. I was lonely and I felt alone.

It was at this vulnerable and lonely time, that Bruce came back into our lives, unannounced and unexpectedly. The children were thrilled to see their father when he turned up on our doorstep, and my heart skipped a beat too. He told me how difficult it had been for him in Italy, although he had the support of his family, he knew how badly he'd treated me, and he had found that difficult to live with, and accept. He told me he still loved me, and begged my forgiveness, he said he'd been through a very dark time in his life, and he could only continue to get better with me in his life. He had had the opportunity to stay overseas, but couldn't bear being away from 'his family' for longer, so he had decided to return to try and regain what he had lost. He had been offered a very good job with a top optometric company, and was looking for accommodation. He'd been so alone, so unhappy, so hurt, he'd had his life turned upside down, and it had been so hard. Of course it had, and I'd been responsible, and my old foe returned, guilt. I chose not to believe, that he was still so selfish. This conversation had been all about his pain and suffering, both of which were self inflicted. He never actually told me he had taken responsibility for what had happened, and that there really was no other way out for me. He never apologised for not sending any money to help support these children he now seemed to love so much. He hadn't been able to, because he'd had to focus on getting better, healing himself, and recover from the trauma of the divorce.

He never asked how my life had been since the divorce, how hard it had been for the kids and I to adjust to our new life, the upheaval and insecurity, the recriminations from the children, their tears and pleas for daddy, the sleepless nights worrying about how I was going to support them. The emotional wounds, now scars, I'd been trying to heal, the seemingly irreparable damage, that sometimes felt like it would never mend. That part of me that felt like I wasn't, and couldn't be, a loved and cherished woman and mother, those parts of me that believed I deserved to be treated the way he had treated me, the child and then adult that understood abuse as familiar, and had so little experience of self worth and value. That part of me, which nearly made up the whole of me, felt sorry for him, and I welcomed him back into our lives.

My parents were unhappy about it to say the least, and I was quite chuffed, as I thought it meant they were concerned for me. Sadly, I believe it was that Emma's attention and focus were on her father more than them now, and my mum didn't like anyone coming between her and Emma, and that included me. They had been very supportive during the months after the divorce, and were thrilled that we lived next door. My mum had taken control again, and in the kindest possible way, she insisted that we have a meal with them every Sunday. The children popped next door often, especially Emma, and she was never sent home, I had to go and fetch her for tea, which she didn't want to eat, because my food wasn't as nice as granny's. She started doing her homework with her granny, especially her maths, which I did become impatient with, and granny said she'd do it with Emma. Emma virtually lived there, and it was always a battle to get her home. It's difficult to explain, because it was so manipulative and cunning. She 'niced' me into thinking it was to help me out, but, for whatever reason, she somehow believed she had exclusive rights to Emma, and I know that her role identity in this relationship, was blurred and distorted. Since

Bruce's absence, she behaved in every way as though she was Emma's mother. This of course left me somewhat in limbo land, and likewise my identity became blurred. My role as a mum had been usurped by my mother, and my identity as a daughter had been replaced by my child. Two's company, three is a crowd, and I was the unwelcome one in this threesome.

Bruce came for meals, he saw the children as regularly and often as he wanted to, and he started to pay minimum maintenance. He'd told me he now had his drinking under control, and when he was with us, he had a glass of wine or two with his meal, and I believed him. He treated me with respect, flattered me, praised me, and in this way, gave me everything I craved. I really believed he'd turned his life around. That sponge in me, that was so eager to soak up his liquid compliments and praise, forgot that as easily as a sponge soaks, it is as quick to squeeze the fluid out, returning it to its original dry dead useless form. For now though, that sponge was saturated.

31

I scoured the papers daily, and there were so few vacancies. There weren't many that I could apply for anyway, with most of them being admin based, and then one day, I saw one for a combined sales and admin person in an office furniture organisation. I sent my CV and references in, and of course the one from Alistair was glowing to say the least, I could have won awards with it. Then, I waited, and prayed. The salary mentioned had been good, and there was commission too, and it was close to where I lived and the children's school. The call came, and I was asked to attend an interview. I was more nervous before the interview than when I'd had to go to Cape Town. This could mean absolute security for me and the kids.

I was interviewed by one of the Directors of the company, and he told me they'd had over three hundred applications for the role. My heart sunk, I didn't stand much of a chance then. They were interviewing ten people over the next two days, and then they would shortlist to three. I felt the interview went as well as possible, but I left feeling quite negative really. One of the questions they had grilled me on was the fact that I was a single parent with two young children, and their concern was that I would take more time off work than the average two parent family with shared responsibilities. I was called for a second interview, and geared myself up to do the best sales pitch I had ever done. I was going to persuade them that I was the best person for the job. I was so nervous, and it all went really well, until that question came up again, about me being a single parent. It wouldn't have been considered discriminatory at that time if they had declined me on that basis. I had to convince them that my dad was retired and on hand for any emergencies, and my mum was often about too. There were friends I could call on for lifts to and from sport and other extra curricular activities; I did my best short of begging for the job. I was introduced to the other staff, and it was a small but very successful company, and there were only two other women there, one of whom was the wife of one of the Directors. They said they would get back to me that afternoon, either way.

I sat willing the phone to ring, and then terrified it would. They could be calling to tell me I'd been unsuccessful, so I swung between optimism and total despair, and when it did ring, I jumped out of my skin. It was like you see in some movies, when you know that at the other end of the line is a life and death situation, and you sit there screaming at the television, 'answer the damn phone for goodness sake, what are you waiting for?'. Well that was me, hand poised, knowing I would be either ecstatic or totally gutted; it didn't occur to me for one moment that it might have been somebody else. I eventually answered, and Martin, the director, told me they would like to offer me the job. I nearly wept with relief and gratitude, and declared I would be the most dedicated employee of all time. I think Martin thought I was a little over the top, but we agreed I would start on the Monday, and now my only problem was transport, as there was no longer a company car. I was blessed and Bruce managed to find me a little blue beetle, the old style, and I started to feel, things were really changing for the better now, and that life would become less complicated. I had just turned twenty nine.

I loved my new job. There was a lot to learn, but the people I worked with were very supportive. There were two directors, Lee and Martin, and Lee's wife Joy worked mornings only. Lee was a big man with an equally big personality, and he reminded me of Alistair. He was a typical salesman, and I think his blurb and charm, spilled over into all parts of his life. I think he'd forgotten how to just be himself, and instead was always promoting himself, his life, his wealth, his supposed sex appeal, but with all this, Lee was all talk, and he adored his wife and children. Joy was obsessively jealous, very vain, and as Lee's second wife, had married into wealth which hadn't been part of her life before. She only bought designer clothes, and was quick to tell us how much they cost, and how easily she could now afford them. Underneath it all she was nice enough. Martin was short and slight, and his personality fitted his build. He seldom closed sales, and relied heavily on Lee to pick up after him. It was obvious he was intimidated by Lee, and I felt sorry for him. Marie and I did all the secretarial and telephone work, as well as showroom sales, and, believe it or not, the bookkeeping was handed over to me. This included the sales figures, banking, and petty cash, in fact anything to do with figures was my responsibility. I excelled at it, which left me more surprised than anyone else, and more than that I enjoyed it.

A number of things happened very quickly during my first two weeks there, some of them temporarily life changing. The first had to do with Bruce. I'd invited him around for dinner, and I saw his car outside when I arrived after work. Both children came running out to meet me, and the first thing they said was 'Mummy, daddy is here and inside and he's drunk again'. The disappointment and despair on their little faces broke my heart. It also enraged me. I stormed in, and he was in the kitchen. He was attempting to prepare dinner, but could barely stand up, let alone cook, and the empty bottle of wine on the table indicated he was still drinking up a storm. 'Get out', I screamed, 'get out of my home and don't come back, you lying bastard'. I was pulling and dragging him out as I ranted. 'How dare you do this to the kids'? I got him to the front door and Emma and Jack were standing behind me, both crying now, as I shoved him out. 'You stupid useless cow', he said, 'you were nothing, you are still nothing, and you will always be a useless nothing'. As he stumbled to his car, he continued shouting the two words, 'useless' and 'nothing', and I thought he missed two out, 'stupid' and 'gullible'. The rest of the evening was spent comforting the children, and listening to the 'I told you so's', from my parents. They, and the rest of the block of flats had heard the commotion. The next day, there were the normal apologies, but I turned a deaf ear, and said we would discuss visiting arrangements for him with the children, and that would be all there would be from now on. That was enough for the familiar Bruce to emerge, and the maintenance stopped. He didn't contact the children for weeks after that, and when he did, and I let them spend time out with their father, Emma came home angry and defiant with me. God knows what he'd been saying, but I refused to be drawn into using the children as weapons of emotional destruction.

In the meantime, I'd been invited to a barbeque at Marie's farm that weekend, which I'd accepted, and looked forward to meeting her family. She is Afrikaans born and bred, and her and her family were of the old type of Afrikaaner. They lived off the land as much as possible, and her husband was living well behind the times. His name was Stefan. He had old fashioned, rigid and very harsh rules about bringing up his boys and his relationship with women. They were there to cook, clean, keep their spouse comfortable and happy, and bear children. They were not supposed to have opinions, let alone voice them, and their priorities in life were, and in order of importance, their husband, their children, and their home. If they obeyed all of these, their reward was a reasonably trouble free existence. For him though, other rules applied. He was to have free will to eat, drink, sleep, and forego a regular job. His wife and sons did the chores so that he needn't be troubled with them, and his days were spent doing exactly what he chose to. They had bought a plot of land, albeit with Marie's hard earned cash, and he was going to build them a house. This was his huge sacrifice, for which they should be grateful, and of course express this gratitude often and whenever he expected another pat on the back. This 'sacrifice' however, was really his pleasure, because he liked nothing more than being out in the open, his time was his own, and he enjoyed building things. He also expected his sons to be tough, and they were never babies or children, as far as he was concerned they'd been born men, and god forbid they showed any sign of what he felt was weakness or fear. They were taught to hunt game, from rabbit to hawk to buck, and what they shot, which was edible, they had to prepare. They learnt to gut and skin these animals, they were taught to fish, and they were taken out into the bush and taught how to survive off the land. They had to know how to make a fire without matches, and to use the sun, moon and stars for direction. Whilst this may sound ideal for some, it was not a lifestyle for anyone sensitive to animals, blood, guts, and sleeping in the rough, freezing cold and hungry, just because dad said so. They weren't allowed any mod cons at all, and there were no luxuries. Marie used to sneak in the occasional sweet or treat, and was sometimes successful in buying them something like a tape player for their birthday or Christmas. Punishment for disobedience of any sort, and that might mean not getting water for the chores on time, was swift and harsh, and mainly physical. Out of the two boys, who were called Roger and Brent, Brent thrived on this lifestyle, Roger despised it, and he was a morose, unhappy boy. It was as though Stefan wanted to preserve his heritage, and continue his childhood through his boys. Brent worshipped his dad, Roger hated him, and both loved their mum.

Obviously I didn't learn all this immediately; it was over a period of time. Marie found me to be a sympathetic listener, and I was always ready to share my negative and sometimes shameful experiences, which encouraged her to open up to me. Anyway, back to the barbeque. It was going to be a celebration of sorts; part of the foundations had been dug, so everyone from work was invited, to celebrate the beginning of their house. I was quite nervous, because everyone at work, had known each other for a couple of years, and from what I heard, they socialised together quite frequently. Because it was a small company with so few staff, they were all quite close, and I was still very much the new person, and it was my first social event with them all. I travelled out alone, and must admit I had my fair share of wine, partly to relax and feel less nervous, and partly because it was a really good evening, and everyone was drinking a lot. Gay got quite drunk, and seeing the bosses wife in a really tipsy state, made me feel that it was ok, to let my hair down and enjoy myself. I met both the boys, and where Brent was an energetic, outgoing, lean, tough looking boy, Roger was plump, slow, sulky and lethargic.

I needed to leave earlier than the rest, because my parents were looking after my kids, and I didn't want to take liberties. I hadn't taken into account that, although Stefan had provided a makeshift track for us all to drive on, just off this, where I had parked, it was rough ground speckled with rubble and soil. Everyone had come to see me off, and as it was very dark, with only torches and the moonlight. It was one of those moments when you want to act really cool and just disappear quietly in your car, into the darkness. Well that was not to be. If I'd just stalled, it would have been ok, but I got myself into a total mess, trying to reverse over the rubble, and although with the headlights on I could see what was in front of me, the reversing lights didn't help at all. Great, I thought, I've got this audience, and I can't even leave with dignity. Stefan came to the window, and told me to shift across, and he would manoeuvre the car onto the track, and I could take it from there. I did, feeling like a complete prat, especially with this male chauvinist. He got in, and in no time at all, he had the car out and ready to roll, and then he suddenly grabbed me, and started snogging me. What the hell was he doing, his wife and all the others were standing just outside the car, and I thanked God for the darkness, because it was likely they couldn't see what was happening. That changed in an instant, when someone shone the torch right into the car, and it was blatantly obvious what was happening. The front of the car was compact, and he was very strong, and when he'd grabbed me, it was a vice like grip on my arms, and I'd been pulled and held against him. When the light shone in, he let me go, but I knew it had been too late, they had all seen what must have looked like a mutual embrace. 'Get out', I hissed. I seemed to be saying that a lot lately, and the cocky bastard, put both hands either side of my face, kissed me full on the lips, and slowly got out of the car. It was so deliberate, and he fully intended for it to be seen, especially by his wife. I got into the drivers seat, and left in a hurry, tyres screeching. I didn't look back, and I didn't know what I was going to do now. I agonised over what had happened over the weekend. How could I continue to work with someone who had seen me supposedly kissing her husband? She wouldn't believe he had initiated it, and nor would she believe that I had tried to repel him. It wouldn't have looked like that, because his hands were gripping the tops of my arms, and that wasn't visible. Aside from that, how hard would it be for her, if I told her that Stefan had basically forced himself on me? I'd been on the receiving end of that kind of confession more times than I cared to remember, and it hurt like hell. I know I'd always tried to believe that it had been the woman's fault one way or another, and I expected Marie to feel the same. The only thing I could do was offer to resign, and then I'd be back to being unemployed, and how would this look on my CV anyway, It wasn't considered acceptable at that time to change jobs, in fact the longer you had been in any one place, the better it was.

I was a wreck by the time I arrived at work on the Monday, I didn't know what to expect from anyone, and Marie was there already. I asked if I could speak to her, and she just nodded. God it was going to be as bad as I thought. There was no-one else there yet, so we had some privacy. 'I'm so sorry for what happened Marie, I don't know what to say, apart from that I will resign today, to prevent you from having to work with me, and hopefully you can forgive me.' I was rambling. 'Forgive you for what?' Marie asked, and I was stunned. 'For what happened in the car', I replied. 'I've been with my husband for a long time', Marie said, 'and I know what he's like, particularly with younger more attractive women', she continued. I kept quiet, while she went on, with tears in her eyes now. 'It's not the first time, and it won't be the last', she was crying now, and so was I. 'I am sorry that he put you in this position, and I certainly don't want you to even consider resigning, if you can continue to work with me, that is', she said. What an enormously dignified and brave lady. She loved this man, despite his philandering and shortcomings, and she was prepared to continue loving him regardless. She had often been embarrassed like this before, and she was grateful that I hadn't pointed a finger at him, and that I had been prepared to leave, out of consideration for her feelings. We talked until the others came in, and a close bond had been forged. She asked if I would still continue to visit, and not let this prevent that, and I said I would. We agreed that when I did, I would make sure that I wasn't alone with Stefan at any time. I understood that Marie had lost most of her friends because of his behaviour, and I wasn't about to let him do it again. The others at work acknowledged our unspoken alliance, and reacted accordingly. Nothing was said, and we all got on as before.

It was shortly afterwards, that Marie was arranging another party for her birthday, and once again I was invited. I was very uncomfortable about going, but wouldn't let her know that, instead I asked my younger cousin, who was nineteen to go along with me. At least that way, I'd have someone with me at all times. There were a lot more people this time, other friends and family, and I did go overboard with the wine. Towards the end of the evening, I was sitting with Sally my cousin, and a strange man came over. He introduced himself as Harold, and Sally recognised him from the golf club, her step father was a member of. They got chatting, and I was quite happy people watching, when Harry, as he was called by his friends, asked why I was so stuck up. Cheeky sod, I was just sitting quietly. The fact that I'd been on egg shells all evening with regard to another man, and the over indulgence of wine, I gave him a sharper than necessary retort. 'If I'm stuck up as you call it, it's because you don't interest me enough to talk to'. Ouch that was harsh. He threw his head back with a mock look of shock and horror, and then said 'I know where you work, and I will come and invite you to coffee when you are hopefully in a better state of mind'. I shrugged disinterestedly, and suggested to Sally that we leave. She agreed quickly, I think she was worried about who else I might insult. We said our goodbyes, and Sally drove us home. The giggles kicked in on the way home, as Sally saw the funny side of my interaction with Harry. He was a nice enough person she told me, and added he was recently divorced. A really charismatic type, a man's man, and the ladies loved him too. Well, here was one lady that wasn't going to fall at his feet, and succumb to his charms. I really believed it at the time, but he did come and invite me to lunch, and it took all of about two hours for me to be completely smitten. Talk about playing hard to get!

To cut a long story short, in no time at all, Harry had moved in, he was between places after his divorce, and this helped me financially too. He was wonderful with the children, and spent extra time with Jack, as he had two girls of his own, and he loved having a little boy to take fishing, play rugby with, all the things most fathers do with their sons. This endeared me to him even more if possible; I was totally in love with Harry. I chose to ignore the fact that he was so recently divorced, and clearly still loved his ex wife. The divorce had been at her request. I chose to ignore the infrequent, but persistent little remarks, about my weight, the fact that he liked blondes and I was brunette, and that he was a 'bums and tits' man, neither of which I had much of at all. I chose to ignore the fact that sex felt like a chore, and was infrequent, and I turned a blind eye to his regular and quite heavy drinking. I don't believe it was conscious ignorance, I think it was more that I was subconsciously slipping into a familiar role, and I truly believed he was the kindest, nicest man I'd met. The words 'rebound and revenge' did come to mind, but I dismissed them as quickly as came. I didn't consider that I was beginning a familiar journey, with an equally familiar type of companion.

My new relationship infuriated Bruce. He wanted company in his misery, and the thought of me being happy in a relationship was just not on. He retaliated by making unreasonable demands on his time with the children, and threatening me constantly with legal action of one kind or another, none of which I believed were valid or applicable. I didn't deny him his visitation rights, and never cancelled the days he took the children out. Those days were a nightmare for me, because I was terrified he would get drunk, not watch them carefully enough, or drive whilst seriously under the influence. I know he pleaded poverty with the children, because when they came back, I asked about their day, as I wanted them to feel it was ok to talk about their dad. I didn't want them thinking that their time with him was anything other than normal, nothing to be secretive about, and for them not to feel they were being tugged or pulled like piggies in the middle. Whatever they chose to tell me about their outings, I took in my stride in front of them, but I understood that 'daddy always has lots of beer', meant he was drinking a lot more than he should be when with them, and I made threats of my own. These weren't empty threats, I told him that if he brought them home after drinking again, I would stop him seeing the children, and he could take me to court. The next time he took them out, he ignored my warnings, and when it came around to his next visit, I contacted him and told him not to bother. Within minutes really there were screeching tyres outside, and he slammed through the front door into the kitchen, screaming and shouting abuse. He came face to face with Harry and I, and then he ranted on, that no other man was going to bring up his children, and that would be over his dead body. I said, 'well at the rate you're going, it will be over your dead body, but it won't be over my children's too', and Harry added fuel to the already blazing inferno by saying, 'At least I will bring up your children, better than you are at the moment'. Oh shit, Bruce was launching himself at Harry. I was not going to tolerate him literally breaking into my home, and going on the offensive, and I was not going to have an all out fight in my kitchen or anywhere else for that matter. 'Get out now', I shouted, 'get out or I will call the police and have you arrested and charged for anything and everything I can throw at you.' Bruce hesitated, and I said, 'I mean it, God help me, I will have you locked up'. He realised I was serious, and with a 'this is not over', thrown over his departing shoulder, he left with as much burning rubber, as he'd arrived.

32

It got worse. I had filed for back pay of maintenance for the year and half that Bruce had been away, and he was contesting it. He was earning a good salary now, and I believed he should be responsible for his children too. He'd stopped paying me anything anyway out of spite, and I'd asked for an order to be served so that I could rely on the additional income for the kids. Emma wanted to start horse riding lessons, and I wanted them to have extra swimming training, which they both loved. I couldn't afford the extras and I didn't feel it was up to Harry to support my children, as he had two of his own he was supporting. This made it worse in a way, because Harry was adamant that regardless of anything else, his maintenance for his children was the first money that went out of his account every month.

It ended up in court, and Harry came with me. I was angry that Bruce had even contested it. I had never claimed anything for myself, this was about the children, and I found it very difficult to comprehend that he would fight tooth and nail not to help them in any way he could. I had and continued to struggle to even keep them in school uniforms. The school uniform industry in South Africa, had a secure very lucrative exclusivity. They knew that parents absolutely had to buy them, and they were criminally expensive, even down to the socks, and I like hundreds of others didn't have available cash, and had to open an account, which had to be paid every month. Credit cards were rare and exclusive at that time, so if you didn't have cash to hand, it was the only way to do it. Bruce knew all this, I had shown him receipts, and the total cost over the last couple of years.

We were directed to the waiting area outside the courtroom, and Harry and I wondered where Bruce was. He arrived just before we were due into court, and he looked worse than usual. He came and sat with us, as if we were old mates, and told us he'd been out the night before, talked about who he had shagged, and then said he was still drunk, and rushed to the toilets to vomit. He still stank of booze, and he intimated he was here under duress anyway. Bruce was interviewed in the courtroom, and what came out of his mouth was unbelievable. I don't know why I was surprised, it was his pattern, his way, I think I'd hoped that if there was only one redeeming factor, it would have been that he'd be eager to support Emma and Jack. He actually cried on that stand, and said he'd been homeless with no income after the divorce because of how it had impacted on his life. His wife had become bored in the marriage and wasn't it there in black and white that the grounds were irreconcilable differences. He'd tried so hard to make it work, and had been absolutely devastated when I went ahead with it. I had destroyed him. He cried that he loved his children and of course he'd pay more if he could, but he was just picking up his own life, and felt that the sooner he became established, the better it would be for the children. He said he'd left me everything when the marriage ended, and he promised that when he could he would help as much as he could. The best one of all, was when he wept about me withholding visitation when he couldn't afford to give me any money for the children. Of course he dropped in that I was living with another man, and made it sound like I had been since the divorce. He called me cruel, cold and calculating.

The judge, perhaps a single father himself, perhaps the victim of a failed marriage himself, looked at Bruce with pity, and looked at me with contempt. What Bruce had failed to mention was that he had not been homeless, he'd chosen to run away and live with his mother in Italy. He'd worked there, doing work on the farms, and at the time had communicated how happy he'd been doing this type of work, and that the salary was inconsequential really, as the most important thing was his well being. He'd also failed to disclose that he was a highly qualified and experienced systems analyst and that had he chosen to stay, he would have continued on a sizeable income. All he'd left me when he moved out was some old furniture, and outstanding bills to pay, and of course the total responsibility for our two children.

Due to legal processes, which I have never really understood, I wasn't entitled to give my side of the story, and although the judge had all the paperwork, which I hoped he'd taken time to review, he ordered that all back pay was disregarded, and he actually reduced the monthly maintenance commitment Bruce was ordered to pay. Case dismissed. Bruce thought it was a victory, I thought it was an appalling tragedy. I couldn't believe he'd celebrate this, but he did, and with a hangover eventually setting in, he came up to me and said 'I told you it wasn't over, I said I would make it hard for you, and I will, this is only the beginning', he added, 'you still won't see any money, and you can keep taking me to court, and I will continue to win'. He turned to walk away, and his passing remark was 'places to go, people to see, and some serious drinking to be done, I'm celebrating'. I was living with a man who would beg, steal or borrow to ensure his children had everything they needed, and the father of my children fought me every which way to prevent helping out in any way at all. I know he was trying to punish me, we'd had this conversation, and I'd tried to convince him that this was not about me at all, it was about his responsibilities as a father. He chose not to get the point.

Harry shared household expenses, and this meant that Emma could have her horse riding lessons, and my parents paid for them to have the extra swimming lessons, so we got by well enough. There were very few luxuries, and the only time we went out for a meal was on birthdays. I had a Christmas and birthday fund, and for Christmas I would buy as many cheap things that I could so the kids would have lots of presents to open.

I loved Harry to bits and pieces; he was different to Bruce in a lot of ways. He cooked and cleaned, and most importantly he spent quality time with the children. We went fishing, and we were out and about most weekends with my two and his two girls. My dream came true one evening when Harry proposed, and I believed that my life was changing now, and things would come right. I was thrilled, and for the first time in a long while, I believed that it could and would work, and that this was truly the beginning of a new and better future for us all. I met his parents, who lived in Cape Town, and we all got on very well, they obviously liked me, and welcomed me into the family. The only regret I had, was that we would never have a child of our own. I was only twenty nine and I thought I wanted more than anything, to have a baby with Harry, but that was impossible, after all, I could never bear another child. Although having a child together often feels like the cementing of a new relationship, particularly between divorced partners, that baby is someone they share exclusively, it doesn't always work out like that. I had this fantasy of a little Harry and Cheryl, but I think deep down I was grateful in a way, that I had reason enough not to have to consider this option seriously at all. I was able to fantasize without having to take action, and fantasies are just that, an idyllic notion of reality, and as we know reality has its moments but is comparatively not as enchanting as our fantasies and dreams.

Harry was divorced because the wife he'd loved had an affair with another man, and left him, and much as I tried to push the thought away, I knew he'd never really come to terms with losing her, and although when I spoke to him about it, he denied it vehemently, I knew he still loved her. I believed time would heal his wounds, and as long as she was with her lover, my relationship with Harry was safe. That was also why I tried so hard, too hard, to try and be everything he wanted and desired. Didn't I know that regardless of my cloning efforts, I couldn't and wouldn't ever be able to replace her, and I would never be loved by him as she was? I was prepared to settle for second best, if it was all I had. I was used to that anyway, so it didn't feel strange or unnatural for me to have to work hard for his love and attention. This was familiar, and I didn't want to see the potential heartache. Why would I expect him to love me the way I loved him, I had never before experienced equality in love, why would I now. This very sadly, didn't feel threatening, it felt normal. This kind considerate caring man was becoming argumentative, short tempered and he started putting me down at every opportunity. He began to criticize the way I looked, what I ate, what I drank, how I spoke, and the worse it became, the harder I tried. It began to feel very much like my previous marriage, and this was a confirmation for me that it was about me. How could two men be wrong, how could it possibly be that out of everyone, I had gravitated towards another abusive man. It couldn't be, he had been such a sweetie to begin with, and that indicated to me that I must be useless and worthless of love and respect. I blamed myself for his behaviour, I excused him and forgave him, and I was terrified he would leave me. I forgot that I could cope on my own, my recently discovered sense of worth and value in surviving and coping with my divorce and aftermath, was a distant and distorted memory. I reverted very quickly into a needy, weepy desperate woman.

In the beginning though it was good and early in the relationship we shared a unique experience. I'd always known that if something weird was going to happen to anyone, it was likely to be me, and one night it certainly did. I stumbled through to the loo in the early hours, and normally I didn't turn on the light so as not to disturb the children. For some reason thank God I did this particular night, and in my still half asleep daze, I turned the light on and went to sit on the loo. I saw something Black down the bowl, and assumed Jack or Emma had been for a poo and hadn't flushed, which wasn't unusual. I sat and was just about to pee, when I heard a noise coming from the toilet bowl. I leapt off the loo, still bursting to go, and looked down the toilet. Good God there was a massive toad in the toilet. For a moment I thought I must still be dreaming, how could a toad get into the toilet? I ran into our bedroom and shook Harry. He woke up, and I said 'Get up; there's a huge frog in the toilet'. His expression said it all. God almighty, she's lost the plot completely, and he shook his head in amazement and obvious pity at my delusional state. 'Harry, for God's sake, there is a frog in the toilet and it might jump out', I was shouting now. He got up impatiently, just to humour me, and prove I was hallucinating or still lost in the ether somewhere. He pushed open the toilet door, confidently and cocky, and bent forward to look into the toilet. My hero! There was a loud 'fucking hell', and Harry moved backwards and out of the loo so quickly it was as though he had a propeller attached to him. 'There's a fucking great frog in the toilet', he said, with a disbelieving look. 'I know', I replied, 'I've seen it too'. I suddenly remembered to shut the toilet door, I had visions of this monster toad jumping out, and cavorting around the place, with us trying to catch it. Emma and Jack had woken up with the commotion, and by now I was in hysterics. I tried to explain to them that there was big frog stuck in the toilet. Of course they wanted to see, so I cautiously opened the door, and oh shit, the toad had got to the seat, and we were met by this squatting Black mass, with two beady evil eyes. 'Mind, quickly', I screamed as I slammed the door. How were we going to get the toad out of the 'hole'. The kids and I all turned and looked at our live-in, newly appointed hero. The colour drained from Harry's face. First we had to figure out how to get it, and then to transport it outside. We were fairly limited in frog catching equipment, but I suggested the colander. That way, Harry could scoop it out, but then what did we do with it. He came up with the bright idea of a dinner plate, and we moved into action. He wouldn't allow us to close him in the toilet with the toad, so I told the kids to be ready to run, if it got out. They were to run into their room, and shut the door, in the meantime, I told them to go and stand on our bed, and God I wanted to be with them, but I was the dinner plate holder, and chief support. Harry went in, and I stayed as far back as I could, and I could hear him squeaking and squealing with fear, as he tried to scoop the toad into the colander. He suddenly came out with this enormous creature in the sieve, and shouted at me to hand him the plate. In one deft move, he slammed the colander onto the plate, and we had captured the monster. It filled the dinner plate, and reached the top of the sieve, it was huge. Watching him run to the front door, holding a dinner plate with the biggest toad we had all ever seen, was too much, and now we were safe, I couldn't stop laughing. The kids and eventually Harry joined in, and we thought it was the strangest, funniest thing to happen. It was, and I discovered that there was building work taking place nearby, and it wasn't unheard of for toads to get caught up in the pipe work. They flattened out when they swam, so to speak, and our one ended up in the toilet bowl. These toads also have teeth, believe it or not, and I realised that I might well have had a chomp out of my butt, it took a very long time for me to sit properly on any toilet seat after that. Well Harry had certainly had a very strange initiation into my little family.

We had Harry's children over every second weekend, and his older daughter and Emma were about the same age. I did spend time with them trying to make them feel welcome and at home, and I'm not sure whether it was because I perhaps gave them extra attention when they were with us, but Emma became very jealous and hated having them over. I couldn't understand really where this jealousy came from, but I learnt soon enough, that as with everything else Emma had spoken to my mum about me being too nice to Harry's girls, and she was encouraged once again to believe that mummy loved everyone else now apparently more than her. I tried to draw Emma in on all our activities, but she sulked and refused to join us, and it started to make their weekends with us difficult. This compounded with the fact that his ex-wife had left her partner, and apparently was very distressed about Harry's commitment to me, started to flaw our relationship. Harry became distant and went out with his mates more often. We hardly ever made love anymore, but even with all this, I continued to believe that it was a phase, it would pass, didn't it always. When she stopped him from seeing his children as often, things really started to go downhill. He blamed me. I was now responsible for all his difficulties and frustrations, and I once again bore the label scapegoat. I was on familiar ground, and I wore it as I had always done, with some resignation, but with acceptance. I tried harder to please him, and things got progressively worse. Bruce must have heard snippets from the children that things weren't going well at home. Harry was out most of the time and when he was home, he was abrupt and dismissive towards me. Give him his due, he maintained his relationship with the children, but the atmosphere was filled with his tension and my compliance.

I wasn't fool enough not to know that things were going from bad to worse, but there had been no mention of him leaving or moving out, and I assumed it was something we needed to work through. I didn't know that he was a coward too, and that he had made plans to leave, but he didn't have the courage to tell me, and hurt me. As it turned out it hurt a hell of a lot more than if he'd told me.

It was close to our annual company shutdown, and we all went out for a celebratory meal a week or so before we all had a well earned three week holiday. This was the only leave we had all year, and by the time it came around we were all desperate for the time off. Marie and I had planned what to wear, and it was a big treat for me, because as I mentioned, I hardly ever got to go out. Christmas was just a few weeks away, and three weeks of lie ins and the beach made it a really special time of year. It was to be our second Christmas together, and my thoughts were full of warm fuzzy expectations. We all met at the restaurant, and there always had to be a dance floor, as Lee and Gay loved dancing. We ordered our meal, and Harry focused a lot of his time on talking to Stefan. This wouldn't have appeared unusual to me, as they were friends, but the conversations seemed to be very private, and when I asked Harry what he and Stefan were discussing, he dismissed me with 'men things'. We ordered our meal, and Harry flirted blatantly with the waitress, to the point of embarrassment to all of us, including the waitress. Marie and Gay were looking at me sympathetically, and I felt awkward. I asked Harry to dance, and he refused, and then asked Gay to dance. He was clearly going out of his way to hurt me, and embarrass me, and it was working. As the evening progressed, he started getting really nasty, and I was confused and angry. He'd known how much I'd been looking forward to this evening, and his behaviour was unkind and unfair, particularly in front of my boss and colleagues. He was publicly ridiculing me. I confronted him regarding his attitude, and he just said he needed some air. I noticed he'd been checking the time quite regularly all evening. I was beginning to wonder what the hell was going on with everyone tonight. Everyone seemed to be in on some sort of secret apart from me. I went back to the table and tried to act as though I was having a good time, and after about a half hour, I went outside to check what had happened to Harry. He was nowhere to be seen. I was about to go back in, when Marie came to join me. She said 'I am really angry and sorry that Harry obviously didn't talk to you before this evening, but he's gone to Mitch'. Mitch was Harry's best friend, and we'd often socialised together. 'Why?' I asked, and 'why didn't he tell me he was leaving the party, is he meeting me at home later?' 'He isn't coming home', Marie said. 'He's left you'. What, I couldn't believe what she was telling me. Apparently he'd been confiding in Stefan, they were also friends, and because his ex wife wanted him back now that her affair had gone sour, she had told him that as long as our relationship continued, she would make it very difficult for him to see his girls. I knew how much he loved them, and I could understand that part, what was left unsaid though was that I believed he still loved his ex wife, and also wanted to reconcile with her. He hadn't wanted his departure to be too traumatic for Emma and Jack, so thought this was the best way for all of us. He would be in touch with me tomorrow to make arrangements to collect his things, and he would be staying with Mitch from now on.

Cowardly bastard, this had nothing to do with saving my children's feelings, and how dare he play the hero card, and suggest he was being considerate to them. This was about him planning and scheming behind my back, and not even having the decency to sit down and discuss it with me. I might have wept and wailed, but I would never have kept him from leaving. I didn't want to be with anyone who wanted to be somewhere else, and apparently with someone else. His behaviour tonight had been calculated and deliberate. I knew he had been as nasty and cruel as he could, in the hope that I would dump him, and then it would have been much easier, for him that is.

He must have felt so frustrated, whatever he threw at me, I just took it, good god he must have appalled at how much I'd let him get away with. Unfortunately for him though, he obviously didn't have a realistic conception of how hardened I was to abuse, and that it was actually familiar to me, so I didn't react the same way that other people did. I took abuse in my stride; it was what I deserved after all. Worthless, useless me, remember.

Marie and Stefan gave me a lift home, and we travelled in silence. They were embarrassed and pitying in their silence, I was mortified, hurt and angry in mine. I thanked them, and agreed to meet up during the holidays, and I went inside. I poured myself a large glass of wine, and sat and wept. I wept bitter tears, angry tears, and heartbroken tears. I couldn't believe it had happened so suddenly and so cruelly, but it had. I had been misled, lied to and betrayed in a horrible way, in front of friends and colleagues, and he claimed it was because he was considering the children's feelings. This impacted very negatively on my once revived, now re shattered, sense of value and self worth. I felt thoroughly used and abused, and I felt so stupid too, everyone else had known, how could I have been that blind to his obvious plotting and planning. I still trusted and believed what people said to me, I was still so naïve and I still chose to latch onto that scrap of kindness thrown my way, and convert it into a feast. I berated myself, I hated myself, it was my entire fault, I was so stupid. Maybe if I'd behaved differently, maybe if I'd done this, or that another way, so many maybes and if only's. I still believed, that to sustain a relationship I had to fill the needs and desires of others, and I thought I had been doing that, but I had misjudged Harry's. I had no concept of mutual giving and taking, that was foreign in my world, and neither did I realise that the constant thought and consideration and planning I put in, in order to try and be a step ahead was soul destroying. I was constantly playing mind games with myself, I was always walking on egg shells, I didn't know what it was to literally go with the flow.

I eventually exhausted myself and by the time I went to bed, I'd put most of it away in one of the pigeon holes in my mind. I couldn't afford not to, I had to tell the children in the morning, and Jack in

244

particular would need a lot of support. Jack was devastated, Emma tried hard to be, but I knew that secretly she was pleased in more ways than one. Her competition had gone, both in the form of Harry's girls, and Harry himself. I think the departure of Harry gave her renewed hope that her father might come back into my life again, because I knew she wanted nothing more than her dad back in her life full time. She missed his obsessive love, and his alliance against me. She still blamed me for his departure in the first place, and there was no sign of forgiveness in sight. My parents said what they thought were the right things to say, 'he wasn't good enough for me anyway', when in fact, I think they meant that, yet again I had ruined another relationship. My mum always said the right person would come into my life, I tried to believe her, but how would I recognise him. I subconsciously gravitated towards abusers, how would I ever meet the right man? What my mum didn't tell me, and what I found out many years later, is that when you are right with yourself in all ways, when you have self respect, value and worth, then, you recognise the 'right person'. In my personal experience it is true, that you will attract people who feed off your weaknesses, and so too will you attract people who admire your strengths. When you respect yourself you won't be drawn to others who show disrespect, and I eventually learnt this, but that's for much later. Back to where we were. Bruce heard through mutual friends about Harry's and my break up, and to say he was ecstatic is putting it mildly. I didn't understand his persistence in remaining in my life at this time, but it obviously had a lot to do with me meeting his needs. I was the ideal victim to a bully and abuser, and believe me, there weren't many like me to be found easily. He was unlikely to find such a perfect victim effortlessly, someone who would satisfy his bullying and cruelty, and he'd already had experience of how good I was in this role, and he missed it. He didn't like being with strong woman, they didn't fulfil his desire to feel powerful. I was his ideal candidate and he'd let me slip through his fingers once before, he wasn't likely to do that easily again.

He wore a different guise, one of confidante, supporter, friend, father, and a shoulder to cry on. He was sympathetic and attentive. He came back into the children's life with a vengeance, and he paid maintenance for the children willingly and regularly. I didn't see or talk to him apart from when arrangements for the children were involved, but during those conversations he was all of the above. When he came to fetch them he stopped to ask how I was, and once he invited me to spend the day on the beach with them. Of course this was the ultimate for Emma and Jack, having mummy and daddy together with them for a day, and I went. It was a very pleasant day, and we all enjoyed it. Bruce didn't drink that day either, what a change! I made it clear to him that there would be no further developments between us, and he didn't take kindly to this. He continued to see and support the children, but he went out and found himself a girlfriend who he appeared to be quite serious about, and I was pleased the pressure was off me. He had moved in with one of his friends Ron, who was also divorced, and from all accounts they were living the high life of bachelors. As long as he continued the way he was with the kids, I didn't really care about the other stuff.

33

I loved my job, and I was doing well with sales, and consequently earning a lot of commission, so my financial position was improving. This was the one part of my life, where I felt competent, confident and self assured. I think it was because there was little if any emotional content involved. Life seemed to have calmed down a little, but then again, it's always calm before a storm, isn't it?

I was given my third opportunity to save someone's life. Jack had made a little friend, who lived right next to our block of flats. They had a house on the adjoining plot, and a fence bordered their garden and the flats. His name was Dirk, and Jack and Dirk had found, and adjusted a gap in the fence, so that they went through there to visit one another, as opposed to walking the long way around. It was late one night, when there was a loud banging on the front door, and I was anxious about who it would be at this time. I opened the door carefully, and was met by a hysterical Dirk. He was basically Afrikaans speaking, so we had a language barrier, but the terror on his face, spoke volumes, and I could understand that he wanted me to come quickly. Emma and Jack had woken, and I told them to go next door to granny and granddad, and tell them where I'd gone, then they were to stay there. I ran with Dirk, and literally fell over the fence, whilst he whizzed through with the agility of a child. As we ran, I was able to understand that his parents were out, and their maid was babysitting him and his younger sister. He ran to where his maid lived. Live-in maids often had their own small homes built on the property. I could hear a man's voice shouting, and a woman's making a mewling sound. Dirk wouldn't go in, just kept pointing towards the door, and telling me to go in quickly. I opened the door, and the sight that met me, made we want to turn and run away as fast as my legs would take me. The mixed race woman was slumped against the wall, and there was blood everywhere, and a few feet away from her was a large mix raced man, standing swaying, and shouting at her, and in his hand was a knife dripping blood. Oh dear God, I thought, he's stabbed her, and by the look of it he's about to do it again. He was clearly very drunk, and she was clearly very frightened, and so was I. I was petrified. I turned to Dirk, and told him to go and call the police, I knew what 'hurry' and 'quickly' was in Afrikaans and I gave him the number and emphasised that he had to call them now!

This all happened very quickly, and then I turned back to the nightmare ahead. I knew I had to do something, as the man was becoming more threatening. I went in slowly, and walked towards the maid, to try and ascertain her condition. The good thing was that she was still conscious and although had quietened down, was still making strange high pitched whining sounds. I got to her, and the man was infuriated by now that a strange white woman was there, and he started to advance towards me with the knife. I tried to tell him it was alright I just wanted to see where the woman was hurt, and although I was shaking like a jelly, I kept my voice as low and calm as I could. She had her hand against her neck, and blood was spilling out, and when she let me move her hand, the gash was obvious. God there was so much blood, and it was coming out fast. Whilst I was checking her, the man was becoming more volatile, and I realised, that in the state of rage he was in, there would be no calming him down, he had no sense of reason or rationale, and it was probable he would stab her again, and me. The only thing I could think of to help her at that time was to stick my fingers in the wound, to try and slow the bleeding, and I did, and with my fingers in her neck, I took the chance of my life. I knew it could go one way or another, and if it went wrong, that would be that, I probably wouldn't come out of this one without injury or worse. He was close now, and I had to rely on fear being his overriding concern, I also had the additional worry about the language barrier. Thank God, I knew enough to make myself understood, and in Afrikaans, I told him the police were coming, and he must get away quickly before they caught him. I tried to make him believe I was helping him. I realised this meant he might escape altogether, and this would mean he wouldn't be accountable for what he'd done, but I believed that was a chance worth taking. Otherwise, it might end up in double murder, and sure, he would be caught, but what good would that do either of us woman. Oh sweet Jesus, he was hesitating, and still advancing. I couldn't run and leave this woman to bleed to death, and then it seemed, my angels stepped in, and we all heard the sound of sirens in the distance. Good boy Dirk, I thought, and prayed this would encourage the man to make the decision to run, I was praying he would. If he chose not to run, he would know that he was going to be caught, and he didn't have anything to lose really, by attacking us both. I didn't even know whether it was the police answering our call, it might have been anything else, but it was so well timed. 'Run quickly before they catch you', I said, trying to persuade him that I was helping him. 'Run', I said again with urgency in my voice, 'Run, the police are coming'. I watched his alcohol dulled mind struggling with thoughts of escape, or satisfying his rage. He turned, and left in a stumbling run. He hadn't made his decision in time though, and he didn't get far, as the police were coming to us, and caught him as he ran out of the property. Dirk had been sensible enough to tell them someone was hurt and the ambulance arrived at the same time. The police were absolutely stunned when they saw me there, and the para-medics were equally amazed and impressed with the action I'd taken. They told me I had saved her life, and that was worth those terrify-ing moments when I had no idea whether I would survive the night. Dirks parents came home to mayhem, and were very grateful, and I reminded them that their little boy had been a hero, I wasn't the only one to save a life that night, it wouldn't have happened if he hadn't had the sense to find help, and call the police. The maid came to visit me when she was well, and said her life belonged to me now. She meant this, and I didn't want her beholden to a stranger, and I also didn't want such enormous responsibility. She was deeply religious and I told her, I had been God's tool that night, and that her life was, and always would be her own, she had been given a second chance, and that was for a reason, and to use this time well, for herself and her family. She seemed happy with this, and with more effusive thanks she left, and I never saw her again. Of course my children thought I was the heroine of all time, and the story was told for years afterwards.

The next incident, if I can call it that, had far more lasting devastating effects, and this time I was outside of what I think can only be referred to as a tragedy. Marie and I never missed work, we had to be desperately ill to skip a day, so when I received a call early one morning from Marie, telling me quite calmly that she wouldn't be in that day. I was surprised. 'Why, what's up?' I asked. 'Stefan was shot last night', she replied. Shit, she was so calm, I realised she'd either been given tranquillizers, or she was in deep shock. She told me what had happened in a monotone voice. They had been asleep in their bedroom, they rented a small place close to their plot, and Marie had woken with the sound of the shot, Stefan's screams and blood spraying everywhere. In the moments that followed, she had focused on locating Stefan's injuries, and trying to control the bleeding, whilst screaming at the boys who were now obviously awake to call for help. The ambulance arrived and rushed him to hospital with Marie, and of course the police came to investigate. They discovered that Stefan had been shot whilst in bed asleep, and that he was very lucky to be alive and also to have avoided paralysis. They also couldn't understand why only he had been shot and not Marie too, because an intruder would normally shoot both, if they were going to shoot one. Stefan had been shot in the top of his thigh into his buttocks, and because it was at such close range, it had blown a lot of flesh away. Because he had lost so much blood, which in itself induced shock, he was critical for a few days. Marie stayed at the hospital whilst he underwent emergency surgery, and she was told, that although he would walk again, there had been such extensive damage done, that he would walk with a pronounced limp for the rest of his life, and there would be months ahead of physiotherapy. Marie was just so grateful that her beloved husband was alive, that she didn't at that point consider the consequences his disability may have. Stefan's life revolved around physical activity, this was bound to have a devastating impact on him. She kept in touch with me, and called me later to say that she was worried about Roger, as apparently he'd gone out shortly after she'd gone to the hospital with Stefan, and he hadn't come back yet. God forgive me for the first thought I'd had, and which for me, now seemed confirmed. When Marie had told me about the shooting the first person I had thought had done it was their son Roger. I had dismissed that immediately. He was still a child. I'd reminded myself however, that neither of the boys had ever been children, as I said earlier, they had been forced to by-pass all of the normal childhood expectations, as Stefan believed that they had to be men, and had treated them accordingly. No cuddles or softness, just a tough hard attitude, and Marie had only been able to give them those gentle moments sparingly and away from Stefan. I knew Roger hated his father, and found it very hard work being his son, but could that anger and hatred be this strong, this big, that he would try to kill his father. He must have been absolutely desperate to rid his father from his life, because although he'd learnt to use guns from a very young age, he surely must have been aware that he had put his mother's safety at risk.

I didn't mention any of this to Marie, as she was convinced he'd reacted out of shock, and fear. I suggested that if he wasn't home within a couple of hours it might be an idea to get a search party going. It was only a few hours later that she called again, it was late evening, and she said that she'd discovered a lot of Roger's clothing and personal belongings were missing, the other thing that hadn't been found by the police was the weapon used to shoot Stefan. She wasn't certain whether to communicate his departure to the police, as it seemed to be slowly dawning on her that there was a possibility that Roger had something to do with Stefan's shooting. God knows how hard that must be, and how easy it would be to dismiss those thoughts with all sorts of excuses. The next day, when Roger hadn't returned and she hadn't heard from him, she had to tell the police, because she was beginning to fear for his safety too. Stefan was conscious, and Marie insisted that he wasn't to even know that his son was missing. He wasn't allowed any other visitors, as he was still critical, so he wouldn't wonder why Roger wasn't visiting him.

The days that followed were a nightmare, and all I could do was support Marie in any way. She spoke to me often and at length because I tried to be non judgemental, which is probably easier for someone not related. Her family were divided in their feedback, some were ready to lynch Roger for his diabolical action, others were sympathetic, as they knew that he had been a victim of prolonged and severe abuse. One thing was certain though, and that was that everyone agreed that he had done it, and until he was found to prove otherwise, Marie

251

craved solitude, away from all the speculation, accusations, and damnations. Roger was found by rangers about ten days later. He had shot Stefan, and cold bloodedly planned it months before. It hadn't been impulsive, it had been calculating, and he was arrested and formally charged.

Marie was devastated, and didn't know which way to turn. She wanted to be with her son as, she above anyone else could understand his anger and fear, but how could she condone the attempted murder of his father, her husband. How had it become so horrific for Roger, that he had taken the action he had? Why hadn't she paid more attention, why hadn't she seen this coming? She was in absolute turmoil. She was terrified to tell Stefan, who was now fully alert and recovering well, and she spent her time between the two. The time came however that Stefan had to be told, and he didn't speak for a long while, then he told Marie that he only had one son now, and that regardless of anything, he would never expect to see Roger again, and no-one was to ever speak of him, or mention his name again. He also told Marie that she was to follow his instructions regarding disowning Roger completely, or she could leave. She was never to see him, or speak to or of him again. What a terrible choice to be faced with. Marie chose to stay with Stefan.

Unfortunately, Stefan did have to confront Roger, as Social Services insisted they meet just once. The meeting went as expected, although Stefan contained his rage and hatred for Roger, it was evident that he would never reconcile with him. This was more about Roger having the only opportunity he would ever get, to try and explain to his father why he had done what he had. He said he was more sorry than his father could ever imagine, that he had shot him, but he also tried to explain that it eventually felt like it was the only way he was ever going to escape his father's rigid control. The child had felt like a prisoner, punished for the crime of being born a gentle, quiet soul, who hated blood and guts and shooting, and the bush, and every day of his life he had been forced to endure everything he hated most, because his father wouldn't allow it to be any other way.

Roger was sent to a juvenile's rehabilitation centre, which included psychological assessment and treatment, and this was run on the basis of a boarding school, which meant he should have been home for the school holidays. Marie arranged for him to stay with her mum, and he also spent time with me. When he was with us, obviously Stefan couldn't know anything about it, and as Marie often visited me, he never questioned her coming to mine. She typed letters at work, which I posted, and his replies came to my address. This was the only way she got to see and keep in touch with her son, and we kept this deception up for the years that I was still there. This was a very anxious time for me, as I had little doubt how Stefan would react if he ever discovered I was harbouring his son and the go-between for his wife's visits and letters.

34

In between all of this, my life was running relatively smoothly, and although I socialised a lot, and had the very infrequent brief fling with a couple of men, I wasn't looking to get involved in anything serious, but life doesn't always go according to plan, as I well knew. Emma and my mum's relationship was as close as ever, and it was now at the point that if I suggested anything to Emma, she had to clear it with granny. Did granny think it was a good idea, if not; well it had to be scrapped. I didn't believe I could fight this, firstly my mum was a strong adversary, but it was also that we lived so close to one another. I couldn't afford to move, and the more I tried to draw Emma into my life, the more she pulled away. She had her granny, and her dad now was still a frequent presence in her life, what more did she need or want. Bruce was still contributing intermittently now, and I understood why, when I had a very unexpected call and visit, which ultimately propelled me on a path I'd never expected my life to take.

I will start at the beginning though. This unexpected call came from Ron, Bruce's housemate. He phoned and asked if he could meet with me, as he wanted to ask for my advice, and it was something to do with Bruce. I told him, I didn't believe I could help him, we'd met only once before a long time ago, and I thought it strange that this request came out of the blue. As Bruce's closest friend, he would have heard me called all the names imaginable, and I was certain, he would believe I had a pointed hat and flew on a broomstick every full moon, and probably expect the customary smoking cauldron and black cat. With all that to contend with, he sounded quite desperate, so I decided to give him the opportunity. Ron came around, as I wanted it to be considered a formal visit, and not a night out for drinks or whatever. When he came in he looked like someone expecting booby traps, and I wondered if he was checking for voodoo dolls or bats clinging to the ceiling. He appeared quite surprised that I lived in a normal environment. The children were asleep, and he told me he was having a really difficult time. Apparently Bruce was drinking very heavily again, and was almost always drunk. He came in at all hours, made enough noise to wake the dead, and whilst Ron thought he could deal with that, there was another anxiety that he felt embarrassed to talk about, but it had now become a major issue.

He took a while to talk, and he felt as though he was betraying his friend, but he said it was concerning him as regards Bruce's health. I thought I knew what was coming, but waited for him to spit it out. It all came out in a rush, and it was about Bruce peeing everywhere when he was drunk. Ron was clearly a meticulous type, and was becoming angry about how his home smelled. His sofa's and chairs had been subject to this abuse, and no sooner had he got everything cleaned, it happened again. Bruce's bedroom positively reeked of stale urine, and as he regarded this as Bruce's space he felt awkward about trying to clean it out, and reduce the smell. He said Bruce's hygiene habits in total were bad and getting worse, and he asked if the lack of control had happened before. I told him about my experience of this 'problem', and suggested that the only thing he could do was to talk to Bruce about it, and let him know that it was becoming intolerable and unacceptable, and see what happened.

We talked a lot, and Ron admitted I was completely different to how he'd imagined I would be after what he was told. Well, so was he, I liked his gentle nature, and his softly spoken voice, Emma and Jack had also talked about him, and liked him, they'd said 'he was a nice man'. I trusted what they said, more than I would a lot of adults, out of the mouths of babes, so to speak. I also believed his concern for Bruce was genuine, but now that any concerns about it being a medical condition had been abolished, I assumed he would deal with it differently. As far as I was concerned that had nothing to do with me, and I told him so. He surprised me as he left, when he asked if we could perhaps meet up sometime and go out for a drink. I said I would like that, but felt it might be awkward under the circumstances, and I suppose I felt suspicious that there may be a hidden motive for this visit and any future meetings we might have. I said as much, and suggested we perhaps wait and see what happened regarding his housemate.

A short while later, when Bruce came to fetch the kids for his day with them, he ranted that Ron had asked him to move out, and although he didn't go into detail, he made out it was all about Ron being anal about his home. That he was being petty and inconsiderate; he also said that if Ron behaved this way, he wasn't a mate anyway, and he would be cutting him out of his life. I didn't let on that I'd met Ron, and as the children had been asleep when he visited, I didn't have to ask them to keep any secrets. Bruce had managed to find a room in a commune type house, which was quite close by too, and he had moved in the day before.

During that next week, Ron phoned confirmed Bruce had moved out, and that it had gone badly. He'd been at the end of his tether though, and the old adage that 'you don't really know someone until you live with them', was true. Unbeknown to me then, this certainly would come back to haunt me in the months ahead. He asked me out. He didn't believe in wasting time then. We went out for drinks, and continued to date after that. I decided to take my time and learn about this man, before I allowed my feelings to cloud my judgement. He was a kind, gentle man, he was also very careful with his money, to the point of possibly being considered mean. I hadn't experienced any meanness, but he obviously took budgeting very seriously, and thought carefully before spending large sums of money. This strangely appealed to me because I had only had experience with men who spent their money as soon as they had it, and it felt secure. He adored his twin girls, supported them financially and saw them at every opportunity. He had filed for divorce, and this was due to them growing apart, they had married too young, and realized after time that they really had nothing left in common, and agreed to go their separate ways. He had a good relationship with his ex wife in so much as they were able to talk about the children and both believed that their girls had as much time with their parents as possible. This was refreshing too, no major drama's there. He was tall, and a bit of a keep fit and health fanatic, a massive fan of cricket which he played in with a local team, and enjoyed quiet evenings in. He had lovely manners, respected and loved his mum, this was always a good sign, and treated me like a valuable object, the kind you take care of in all ways. One of the best things was that we talked a lot and laughed together even more. This all seemed to be a dream come true, the opposite to anyone else I had met, and I started to fall in love with him. This time it was slow and cautious, and when we eventually made love, he was a considerate and experienced lover and I couldn't believe that at last I had met someone like him.

We saw each other every evening, and agreed that he wouldn't stay over, until we knew where the relationship was going, so as not to disrupt my children. I'd met his twins, and they were certainly both wrapped in cotton wool by both parents to the point of being spoilt, petulant and very whiny. They were still very young, and I wasn't going to hold this against him, each unto their own as far as parenting goes, we all do what we feel is best and not everyone is going to agree with other's methods. Enough rambling, after a sensible time, we decided we wanted to live together, and as Ron's house was about as small as mine, we started looking for a bigger house. I must of course mention that our relationship drove Bruce to more drink, if at all possible, it absolutely enraged him, and every time he came to fetch the kids he had a good few scathing things to say about Ron, and of course me too, for being involved with him. I turned a deaf ear, as it was only to be expected, this must be quite a betrayal for him, his ex wife and his ex best friend together, doesn't get much worse really.

Needless to say, my parents were distraught. I was moving away, and that meant their time with Emma would now be limited. I still had this compulsion to seek their approval in what I did in my life, and it was important that they gave me their blessing. I was unable to break the habit of my lifetime, and I still desperately craved their love and support. I would have walked on broken glass for them to tell me they were proud of me, regardless of how my life had turned out, but I knew they were still disappointed in me. My choices in partners had not been good, as far as they were concerned, and they didn't meet this obvious flaw with kindness, but with contempt, and impatience. 'There she goes again, involved with another misfit'. They had their own guidelines as to who would be suitable and it seemed I just wasn't conforming yet again. It was confusing though, because although they expected so much more from my choice of partner, I found this contradictory to how they felt about me. If I was such a disappointment and failure, why did they set such high standards in my choice of men? Surely it was more realistic to assume, I got what I deserved. As much as I continued to follow a certain pattern, so did they, and I don't think there was anything that I could achieve which might change the way they felt about me. They were as stuck in how they felt about me, as I was, in my sad desperate need for their approval and love.

It was also at this time, that the owner of the flats tragically lost his twenty-two year old daughter. I had met her a few times, and she was a beautiful girl. My dad had told me that her boyfriend had broken up with her, and she had taken it very badly, and turned to alcohol. Her father was distraught, and didn't know how to help her, and he often confided in my dad. My dad was very sympathetic to both his and his daughter's despair, and told me how very sad it was when someone was that despairing of life that they felt they needed to hide from it, using whatever substance they found helped. One morning when her father had gone to wake her, he'd found her dead. She had apparently choked on her own vomit. He was obviously distraught, and my dad felt that perhaps he could have done more for her, and for a long while he lived with this guilt. Sadly, as this time, I didn't realize how this would come back to haunt me in the future.

We took our time looking, and found a house with a lovely large garden. There were enough bedrooms for Emma and Jack to have their own room, which was something I had insisted on, as Emma was growing up, and needed to have her own space. The children liked Ron, although they had indicated he was a bit of a fuss pot, and was over protective towards me. He fussed over me like a mother hen, and was particularly considerate regarding my feelings, my general well being, and my safety. With my history of less than caring men, this was a very welcome change. One thing I haven't mentioned yet, which for me was a huge achievement, was I'd given up smoking. When I was on my own I really became anxious about damaging my health, and I was terrified of getting ill or worse, and leaving my children. My doctor had advised that I couldn't use any of the nicotine replacements on offer at that time because of my hypertension, so after about fifteen years of heavy smoking, I did it absolutely cold turkey. My GP was blatantly sceptical when I told him I was quitting, and equally shocked when I went through with it and succeeded, talk about a lack of support, anyway that probably spurred me on I was determined to show him and all the other sceptics that I could do this. Mind over matter, it worked. Since then I'd become more health conscious and started jogging and all sorts. I felt really good.

Anyway, we moved in, and it was lovely having all this space and such a big garden for Emma and Jack to play in. We had a moving in party, and my friends seemed to like Ron, although they found him a bit strange in his extra attentive behaviour towards me. I basked in it. We settled down, and Ron's girls came to stay regularly, and Bruce appeared to have accepted us being together, because he continued to fetch the children on his days with them, and I was noticing a surprising change in him. When he came to pick them up now, he seemed calmer, and he was actually pleasant. He always asked how I was, and it seemed to be genuine. I wasn't going to be fooled by this change though, and remained suspicious of his different behaviour. I had also noticed he'd lost weight, and the children eventually told me why he seemed so dissimilar. Bruce had given up drinking. I didn't believe it at first, but as time went on and he continued in this new and likeable way, I asked him. He said he had, and he'd never felt better. I was very surprised that he hadn't volunteered this information as this must have been a personal victory, and that in itself spoke volumes to me, that he had truly changed.

We began to have little chats when he fetched and returned the children, and I found myself warming to this new person. This was a Bruce I had never seen before, and how sad, that this likeable and caring man had never been visible during our marriage. I began to believe it would have all turned out very differently for us if only he'd given the booze up earlier. Don't get me wrong, I was waiting for him to regress and go back to the familiar bastard, I didn't believe this would last, but I enjoyed the time it did. It was the first time since I'd known him, that I felt comfortable being in his company, I didn't feel like I was doing the eggshell thing. Gone was the aggressive, unpredictable, angry, cruel man, instead, a real gentle butterfly had emerged from its alcohol saturated cocoon. He wasn't dismissive, nor was he derogatory, he listened to what I said, and he treated me like an intelligent, sensible person, and he even began to praise me as a mother. Dear God, it was hard to accept, but, I cautioned myself, it couldn't last. The children were happier during their time with him, than I had ever seen them before.

During these months of transition for Bruce, my relationship with Ron was changing too, the cracks were showing. Well, what's new? The qualities that had endeared me to him early on in our relationship now began to irritate and frustrate me. I did like being taken care of, but I didn't like being smothered. I couldn't do anything or go anywhere without him trailing after me, making sure I was warm enough, had eaten enough, had enough to drink. Was I tired, couldn't I sleep, what was worrying me, was I happy, was I sad, was I calm, was I irritable, it went on and on, and it felt like I had to give him a second by second account of how I was. This sounds like I was ungrateful for the very thing I kept saying I craved, it wasn't that at all, there is a happy medium, surely, being cared for, and treasured is one thing, being totally smothered is another. He called me about ten times a day at work, and it was becoming a problem. If I was five minutes late home from work he was moments away from calling out the armed guard. I couldn't walk around the garden at night unless he was with me, what did he think was going to happen, alien abduction. He sat with me whilst I was in the bath, in case I slipped, or bumped my head and drowned, or possibly got flushed down the loo. What was I reading, why was I reading anyway when I had his company, what was I watching on tv, could he watch with me. He even insisted he do the children's homework with me. If I went to the loo in the middle of the night, he would leap out of bed to switch the light on, and when I did wake during the wee hours, it was normally to see his face directly above me, watching me. Good God, the man didn't sleep. From what he wore, to what he ate, to where he went, who he spoke to, he had to confirm I agreed with his every action and activity. It was like having an adult child, so needy and demanding it was becoming very wearing.

Things got bad, when he didn't want me to socialize with my friends, and he was constantly telling me that I was far to close to Marie, and Jill, another very good friend of mine, I was exclusively his. My friend Jill had introduced me to a group of women who had a regular meditation evening, and I was determined to join them once a week. This caused mayhem. Ron went on about it days before, and because he didn't believe in this sort of 'hocus pocus', as he called it, why should I? If he thought he would wear me down with all the nonsense that went on prior to my evening out, he was mistaken, it only made me more determined to go, and besides I thoroughly enjoyed it.

As usual, I hung in there, berating myself for being ungrateful. I had finally met someone who obviously cared for me deeply, and even that didn't make me happy. Off I went on one of my self hatred trips, and consequently put up with this suffocating, cotton wool existence. I really tried hard to feel less stifled and more appreciative, but it was becoming quite a struggle. I'd got to the point where I wanted to scream at him to leave me alone. Just for five minutes, and as the only time I had any space at all, was when I insisted that he absolutely could not join me when I went to the loo, I had prolonged bouts of imaginary diarrhoea, which worked against me, as Ron became worried that I was ill, with all the time I was spending in the toilet, and he insisted I go to the doctor, because he couldn't bear for me to be sick, the diarrhoea stopped. All this impacted enormously on my relationship with Bruce, I felt like I was talking to a normal person, when we had our chats, and it had the potentially damaging effect of me making comparisons, and god help me, Ron wasn't in the leading position.

I'd also discovered when we lived together, that he was obsessive compulsive. You couldn't move anything, and it was straightened to an exact degree, he was constantly rushing about picking up, tidying up, straightening up, and I wasn't an untidy person anyway. He also had a lot of little rituals, and again, these once endearing little quirks were becoming hugely annoying. There was absolutely no spontaneity, the hours, days, weeks, months ahead had to be planned within minutes, and I felt like I was fifty, not thirty.

It got worse if possible, and now, as far as he was concerned, I wasn't going to a meditation group, I was having an affair. How could I do this to him, and how could I hurt him like this? What, he ranted, had he ever done to drive me into another man's arms. What? Where in gods name had this come from? I spent hours trying to convince him that there was no-one else. I told him all about the sessions on my return, and he said I'd always had a good imagination therefore; it was easy for me to make all this ridiculous 'hocus pocus' stuff up. This was making me really angry now, and when he phoned Jill behind my back to confirm that I wasn't seeing anyone else I was furious. What made it absolutely infuriating was, that even after she'd confirmed with him where we went, and that we did just meditation, he still chose not to believe me.

That good old straw that breaks the camels back happened late one night. I'd woken up, as one does, and he was rummaging in my handbag. 'What the hell are you doing?', I asked. 'I know there's going to be some evidence of your affair, and I'm going to find it', he replied. I felt sick, this was madness, he wasn't going to believe me, and how do you convince someone when they choose not to believe you. No matter what I did or said, he was absolutely convinced there was someone else, and it was driving me mad. One night he followed me to the house we met at for our meditation class, and I knew that I had to end this relationship. My friends thought he was a nutter when I spoke to them about his behaviour, and the one person who empathized with me was my ex husband. He'd lived with Ron, remember. I started confiding in Bruce about finding somewhere else to live, I felt like I was becoming a nomad, and he offered to help me, as I had to scour papers at work, away from Ron's prying all seeing eyes, and my lunch hour was often taken up with clients. Bruce really went out of his way, and eventually found a small maisonette that was vacant. As it would have created suspicion if I'd gone out with the children, I relied on Bruce to take them to see our potential new home, during his day with them, and they loved it. I decided that I would need to make the decision to move on before things became unbearable, and affected the kids.

I sat down with Ron one evening and in the nicest possible way told him how unhappy I was about his constant suspicion, jealousy and obsession with me, and that I thought it would be a good idea for us to go our separate ways. I really tried hard to be kind about it, but he wasn't having any of it, and all he said was 'I won't allow you to leave me, if I can't have you, no-one else will'. This was said in a flat, cold tone, devoid of emotion, and it was horribly scary, more so than if he'd ranted and raved. I felt like a character in a film, it sounded as though he'd rehearsed this line, I did take him seriously though. It wasn't a threat, it was a promise, oh God what had I got myself into this time. I didn't want to be dramatic and believe he would actually carry this threat out, but his behaviour was becoming more unstable by the day. He was having major mood swings, from a hysterical, completely over the top happy persona, to an almost manic moroseness. He was totally unpredictable, and whenever I tried to broach the subject about our relationship, he'd started to cover his ears with his hands, and start whistling or singing, so as not to hear me. It was really scary, and I wasn't alone in this environment, my children weren't immune to Ron's erratic behavior. I managed to find the time to talk to them when Ron was at work one Saturday, and told them that we were going to move to the place they'd seen with Daddy. Emma said Daddy had told her he was helping us, and she was over the moon that he was involved. I confirmed he was, and as their relationship with him had become more stable and secure, it gave them a sense of comfort and unity, that mommy and daddy were working together on this. I told them that we would have to keep this to ourselves and it was going to be an adventure. It was important for them to see this as an adventure, I didn't want them to know how serious it was becoming, nor explain why we were now impelled to move in secret. I had also noticed that I was missing belongings and possessions that had particular sentimental value to me. The stuff I would never leave behind nor intentionally misplace. Things like my photo albums, the only record I had of my childhood, and all the captured memories of my babies and the years in between. I had always said that in the event of a fire, I would always try and save these, as my photographic history of my youth, was encased in these albums. Ron knew this, and they were nowhere to be found. He obviously had suspicions that something was afoot, and he was doing whatever he could to keep me there. I searched everywhere, and discovered that the garage was locked, and my key for it had been removed from my key ring. It didn't take rocket science to know that he was obviously hiding all my precious things in there, the problem was I couldn't get to them. I couldn't just ask Ron to let me in to remove them, because that would intensify his suspicions, and I was increasingly concerned about his behaviour. He was so intense and hyperactive, always bordering on hysteria. Although I didn't think there was too much risk attached whilst we were there, I didn't want my children affected in any way. They'd been through enough already, and I wasn't about to have any major rows or upheaval. We just had to include this in our plans.

35

I couldn't achieve this overnight, as once again there were a couple of weeks before we could take occupancy. I kept the secret going with the children with conspiratorial winks, and whispered plans when I put them to bed, they were excited rather than anxious, and I encouraged this reaction. Bruce and I spoke often during the day, and he helped enormously. He organized all my utility accounts, and did everything possible to make the transition as smooth as possible. I'd asked him what had made him give up drinking, and he said he'd been out one night as normal. He'd got totally drunk as normal, and the following morning had a couple of beers for breakfast. That wasn't unusual. He'd been driving to one of his haunts to drink up a storm all over again, and had stopped at red traffic lights. When they turned green, he hadn't reacted spontaneously, and a police car had spotted this lack of concentration and pulled him over. Needless to say they noticed very quickly that he'd been drinking, and he was arrested and taken to the police station, where they'd confirmed he was excessively over the limit. To cut a long story short, he'd been charged accordingly, had to go to court and received a very heavy fine. When he'd eventually been allowed to go home, and that was a couple of days later when he'd sobered up, he'd had a very serious fright, and hadn't liked being in a cell. This obviously encouraged him to consider changing his life, and that experience had achieved more than I'd ever been able to during our marriage, and he hadn't had a drink since he'd been arrested. He said he felt absolutely marvellous in every way. Both physically, and emotionally, and said it was the first time since he was a teenager, that he felt in control of his life. He was far less angry at the world and everyone in it, and the one I really was shocked at, was that for the first time, he admitted he'd cocked up monumentally in just about everything he'd done in his life, and realized that he was responsible for the way things had turned out. It wasn't everyone else's fault. He'd obviously done a great deal of soul searching, and I think it was the first time he ever had, because even though he'd been sober when he'd become deeply religious, I don't think he'd searched his soul then, I think he'd sold it. When that had all gone horribly wrong, he'd hit the bottle harder than ever before, and increasingly seemed to lose all perspective. I suppose this was the person I'd had some sense of, but who had been suppressed by the anger and private torments that the alcohol had fuelled. The person I had observed very rarely, and although he was vaguely familiar, I didn't know him at all. He was so totally and completely different to the Bruce I had been married to, they could have been complete strangers. We had the shared bond of the children; otherwise I think I would have run a mile and then some, because I could easily grow to become very fond of this person indeed. The monumental brick wall I'd built myself, to guard and protect me from any feelings for Bruce, was starting to crumble, and it frightened me and excited me at the same time.

We'd set the date to move, and I had explained my situation to my boss and colleagues. They were caught up in the adventure, and I was given a very rare extra day off. Lee also offered me the use of the company van and staff, and as their daily job was moving office furniture, this was an enormous bonus. We could move all my furniture out quickly and expertly, and this was a real comfort with the time constraints we were working under. I would take the children to school as normal, so they wouldn't be involved if there were any problems, and my dad would fetch them and take them home with him, and as far as Ron was concerned I was following my normal routine, and at work. If he phoned, Marie was primed with as many excuses as necessary, as were Gay and the others. We had organized storage for my belongings and I would be staying with my parents for a few days until my new home became vacant. Needless to say they were less than pleased, at yet another failed relationship, and the fact that Bruce was helping me enraged them. None of us were looking forward to our stay there. The furniture part would be the easiest, all the clothing, and linen, and ornaments would just have to be thrown into bags and taken. Every evening I'd tried to make a mental note of where everything was, so that I could get it all packed quickly. Most of the stuff in the house belonged to me, and I was determined that I wouldn't accidentally take anything that was Ron's. I was going to be very particular about this, because he was obsessive about everything he owned, and I didn't want to add to his anger and pain, when he came home to a nearly empty house and an extinct relationship.

It was very difficult trying to maintain our relationship during this time. Ron was more confident and arrogant, and overbearing because he thought my change in attitude was attributed to me accepting him and a life with him. He frequently alluded to marriage, which sent shivers down my spine, and I think he believed I was the luckiest woman alive to have his devotion. Good God, let me get out before he goes down on bended knee. I couldn't go through with the pretence of accepting his proposal, and the alternative would be unimaginable. I made all sorts of excuses to avoid sex with him in the nicest possible way, when all I really wanted to say was 'Fuck off, don't touch me'. He literally made my skin crawl now, and even the customary kisses of greeting and leaving turned my stomach. He sensed I was withdrawing, God, I was doing a reasonable job pretending, but I wasn't in line for any Oscar's and this just made him more obsessive, possessive and intense in his feelings towards me. It really was a nightmare time, and I quaffed huge quantities of wine in the evenings to see me through.

Bruce and I spoke often during this time, and even met for lunch. I had to lie about that too, as I had told my work mates all about what an utter bastard he'd been, and now I was socializing with him, I kept my changing feelings from anyone and everyone, and tried to deny them myself, but they wouldn't go away. I knew they were reciprocated, Bruce had never made a secret of the fact that he would do anything to be reunited with me and the children, and this made it harder for me to distance myself from my growing fondness for him.

The day came, and driving the children to school, I was an absolute bundle of nerves. Anything could go horribly wrong. Ron had gone home unexpectedly from work before, either to pick up something, or during an extended lunch hour, and it didn't bear thinking about, that that might happen today. He would be met with the woman he loved and wanted to marry leaving him secretly, and worse than that, being assisted by her ex-husband, and his ex best friend, the despised enemy. Bruce had his friend Grant with him, to help with the move, and to keep watch for any sign of Ron. Grant was a nice enough person, but from what Bruce had told me, he was involved with a gang of drug dealers, and the most worrying aspect of it all was that Bruce and Grant were all carrying guns. Most people had their own pistols illegally or legally, and Ron's had been missing from the cupboard he kept it in for a while now. I had checked that a while back and assumed he carried it with him now, and if Ron came home to this, I was reasonably certain he would use his gun. It would enrage him that I had planned this with his arch enemy behind his back, and the fact that the people he despised most, were walking freely about his property, and in his home would eradicate any thoughts of sanity or reason. I was petrified, and moved as quickly as I could, throwing things into bags, or just throwing them into the car. It could all be sorted out later. I ran around the house frantically collecting my stuff, my heart thumping, dizzy with fear. Bruce and Grant had to break the padlock to the garage, and sure enough there were all the bits and pieces that gone missing over the last weeks. The staff from work loaded up my furniture as quickly as they could, but it was inevitable that they would have to come back for another load. Shit, this was madness, I was running around like a mad thing, flinging things into any available vehicle, shouting instructions to everyone, expecting them to do ten things at once, and then yelling at them when they didn't achieve the impossible. I had this vision of Ron arriving home, and having a shoot out with Bruce and Grant, guns drawn at dawn sort of scenario, with me in the cross fire getting shot to bits by them all. I couldn't easily shake this image, and I rushed about on fast forward.

I kept in contact with Marie, and Ron had called twice so far. That wasn't unusual; me being unavailable every time he called however could make him suspicious. I knew that it was highly unlikely that he had any idea about what was happening whilst he was at work, but it was my guilt and fear that made it feel as though he could read minds suddenly, and would be alerted to the situation. Time was running out, and although we'd worked frantically all morning, it was getting ever closer to when he would be leaving work to go home. The last of the furniture had gone, and after countless trips with all the other bits, there were the last loads to be taken. How none of us got speeding or careless driving fines that day I don't know, because every load we'd taken to storage had been at high speed and high risk. The last of it was ready to go, and I rushed through the house checking I'd got all my stuff. I knew that whatever I'd missed, I would never see again, as I couldn't expect Ron to be considerate to my needs after this. I'd written a note explaining my departure, and apologizing for how I'd deceived him, but it had been the only way, and I left that clearly visible, and then locked up. I put my keys in through the letterbox, so that I didn't have to hand them back to Ron.

We made the last trip to my parents and offloaded. I felt sad that I'd been unable to end this relationship normally, but I also felt free, and enormously relieved. My parents had been primed that I wasn't contactable, and I would just have to sort things out at work, if he tried to contact me there. I expected anger, bitterness, and loathing, what I hadn't anticipated was despair and heartbreak. Ron was devastated, apparently in his own little world he'd thought things were ticking along nicely, and of course in the past weeks I had worked hard at him believing this. He phoned my parents constantly, and he cried on the phone to Marie. She was covering my calls. He turned up at work unexpectedly, and thank God, I'd seen his car, and managed to duck into the basement and hide. I was a total coward, and couldn't face his utter misery. The anger and everything that went with it would have been easier to deal with and I relied on the hope that this would soon take over from his misery. It did, and that I could deal with. Eventually the calls lessened and then stopped, and in the meantime I had moved into a lovely maisonette with Emma and Jack.

Bruce was a constant presence in our lives, he no longer took the children out for days on their own, I went with. We went to the beach, as we had done so often before, but this time, instead of those days being filled with drunkenness and nastiness, they were filled with kindness, consideration and laughter. He wouldn't let me do anything apart from relax and read a book, or just enjoy the sunshine. Whilst the kids were playing or paddling, we talked like we never had before, and he spent quality special time with Emma and Jack. He was considerate in every way possible, and he began to visit every evening. He cooked and cleaned up, helped the children with their homework, refilled my glass with wine, whilst he only drank tea or coffee, and read to Emma and Jack, and then would spend time telling me how very sorry he was for the past. He would do anything to make it up to us, and he knew how his drinking had affected and influenced his life, and if I would only consider reconciliation, he knew he would never drink again and forfeit all this. He bought me flowers and little surprise gifts. He sent me mushy loving cards, he left me little notes, and for example when he put the kids to bed he would put a note on my pillow, so that I'd find it when I went to bed. He took me out for special romantic dinners. One of those evenings brought home to me how very much he'd changed. He wouldn't tell me where we were going, and it turned out to be my favourite place, he'd remembered me mentioning it. He'd booked the best table, and when we got there, there was a beautiful display of red roses on the table. He'd taken them to the restaurant just before he fetched me. I was touched to my core. He bought the children clothes and shoes, and games and toys, and he devoted all his spare time and attention to us. He laughed often and easily now, he was a happy man, happy in himself, and happiest when he was with us. I knew I was falling in love with him, and I tried so hard to remind myself of how bad things had been before, but this man was so completely different to the Bruce of before, that I had difficulty believing they were one and the same person. Of course I was cautious, and scared, but the biggest difference of all was that I could talk to Bruce about my feelings, and he understood, he just said, if it took years to convince me, so be it, but this was who he was now, and for the first time he actually liked himself, so there were would be no reason for him to revert to his destructive and emotionally vacant past. He wasn't going anywhere, unless I asked him to, he wouldn't ever be the cause of unhappiness for me again, and he wanted to devote the rest of his life to me and the kids. One of the most important aspects of our relationship was our history. Not only the children we shared, but our pasts. We shared memories of a wonderful country, and the upbringing that went with it, we shared the traumas of a war, we remembered our flight from that country, and all that went with it, and we talked about these memories superficially, with the fondness and nostalgia of people who know they can never regain those lost years, and believe they were happier and better than they actually were.

I looked forward to him being there every evening, my heart skipped a beat when I saw him; I loved the way we talked and laughed together. I saw Emma and Jack's absolute joy in having this new wonderful father in their lives, I didn't like to think about him leaving our lives, and I hated the possibility of him meeting someone else. I was in love, and I was loved like I'd never been before, it was time to draw a line under the past and move forward. Everyone deserved a second chance didn't they? My family and friends were understandably sceptical, but they had experienced the difference in Bruce, and we'd been seeing each other for over a year now. He'd convinced us all that this was how he wanted to be, and it was believable because he was happy in himself, he hadn't changed to suit anyone else but himself, and that's always the best motive.

Things were changing at work. Marie's cousin had joined the team, and was a junior member of staff, and she openly coveted my job. Whilst Marie and I were still friends, blood is thicker than water, and I was asked to show Katie the ropes. Both of us couldn't share the same role, and I wasn't prepared to be demoted due to nepotism, so the atmosphere became uncomfortable and the rivalry was obvious. I was on a level now with Marie's level of expertise at work, and my sales figures had surpassed hers every month now for a while and she hadn't taken too kindly to this. There was another element to their different attitude towards me, and that was me being back with Bruce. Over the years I had talked about what an absolute bastard he'd been, and I knew they found it hard to accept that I had let this all go to be with him again. Marie and I had discussed it and she relayed their concern regarding this. I'm not sure that the concern was on a personal level, from what she said, I understood it to be more about them losing respect for me. I could appreciate that, but I was dismayed that people whom I regarded as friends, couldn't respect my decision. These people that I had worked with, and socialized with, didn't put any value on the very careful consideration I had given to this decision, and if they couldn't respect that, they didn't respect me anymore. It wasn't hard to put two and two together, and I felt they were trying to ease me out.

Lee and Marie had developed a very close relationship over the years, how close, I wasn't sure, but I knew that Marie was confidently very secure in her job. They were obviously faced with a dilemma, their respect for me had gone, and consequently our friendship was waning. The atmosphere was strained and I think they had tired of the never ending drama of my life. Marie also wanted me out due to my continuing success with sales, and then she could move Katie into my job as a junior, who would soothe Marie's dented ego. You can't however sack someone for doing too well. Unknowingly Bruce gave them the opportunity. One of my favourite international bands was playing in Cape Town, and Bruce secretly bought tickets. It would mean I'd have to take a day off work to travel there, and he had phoned Lee to ask if I could have the leave before he bought the tickets. He told him it was a surprise for me, and Lee agreed that I could take the time off. Bruce had to tell me where we were going a couple of days before, because the children knew and they were struggling to keep their excitement for me a secret, and the day before we were due to drive to Cape Town, whilst at work, I went to thank Lee for giving me the day off. He said he hadn't, and that if I wasn't at work the following day, I was fired. I told him Bruce had said he'd agreed to it, and Lee asked me why I would believe anything 'that lying bastard said?' I trusted Bruce and I loved him, and I knew he wouldn't have made this up. I told Lee I would be going to Cape Town the following day, and not to expect me at work, and he suggested it would be best for all of us, if I left. I phoned Bruce who came to fetch me immediately, and he took me for a coffee at one of our favourite places. I was distraught, I had worked for the company for years, and I had worked hard. I couldn't believe it had ended like this, Lee agreed to accept 'my resignation', and pay me a month's notice. I insisted on the reference which I believed I deserved, and it was to be work related not based on how they felt about my personal life. I insisted this was written there and then, otherwise I would seek advice regarding my unjustified dismissal. I was utterly disappointed in the man I had respected all these years. Whilst I sat and cried, Bruce comforted and soothed me. I wasn't to worry about anything, he could organize another job for me in the organization he worked for, and anyway he would look after us, and then he knelt in front of me, and said 'I love you with all my heart, please give me the chance to look after you for the rest of your life. Please marry me?'

271

Oh God, my mind was spinning, I was jobless, I was scared, I was tired of struggling on my own, I loved this Bruce, and if I could believe he could be like this always, I had a chance at happiness at last. The children would be thrilled, and this would give us another chance to be a family. I had to trust and I had to hope, and surely I deserved a break, this couldn't be wrong, it couldn't be a mistake, and I said yes!

36

I wasn't prepared to get married any time soon though, and said we would live together for sometime, before we made the commitment. Needless to say, the children were thrilled, and Bruce moved in with us. My parents were pleased that things eventually seemed to be working out for us, and we all just had to hope and pray that things stayed as they were. They did for a while, sadly however utter anguish and despair and confusion, was ahead, and this time it would impact on my life forever.

Jack had suffered from a urinary tract infection which my GP had treated with antibiotics. One morning he came and told me it had started again. When I called my GP's surgery, I was told he was out of town for a couple of weeks. GP's often worked single handed, so there wasn't a partner to take him to. Bruce was with another GP, and I asked him to make an appointment for Jack.

Jack saw the GP, and was referred immediately to a Paediatrician, because it was unusual for a child of his age to have this type of infection twice in a short space of time. We were able to get an appointment the same day, and when the Paediatrician examined Jack, he was very concerned, and scheduled him for an MRI scan the following day. He explained to us, that upon examination, there was no indication that Jack's testicles had descended, and this should have happened years ago. He was shocked this hadn't been detected before. He didn't explain the consequences of this, as we had to wait for the

273

scan and the results. Jack had the scan, and the results confirmed the Paediatrician's worst fears. Sometimes only one teste will descend, whilst the other doesn't, in Jacks case neither had, and they were both very high up. He explained that my little boy would have to undergo urgent surgery, as the position of the testes were very irregular for a child of his age, and there was the very high risk of cancer, if it wasn't present already. My poor baby, dear God, please let him be alright, please let him be cancer free, oh Jesus I was so scared. Jack and I had always shared an unusual closeness, from the day he was born, and when his little eyes had opened instinctively and met mine, my heart and soul had opened up to my child in a way it never had with any other person. We shared our birthday, and the bond I had with my little boy was stronger than any other in my life. I adored him, and it was reciprocated. We had two days before surgery, and I couldn't sleep, or eat. I didn't want to be too emotional or distressed in front of him that would frighten him, so I talked to him about the forthcoming operation, soothed him and comforted him, and told him it would be alright. Regardless of my continued terror around surgery and hospitals, I would gladly have taken his place, the thought of what he had ahead was more painful than my fear, and the fear I felt right now was greater than any I'd experienced before.

What was strange was that I couldn't communicate this emotional turmoil to Bruce. It was as though I didn't feel he had the right to share this with me. The anxiety and anguish I was feeling about the situation was mine, and mine alone, it felt as though I needed to keep it safe, if I shared it, I'd be letting it go, I'd lose control of it. I shut down to everyone but Jack. I needed to focus everything on him, and there was nothing left over for anyone else. I felt that my infinite love for my child could keep him safe, and make it all better.

The worst of it was we had been told that there would be two bouts of surgery; they could only operate on one side at a time. This was because it would be extremely painful, and impossible for a child, or adult for that matter, to recover speedily if both were done at the same time. There would be an incision just above the groin, and then they would have to stitch the teste into the scrotum, which is obviously an extremely sensitive part of any male body. He would not be allowed to walk, or stand unaided for the first two weeks, and then it would be a matter of time.

Whilst he was in surgery for the first operation, I sat and prayed, please don't let there be any cancer. I offered God and the angels anything and everything, just please let it be alright. They answered my prayer as regards there being no cancer present, but apparently the teste had been too high to be stretched into the scrotum, they had to cut the main blood supply and bring it down that way. My understanding of the medical terminology and technology is that of your average person, and that was the way it was described to me. This meant that if the blood supply on the other one had to be cut too, my little boy would never father children. He would be permanently and totally infertile. They were confident though, that they had very seldom, if ever, found both to be that critical. I knew my son was very special, and he confirmed this with the way he dealt with his recovery. He was nine years old, and he was in enormous pain, but my little boy didn't cry much, he kept telling me he wanted to get better quickly so that he could get the other one done, and then it would be over. It's hard enough for anyone to undergo surgery, and experience an exceptionally painful recovery, but when you know that six weeks along you have to go through it all over again, that could floor even the toughest of us.

The Paediatrician had spoken to us, and explained that if during surgery they came across the same situation, it would be up to us to give the surgeon the decision on how to proceed. He would come out and speak to us, whilst Jack was still in theatre, and we needed to consider our answer now, as he would need us to respond immediately. He again said it would be unexpected and highly unusual for us to have to make this decision, but in the event of it happening we needed to be prepared. Bruce made it clear that he couldn't and wouldn't be involved with this decision, it was mine to make. I sympathized with this initially, believing it to be about my closeness to Jack, a 'man thing', and probably too painful for him to consider. I chose not to bring my nagging little thoughts to the surface, that in fact it was cowardly and that he didn't want to take any responsibility for any future repercussions from Jack. He could say it had nothing to do with him, that I had made the decision alone. I agonized over this alone, again.

Ultimately, if it was the same as before and their only chance at bringing the teste into the scrotum would be to cut the main blood supply, we would have to decide whether they were to go ahead with it, which would mean that Jack would never biologically father a child, or if it was left, the risk of cancer at any time in his life was higher than ninety per cent. Of course, he may never get cancer, but the very high risk was there. What they could confirm for me was that the risk was ninety nine point nine percent, because they never say one hundred per cent and that apart from a future miracle of medical science, he would never father a child. I suppose on the surface of it, it seems fairly straight forward, of course you are not going to put your child at risk of cancer, but then who is to absolutely guarantee that he would get it. On the other hand if you decide to cut the blood supply, you are absolutely taking any and every opportunity for that little man to father a child. How do you predict a nine year old boy's future. How do you leap ahead in time and understand or know that either being a father was really neither here nor there for him or that it is ultimately the thing he wants most in the world, children of his own with a woman he loves. How do you feel his pain when he falls in love, and has to tell this person, that whilst he wants to spend the rest of his life with her, she can never bear his child? How do you believe that there will be that very special person that will accept this, and love him, and of course I knew about artificial insemination, how and would he be the young man that could cope with that?

I did consider the positives, and yes, I also thought that, of course there are women out there who don't want to have children, and he could fall in love with someone who felt that way, I also considered the leaps and bounds that medical science is making in every way, and there was time on our side. How would this affect him later in life, how would it impact on him emotionally and mentally, and above all how would I tell him. How do you sit your child down when he's older and past the age that girls are just 'yuck', and whilst you are discussing the birds and bees tell him, not to worry, you wont' be able to have children anyway, so no need to go into all that. Mummy made that decision on your behalf.

What if it was left where it was, until he was old enough to produce sperm, and we could have it frozen? Simple, I don't think so, how do you explain to a thirteen or fourteen year old that he may need to go and masturbate in a clinical environment, so that he had the chance to father a child in the future, and then you need to go and have another one of those very painful operations so you don't get cancer. But what if, in between that time, the cancer came anyway. There was no time frame given for this risk, they had explained, he could get cancer at any time if the testical remained where it was. Even with them both sewn into the scrotum, Jack would always be at a higher risk of testicular cancer than is considered normal, but it would be dramatically reduced from where it would be if it wasn't corrected.

I went over and over all of this in the weeks before the next operation. I didn't allow Jack to suspect it was anything other than the routine surgery that had been described to him. He knew he had to have it done, and it had been explained to him, that it was normal for boys to have the testes in the scrotum at his age. His biggest concern was that although he'd never noticed before, he felt that he might look different to his friends if it wasn't done, and he was happy that the operations would remedy this.

In between all this was the self recrimination. I'd asked if it was something I should have detected, should I have known there was a problem when I bathed him as a young child, had I not been attentive enough to his little body, had this been my fault. It was clarified that it's something that should be regularly checked by the GP, and it's not something I would have picked up without knowing how to examine Jack professionally. The Paediatrician and Urologist had asked for my GP's name, and whilst I knew that I would follow this up, it would have to wait until after the operations because I needed to focus all my energy and attention on Jack. There would be time later for answers and explanations, and my simmering rage at this implied negligence.

Six weeks after the first operation, Jack was admitted for the second one. My poor baby was scared this time, because he knew what to expect when he woke up, he'd experienced the agonizing pain, he knew he had to go through it all again. Just before he went in, I held him close to me, I wanted to go into his little body and take it all away, I wanted to absorb it for myself, and as I held him I prayed as I never had before, that he would be cancer free, that they could stretch the teste down, and I wouldn't have to decide my son's future, but mostly bring him back to me. I told him how much I loved him, how brave he was, and that mummy would be right here, and I would be with him when he woke up.

The surgeon had told me where I needed to be in case he had to speak to me, and I didn't budge. I didn't want to see him walk through the doors, until the operation was over, and as the minutes ticked by, my hope grew. That meant it was all going to be alright, they'd managed to remedy it without cutting the blood supply. Then, I saw the surgeon approaching, it was too soon for them to be finished, and I knew. He spoke quickly, the very good news was that Jack was cancer free, and then he explained they had tried everything to stretch the testical down, they couldn't, it was both permanent and irrevocable sterility or that, above ninety per cent risk of cancer. Jack my precious child forgive me, but I can't put you at risk, I need you in my life, I need to give you the best possible chance at a healthy life, I love you so much. 'Cut it' I said.

When my little boy woke up, I was with him, and I was crying quietly. 'What's wrong mum', he said 'why are you crying'. 'I'm just glad it's all over now, and we can get you better, no more operations', I replied, and whilst he slept again, I wondered about the future. Would my son understand one day why I'd made this decision, would he hate me for it, would he know that whilst I had met my needs, to give him the best possible chance at life, and keep him with me, I had hoped that would have been his choice too? I indulged myself for this short while with these fears and possible recriminations, and then put it away in one of my pigeon holes. That was then, this was now, and it would be sad if I took away the very thing I had just given to us both, another chance and time, by wallowing in guilt, and grieving his loss on his behalf.

Jack recovered with the resilience of the young, and his scars healed quickly. Mine didn't. A part of me had shut down to Bruce, and it wouldn't resurface, he'd left me to go it alone, and continued to do so. It was as if he couldn't bring himself to discuss what had happened, and when I told him I was going to investigate the negligence behind this, he didn't want to be involved. I'd spoken to Jack's specialists, and they had confirmed that the checks done on baby boys, and as they grew were a standard procedure by the child's GP, at any visits. If there was any indication of abnormality in accordance with development, it should have been highlighted and investigated immediately. Jack had been with the same GP since birth, so I needed to talk to him. I did, and when I got to his surgery, I was enraged that this could all have been prevented if he'd done his job properly. I stormed in, and was told he was with a patient, and I could wait. Well that wasn't going to happen, and I barged into his room shouting and yelling like a mad woman. He hurried his patient out with apologies, and when he was eventually able to calm me down enough to talk to, he offered his explanation. Sometimes I wish I'd never gone to see him. Before he spoke to me, he went and got Jack's patient card. He said he'd been aware of the problem some years ago, when Jack was about three. Bruce had brought him in with a bad cold, and he'd done the routine examination for descended testicles. He'd mentioned to Bruce that he needed to investigate this further, and when Jack recovered from his cold to bring him back and he would explore it further. Bruce never brought Jack back, and he'd assumed at the time that he'd taken Jack to someone else. I know there had never been much of a rapport between Bruce and my GP, but why hadn't he told me? He showed me the card, and there in black and white were his notes, and it was exactly as he said. I was absolutely shocked, devastated, angry, confused, and an enormous pain swept through me. What was he telling me, that Bruce knew, he'd known about this, and he'd done nothing about it. I scrutinized the patient records, I needed to check if he'd put this in recently to cover himself, because I knew the specialists had already been in contact with him. He couldn't have done this recently, all the other visits over the next few years were recorded after this, and even if it had been a very clever piece of forgery, he hadn't known I was coming to see him, and I hadn't wasted any time in getting to him to confront him, after he'd been alerted to the situation. It would also stand up in court as evidence. He then reminded me, 'Cheryl, remember that Bruce was drinking very heavily at the time, and he might have forgotten'. 'Then why the fuck didn't you say something to me when you next saw me', I retaliated. I knew that regardless of what evidence he had that he'd noticed the problem, he'd been seriously negligent in not bringing it to my attention. Dear God, I was seeing him often enough at that time. I said all this to him, and he said he had a lot of patients, and of course he didn't remember isolated problems, he'd also thought that Jack had gone elsewhere, which was possible and probably considering that Bruce clearly didn't choose to be a patient of his. Fine, I went along with that, but why hadn't he told me, I kept asking him, why hadn't he just mentioned it to me, and why hadn't he checked Jack after this when I brought him, to see if anything had improved or changed. 'I will not accept that you are not partly responsible for this', I shouted, 'and I will make you pay for your neglect of my child', I went on. 'You will hear from my solicitor', I added as I walked out, and I slammed his door, as hard as I could in the hope it would come off its hinges.

I went home, and Bruce met me at the door, ready for a kiss and hug. 'Don't touch me', I hissed, I will talk to you later. The children were there and we had Bruce's family visiting, and I wasn't prepared to vent in front of anyone else.

Later when we were alone, I told him what had been said. I was drained of emotion, and my voice was cold, distant and flat, when I said 'don't say anything now, there is nothing you can say at the moment that will make me feel better', I went on, 'consider your answer very carefully, don't lie to me, and don't make excuses, just tell me exactly how it was'. He started to cry and tried to speak, and I said 'don't talk, I don't know how I feel at the moment about you, I need time to think, we will talk soon, and in the meantime, God help you if you let the children feel things are different between us'. I added, 'I don't want you to touch me, in any way, just don't come up to hug me, because I don't want to have to push you away, and make it obvious things have changed.'

We spoke a few days later. Bruce said he vaguely remembered the visit, and that he thought he had to take Jack back for some reason, but he'd decided it was for a check up to see whether his cold was better, and as Jack was fine, he didn't think it was necessary. He'd forgotten to mention it to me. He was upset, whilst he told me, and he said it reminded him why he'd given up drinking. He would never be able to forgive himself, and all he could do was try and make it up to me and Jack. I needed to think. I still felt flat and dead inside which was probably a good thing because I was able to consider all this more rationally, otherwise I think I would have just ended it all again, and asked him to leave. Neither Emma nor Jack knew anything about what had been going on, and I wanted to keep it that way as long as possible. They were the happiest, and most settled they'd been for a long while. They had the best relationship with their father they had ever had, they were so content. I could destroy all that in a moment, and I could explain to them that I had asked their father to leave because I knew he was partially responsible for Jack's recent ordeal, and I could tell a nine year old boy, that Daddy could have prevented all this just by being sober, and remembering to tell me what the doctor had said, or made another appointment. That would be for Bruce to tell Jack one day. I could create upheaval in their lives again, in an instant, and I could also set their father back on the path to nowhere.

I knew I couldn't do any of this, I also knew that I'd never be able to forgive Bruce for this lapse, just like I would never forgive my GP, but I wouldn't be able to forgive myself, if I destroyed everything my children now had because of my anger and pain, and revenge may soothe me, but ultimately it wouldn't change anything now, it couldn't make amends, it would be destructive, and cause great unhappiness for the two little people I loved most in the world. I knew I couldn't forgive and forget, but I could learn to live with this. Hadn't I asked the angels to keep my child safe during surgery, that he was cancer free, they had answered my prayers, and I didn't think that I could repay this by plunging him and his sister into another cycle of loss, change and confusion? I told Bruce I couldn't forgive him, I would try to live with this, and we would continue on the understanding that this would be something I wouldn't talk about again until the time came that Jack wanted more answers than he did now. This had happened before he turned his life around, and if I brought all of that past into the present I would still believe I was with the old Bruce. He was a different person now, and I would respect that, I'd been prepared to give him a second chance, on who he was now, and whilst I'd never anticipated this, I hadn't been conditional about, this second chance, it had to be based on the person in my present. Part of my new love for Bruce had died, I believed the balance would sustain us, open wounds become scars, they heal in time, but they never disappear.

Things changed between us, Bruce accepted my reservations, and I did my best to move on. It was still alright between us, just different and Bruce continued to be a devoted partner and dad. I knew I'd made the right decision as the children were flourishing in their new life.

37

We set a date for our wedding which was the 5th November, Guy Fawkes day, no better way to do it than with a bang. We planned a 'honeymoon' in Zimbabwe, obviously with Emma and Jack, and we were going to spend three weeks touring the country. Most of it we would be camping, and it also gave us the opportunity to show the children where we had been born and grew up. We were driving there, and this would mean long hours in the car, but it would be part of the fun, and we were all very excited about it. The wedding was going to be small and intimate with close friends and family, and we'd arranged for the minister to marry us at home. We'd moved yet again, to a bigger house, with a lovely garden, and we had adequate space for entertaining.

A couple of months before the wedding I had a life changing experience that proved to be very profound in many ways in the years to come. What happened in an instant would change all our lives enormously.

It was a Saturday, and Bruce, Jack and I had gone grocery shopping in one of the large supermarket chains. We'd finished and were at the till, when Bruce realized he'd forgotten his favourite sweets. I offered to run back and get them whilst he stayed at the till, and Jack came with me. We were rushing along, giggling about dodging people and seeing how quick we could be, and as I ran around the corner of a row of shelves, my feet flew from under me and I came down in a sitting position, and I heard the crack, as the base of my spine hit the metal shelving jutting out just above the floor. Agonising pain shot through me, and although I could see, everything was hazy and weaving in and out of focus, I felt cold and wanted to vomit. As I'd landed, Jack and other people had turned, and I tried to ask Jack to help me up. I couldn't get the words out, I was so dizzy. Jack was looking embarrassed and then frightened when all I could do was stretch my arm out towards him, and he came forward at the same time as a couple of other people to help me up. I managed to stand although the pain was terrible, and I kept feeling as though I was going to pass out, I just wanted to get back to the till, and Bruce could help me then. I didn't want to frighten Jack more than necessary, and he and someone else helped me shuffle back to the till. I obviously didn't know what I looked like, but Bruce turned as we approached, and his face registered shock and terror, so too did the lady's behind the till. I must have looked like the shuffling dead. Apparently I did. I was a horrible grey colour, and the staff member called for a wheelchair immediately. I was wheeled into their first aid room, and all I could tell them was that one minute my feet were on the ground, and the next they shot out in front of me, and I went down. I knew I'd hurt myself quite badly, but I wouldn't let them call an ambulance, that meant going to hospital. I just wanted to go home and take it from there. Whilst we were there, another member of staff came in, and mentioned that I'd slipped on some spilt syrup that hadn't been cleaned up.

When we got home, Bruce called his, and now my GP who said I had to have an X-ray, and I only agreed to this on the condition that it did not mean I had to stay in hospital regardless of the results. He agreed, as he knew there would be no other way to get me there. We went to the A&E, and the X-ray clearly showed the fracture just above the base of my spine. They gave it one of the unpronounceable medical names, and said I had effectively broken part of my back. Then there were all the suggestions for recovery, and a lot of them sounded like a stay in hospital. I refused. I would follow any and all of their instructions, but I would be going home. They couldn't force me to stay in hospital, and at the end of the day it was my spine, and if I was refusing specialized care, I was an intelligent adult who clearly understood the consequences and my recovery ultimately became my responsibility. I followed all the suggestions of medication, bed rest, exercises, and even wore the back brace, and perhaps it took slightly longer than it should have, but I worked hard at getting better, after all there was a wedding and holiday weeks away. During this time we contacted our solicitor, who was currently dealing with Jack's case, and told him we had more work for him. Talk about a family in chaos, we were a solicitor's dream come true, especially this last incident. It was pretty much cut and dried, there had been witnesses to my fall, and they had also seen the puddle of syrup, which I hadn't noticed, and there was no question of contesting liability. We just had to allow the legalities to run their mandatory course.

I had to get another outfit for the wedding, because of the brace, but I managed to do that, and the wedding took place without a hitch. I was in terrible pain still, but I saw the day through as best I could. I wasn't ecstatically happy that day, I think the only way to describe my feelings are that I felt content and settled, and I hoped that all the dark days of our past life together were put to rest now. New beginnings and all that. The children were ecstatic, and even my parents were happy things seemed to be getting better for all of us, and the only comment my mum made to Emma was that she hoped Emma's father stayed as he was, and never started drinking again, otherwise she'd be after him. Emma apparently said 'don't worry Granny, you won't have to, I'll be there first'.

We went ahead with our holiday to Zimbabwe, and I wore the brace for the first day, and then packed it away. Aside from anything else it was about thirty five degrees Celsius on a cool day, and they made me unbearably hot, and they restricted my mobility. I decided to take my chances without them, be sensible and cautious, but I was going to enjoy the holiday as I had originally intended before I went skating on syrup and throwing myself onto pavements.

We had a wonderful time, and visited all the old haunts. When we went back to the street and house I had grown up in, I tried hard to conjure up the same feelings my parents and brother were displaying. They had also gone to Zimbabwe at this time, as my brother and sister in law had travelled from the UK to be there too. It was Christmas, and a family reunion. I felt slightly nostalgic, but my memories were mixed. I'd had some very good times, and I'd had some very bad times, and that left me in quite a neutral state. It was nice to show the children the schools I'd attended, and the places I had frequented as a child and teenager, and Bruce had the opportunity to show them his hometown too. We camped under the stars, and we were together twenty four, seven for three weeks. There were no dramas or traumas and this time together was important in different ways for all of us. Emma and Jack had quality time with us, and I used it as an emotional settling in period after the upheavals of the last year.

38

My court case came to an end in June of the next year, it was 1995, and I was offered quite a large sum of money in compensation from the supermarket chain, and I had already given it a lot of thought, as to what I'd use it for. Bruce had suggested we put a deposit down on a home of our own, but I had a different dream. In South Africa, the children don't sit GCSE's they sit an exam called Matric. It is somewhere between O and A levels, but it isn't recognized anywhere else in the world. That was my first consideration towards my suggestion on how we use the money. The crime rate was climbing steadily in South Africa, and car jacking and burglary were a way of life. That was my second consideration. The third was regarding travel and the opportunity to see the rest of the world. You have to have a lot of money to travel abroad from South Africa, which is mainly due to the exchange rate of the Rand to international currencies.

I wanted the children to have the opportunity to achieve an internationally recognized qualification, and I also wanted them to be able to see a lot more of the world apart from Africa. I wanted to use the money to start a new life for us in the UK. I had my own motives too, ever since I'd visited there on holiday as a child, I'd felt like it was home, I'd always felt a very strong pull to go back, and I had never believed it would be possible, until now. It would mean selling up, and we didn't own property, so basically that would be everything else,

286

our cars, furniture whatever we could really. We couldn't afford to go over and secure jobs, investigate schooling, or have a look around as to where to live, we would literally have to land in London, jobless and homeless, and take our chances. The most difficult part would be leaving family and friends and everything familiar. Bruce and I had done it before, but we were much younger then, and it hadn't exactly turned out how we'd believed it would, but the children would find it very difficult leaving their friends, their grandparents, their schools, and the adjustment for them would be enormous. They would be thrown in at the deep end regarding education, a completely different syllabus, and of course it's every child's worst nightmare going to a completely new school where you know absolutely no-one.

Although my brother and sister in law had been living in London for some years now, when I contacted them with my plan, my brother couldn't have been more negative if he'd tried. He told me I had absolutely no idea what I was letting us in for, and I was totally insane to even consider coming to England. The weather was awful, the commuting was awful, the crowds were awful, there were no jobs, all the kids were either drug addicts or criminals, we would have to adjust to life in a high rise council estate, and it was just total doom and gloom. I think he was terrified we would arrive on his doorstep and expect him to support us. Well there was no positive feedback there then. I had a few other contacts there, and although their feedback was less depressing, it certainly didn't paint a pretty picture. I wasn't deterred; I believed it came down to attitude. I was committed to doing any type of work that was available, and I was prepared to work hard. I knew that there were alternatives to high rise flats, and it was impossible that the youth in the UK, could be that different to here. I also took into account, that Peter had probably checked the latest mugging statistics or something for his view, and against the crime rate in South Africa, it would be considered safe as houses.

Bruce and I discussed the pros and cons in depth, and he agreed with me, that this was our opportunity to start a new life, and give the kid's the chance at one too. When they completed their education, and were old enough to leave home, they could travel the world, and they could choose where they wanted to settle. If we stayed in Africa, they could still travel overseas, but only on a limited stay basis, their options would be restricted. Although we called a family meeting, he left it up to me to tell them what we had decided. It wasn't about them being given a choice, because I knew that they would obviously choose to stay. It was about telling them we were going to do this, and why, and then supporting them through their anxieties, their questions, their fears, their excitement hopefully. It went pretty much as I'd anticipated. Jack thought it was a wicked idea, and he enthused about living in London, and the flight over would be the best. Emma was absolutely devastated. She was just thirteen, and this was a difficult age at best, and she couldn't believe that I, not we, I was taking her away from her friends and especially her granny and granddad. There were days of sobbing and she told me she hated me, so often, that it became meaningless. She threatened to leave home and go and stay with her best friend Joanne, and she threatened to tell people that I, was kidnapping her. I knew this must be very difficult for her, especially a teenager, and girls experience friendship differently to boys. For them, their best friends are who they live and breathe for, and she was leaving them all. I didn't know how to persuade her, that I did truly believe that one day in the future, she would understand why I was doing this, and be pleased about the opportunities she would encounter in the UK. I didn't achieve this, her friends did. When she told her friends, after the initial highly dramatic sobbing that is so typical of thirteen year old girls, they all thought she was so lucky, going to live in London, and she'd be able to see the queen, and all the shops that were there, she'd be so sophisticated and grown up. They were so jealous, and wished they could go too, and they were going to ask their parents if they could go and live in London as well. Of course if they had to stay, Emma could fly back and visit them often, and she was their absolute heroine. This changed how she felt, and now she told anyone and everyone, about us leaving. There was an enormous amount to do in not much time, as I'd discovered the British school year was different to ours. They started a new year in September, ours was January. That meant that had to get there as close to September as possible, so a difficult transition for the children wasn't made more so. As we were into July now, we had about two months to leave. Bruce handed his notice in at his job, and I told them when I'd be leaving, I was temping so it was flexible for me. I had to make appointments with the kids teachers and Head teacher to inform them they would be leaving, and to request testimonials. We had to have full medicals and x-rays to check for TB. Bruce and I had right of abode in the UK, as he had a British passport through his father who had been born there, and I had an Irish passport through my granny. The children however had South African passports, because although they were entitled to British passports through their father, he hadn't registered them with the British Embassy within the stipulated time frame, after they were born. They could live with us, as minors for two years, and then we could apply for citizenship for them. This was probably the biggest risk we were taking, because there were no guarantees they would be granted citizenship, we had however, agreed that if this happened, we would ultimately have to come back, and at least we would have all had a taste of another life.

We had to book our flights, and we had to get rid of all our bits and pieces. I was ruthless, and sold or gave away just about everything we owned, apart from our clothes. I only kept the most special items of sentimental value, and of course my photo albums. None of us had ever owned a coat, in our lives, let alone a scarf or boots, other than plastic fashion ones, and you couldn't buy the right stuff anyway, that would have to wait until we arrived in the UK. It was a mad couple of months, and I think it was a good thing because the children were caught up in the plans, and didn't have much time to worry about the uncertainties ahead. I was so excited; I was like a mad thing. I gladly rushed here and there sorting everything out, whilst Bruce continued to work. We would need every last Rand, because the exchange rate was going to make our nice sum, look pathetic. It eventually converted from about R28,000.00 to £4000.00, and that was all we had with us, apart from our clothes.

There were so many different farewell parties, but each one collectively had the same message. Everybody believed we were completely mad, and would be back with our tails between our legs. We had absolutely burnt our bridges, and would have nothing to come back to; we were taking an incredible risk. Of course if this did happen, the responsibility would be mine, because after all this had all been my idea.

I forgot to mention that about six months previously I had decided to join Bruce as a complete non drinker, for a couple of reasons really. I just felt it was a good time to go on a bit of a health kick, and also to support him. It was at one of these farewell parties that Bruce decided to have a beer, and when I saw him drinking it, my stomach lurched in absolute dread and fear. Dear God above, please don't let him start drinking again now. How would I possibly cope with all that again, and with us leaving for a strange country in a few days, I was absolutely terrified? I told him later how scared I had been, and said he'd only had the one, and hadn't even enjoyed it. I thanked the angels, and thought it was probably a good thing he'd tried it and disliked it, that was really very positive.

We moved out of our house, and in with my parents, yet again, and it was awful. My parents were as angry with me, as Emma had been, and as she'd become accustomed to the idea now, things weren't quite so difficult. That was until we spent the last few days with her granny and granddad. My parents didn't try to subdue their utter misery at losing their granddaughter, and the rest of us I think, and although I'd been over and over the validity of this move, all that was disregarded in these last few days. It just made it so difficult at a time, when I was hoping I could have focused on the excitement and thrill of this wonderful adventure to help the children through the emotional and tearful goodbyes. It wasn't to be, and I had Emma and my mum treating me like some sort of child snatcher of the worst kind. The day before we flew it all exploded. Emma became hysterical and said that she absolutely would not be getting on the plane, she had spent the day before with her best friend, and that upset her granny because she felt neglected by Emma. I went to fetch her, so she could spend time with her granny, and I literally had to drag her kicking and screaming into the car, and when we arrived back at my parents, my mum rushed to her, telling her she understood how badly she felt, because granny's heart was breaking too, and of course she didn't want her little girl taken away from her. Well, that was really supportive, my mum encouraging Emma's last minute rebellion. If that wasn't bad enough, Bruce joined in, and had a tantrum of his own. How could I think I was doing the right thing, look at his daughter, she was absolutely distraught, and he wasn't going to put her through this kind of trauma. Didn't I see how upset she was, what was I made of, stone. He got in his car, which was being left at my parents until it was collected the next day by the buyers, and drove off, saying he wouldn't be back. Shit, didn't they think I was as scared as they were, did they think these farewells weren't hard for me, and to top it all, I was now carrying the full responsibility for everyone's misery. This was wonderful, just hours before we were due to fly, and I was sitting in the bedroom with Jack. 'I'll still go with you mummy', he said. 'We can go, and it will be fun'. Bless his little heart, he'd been left out of the loop by his grandparents and father yet again, and it was one of those out of the mouths of babe's profound moments. I had a choice to make; I could wallow in self pity, or say 'fuck them all, we were going'. I was not going to be emotionally blackmailed, and the last day, on which everyone should have been using positively and taking advantage of their time together, they were turning into an absolute nightmare.

Bruce, Emma and my parents really believed that I would call it off, the louder they shouted the more miserable they were, the guiltier they tried to make me feel, and they believed they would wear me down. I was so angry now that I was determined that regardless of what they did, Jack and I would be on that plane in the morning, and we would take our chances. I know I was being totally irrational and mad, thinking we would or could do it, but then I didn't feel very rational, and in fact I didn't think much further than my anger at all this last minute mayhem. I walked into the lounge where my parents and Emma were sitting. They actually looked quite pleased with themselves when they saw me, and my mum asked if I'd reconsidered. Bruce could get his old job back, and we could stay with them until we found a house, it's not too late to call it off. 'You can do what you like', I said to Emma, 'and if you want to, you can stay here with your father, that will be up to you. I will not be responsible for making you and him this unhappy'. I went on, 'we have discussed this every which way for the last two months, and if you have now suddenly changed your mind, then stay', and I ended with 'Jack and I will be getting on that plane tomorrow, and I would love you to come, but I won't force you'. With that I started to walk out, and added, 'If your father phones, you can tell him that too'.

I went for a walk with Jack, and when we got back to the flat, Bruce was there. The anger and frustration had obviously gone out of him, and I think he felt stupid at his very childish temper tantrum; I wasn't going to make it easy for him though, I was still really angry. I waited for him to initiate the conversation, and he said 'I'm sorry I went off like that, it all just got to me'. I replied, 'don't you think I'm feeling just about everything you are, but what good would it do if I crumbled in a heap too', I was in full flow now, 'I have told the others, and I'm now telling you, that I am sick and tired of trying to keep you and Emma positive, you can stay here, I couldn't care less anymore, but Jack and I are going'. I started to walk away, and he knew I meant what I was saying, I wasn't playing mind games, I was well and truly fed up, and didn't give a shit anymore. 'Of course I'm going with you', he said, 'We're doing this as a family'.

Bruce took Emma into the bedroom to chat to her, and not long afterwards, she came out all smiles, and eager to go. If only he'd worked with me on this, months ago, it was so easy for him to control our daughter, and I realized he knew that, which made me realize that he could have helped me or the family a long while back. He wasn't drinking, but he hadn't lost his taste for power and control and the mind games, and I believed that he had deliberately made it as hard as possible for me. He still liked to see me work hard for everything, and hadn't he just rewarded my perseverance and obstinacy. The rest of the day was miserable. Everyone now tried to be cheerful and excited, but it was so contrived it was nauseating. I just wanted the morning to come, and to get away.

It did come soon enough, and we had a lovely surprise waiting for us at the airport, which got the tears flowing. Emma and Jack's classmates, and a lot of our friends were there, with banners and balloons, wishing us well. Emotions were high, and we all cried buckets. I hugged my mum, and told her I loved her and would miss her, oh God I still craved her love, maybe time and distance would bring this to me, and maybe making a new and prosperous life for us, would gain me her approval. She clung to Emma as though her life depended on it. We were all crying when we boarded our plane, this was it, we were on our way, a wonderful new and exciting life awaited us all, and I had no doubt it did, that all changed on the flight over.

We were flying via Athens and staying there overnight, this had been our cheapest option, and I'd arranged for my brother to meet us at Heathrow the following morning, and we had a reprieve in finding accommodation. My sister in law was heavily pregnant with their second child, and they were moving out of London to a place called Redhill in Surrey after the birth. They had rented a flat there in the meantime, and we could use it for a couple of weeks. It didn't give us much time to sort ourselves out, but it meant we wouldn't have to spend any of our precious cash on a hotel or B&B.

The children had never flown before, and the take off took their attention away from the trauma of the goodbyes, and they loved looking out of the windows, and every bit of turbulence was cause for celebration. It was cause of great terror for me, I hated flying now, and every little noise or movement meant we were going to crash. The kids enjoyed their new role of looking after mummy, and wasn't she such a baby, it was so cool when the plane went up and down like that, and everything rattled, and the seat belt light went on, for me everyone of those was a heart stopping moment. Out of a desperate need to calm my nerves, I had some wine with my meal, and Bruce did too, only he didn't stop there; he drank steadily throughout the flight, and got totally drunk. This scared me more than anything, and I felt as though it was all over before it had even begun. There was absolutely no turning back now though, so I had to try not to think of the bigger picture and just hope this was a one off, deep down though I knew it wasn't, and I felt as though I'd been well and truly had. It felt too coincidental that he'd been so strong and stuck with it for as long as he had people to impress with the way he'd turned his life around. He'd known that I would have left him in an instant if he'd started drinking again when we were back home, now however it was totally different, I was perhaps at the most vulnerable point of my life, and regardless of my earlier bravado, he knew without a doubt that I couldn't really survive in the UK without his income and support. We were on a one way ticket, we had £4,000 between us, and he knew that it would be impossible for me to find work, a home and support two children in this strange and new country within the very limited time we had, before the money ran out. Most of all he knew I wouldn't leave him, because this was an enormous upheaval for the children without their parents separating yet again. I'd forgotten how clever and manipulative he was, I had thought all this and the control and mind games had ended with the drinking, I had been so gullible yet again, I remembered how he plotted and planned, and on that flight, I knew I had been totally had, and he really had me between a rock and a hard place. This was a no win situation, and I would have to once again accept whatever life threw at me.

39

As we came into land the following day, I cried, I had the overwhelming feeling that at last I was coming home, the fears of the last day felt less devastating, and I knew that here, in this wonderful country I would find peace and happiness at last. This feeling was strong and at soul level, and there was no logical or reasonable explanation for it, after all realistically I didn't know what the immediate future held, apart from enormous challenges in every way. I stepped onto English soil with a sense of profound peace and a strange feeling that there was someone here waiting for me, that I would meet the soul that I had been searching for all my life, and my life would become complete here in a way that I had never before experienced.

We were absolutely shattered, and my brother was there to meet us. He hadn't changed his opinion about us coming to live in England, and he thought we were wasting our time and our money, and being very foolish disrupting the children's lives like this. He'd continued to send us negative feedback whilst we were in South Africa, and this was his motivation for the way he introduced us to our new life. All our suitcases were extremely heavy, and as we had packed all we were bringing with us, we all had backpacks that were equally heavy. It was exhausting even getting them from the baggage section to arrivals, and I was looking forward to getting into a cab. Andrew had other ideas though, and we travelled from Heathrow to Earls Court by train, and tube, and then by foot. Their flat was on the second floor, and there was no lift, so we had to haul everything up the stairs. I couldn't believe he had been so unkind. He must have known how exhausted we were, but he said that if we wanted to live here, it was best we met it head on, so to speak. I didn't take this view, but I seethed in silence. The children had never been on a tube before, and everything was so new and exciting for them that the arduous and unnecessary journey hadn't impacted on them. We couldn't haul all the suitcases to Redhill, as Andrew still refused to use any other mode of transport other than tubes and trains, and he'd wanted us to see Jane, hence the trip to Earls Court. We had to separate out what we really needed, and then we had to walk back to the station with our luggage, and get to Victoria Station to pick up a connection to Redhill. When we arrived at Redhill, we were all now absolutely finished, the excitement had worn off, and sheer exhaustion had taken over. Andrew said it was a short walk to their flat from the station, but it wasn't that short, and by the time we got there, every part of me ached from lifting and pulling the luggage all over the place. Still, we were grateful for the flat, and when Andrew left, we were too tired to eat or anything else for that matter, and collapsed into our beds. That was our first night in our new country.

Our priority was to get the children settled in a school, and we had decided that we would make our home around this. I didn't want to waste time, and got a list of the local schools from the library. We also had to consider that we didn't have a car, so for now, it had to be close enough for the children to walk to school, until we understood bus routes. We enrolled the children into a local school, and I expected to pay a large sum of money for their uniforms, and their schooling. The jumpers and tie were unbelievably cheap, and we didn't have to pay anything for their education. What a wonderful surprise. Emma and Jack started school the following day, and I was probably more nervous than they were. Bruce and I went and bought as many local papers as we could, and I realized that I would need to gain computer skills to improve my opportunities. The only work I had done on a computer before was data input, and beyond that, my knowledge was zero. I discovered a self-teaching course at the library and booked my time in.

We also had all this money in traveller's cheques on us, and we had to deposit it into a bank. Opening a bank account was difficult, and eventually we were only able to achieve this using my brother as a guarantor of sorts. During these first few days, we had to look for somewhere else to live too. Fortunately I had brought over references from previous letting agencies, and we were able to find a fully furnished and equipped little house. We knew nothing about the different areas, and the significance of post codes, and I had never heard of a council estate before. We also had to find a GP, as I was still on medication for hypertension, and would need my prescription renewed.

Besides that, there was so much to learn, and most of it was class related. Upper class where I came from was lower middle class here, and it was advisable that you knew the right area to live in, the proper newspaper to read, shops to avoid or at least never admit shopping in. Even though they were the ones that offered the best value for money, you made sure you went there in disguise, and never ever kept those carrier bags, let alone display them. You needed to know designer labels and do the associated name dropping. From what you ate, to where you lived, to what you read, to where your children went to school, was relevant to where you were in this class structure, and it was crucial to how you were received and related to. Most important was which football team you supported, and which political party you followed. These could make or break you in an instant. Good God, this was complicated, so much for a simple life.

There were boroughs and counties, the 'high street', the currency, the markets, and of course you're 'local'. What the hell was a 'local'? Perversely you needed to owe money or at least have a loan or credit card, before you had a credit rating, and if you didn't have either of the above, you had no credit rating, and therefore you weren't eligible to borrow? There were the different modes of transport, and we thought the rail system, and the buses were fantastic, there wasn't anything like this in South Africa, but here apparently it was awful, and everyone complained about it. Then there was this totally new concept of the obsession about the weather. Why? People found it incredible that we would choose to live here rather than in all that lovely sunshine. Well living in over thirty degrees, with humidity for nine months of the year, is really not that great. Sure if you don't work, and spend all your time on the beach it might be fun, but there's no season definition really apart from summer leaping into winter. The opening line of conversation always seemed to be 'so, what do you think of the weather'. Not, 'what do you think of this wonderful country, the free health service, the vast and efficient transport network, the free education, the wealth of opportunities to work, and you could find a job in an instant if you were willing and prepared to do anything'. We found everything so cheap in comparison to South Africa, once we got out of the habit of converting the pound to the rand. If you related it to your earning power in pounds, it was unbelievably reasonable; you could buy a t-shirt at the market for one pound! Oops, you shouldn't be seen to be buying anything at the market. The police here didn't walk around armed to the teeth with automatic rifles; all they had was this little ineffectual looking baton, so much for the dangerously high crime rate. There were no high rise blocks of flats in Redhill, it was a lovely town surrounded by the most beautiful countryside, and we spent most free days walking as much of it as we could.

It took a while for us to adjust to the different climate, and we had arrived in what was described as a lovely warm October. We were freezing, we still had our African bodies, which were accustomed to high temperatures for most of the year, and whilst everyone was wearing t-shirts and shorts, we looked like Eskimo's in our newly acquired coats, scarves, boots and anything else thermal.

After much faxing and calling our letting agents in South Africa, we were considered acceptable to rent a local property, and we moved our meagre belongings in by cab. It took a couple of trips, and we were done. This was cause for celebration and concern. We celebrated that we had our own little home, it was now critical, however for Bruce and I to start earning as the deposit had taken a huge chunk out of our funds. I'd put in as many hours as I possibly could learning as many computer skills as possible, and I couldn't waste time, so I enrolled with a local recruitment agency, and got through the basic tests. I was soon offered a temping position at a local insurance company. I was thrilled and terrified. The first day was an eye opener. I was working for an old, well established, very large firm, and its foundations were built on snob value. At my interview, my post code was scrutinized and it was only when I confirmed that this was a short term rented property, and revealed my ignorance about the relevance of where you live, was I considered acceptable. I didn't know this at the time, it was only revealed to me later. Of course I learnt about 'street cred' too, and how important this was to establish and maintain.

Isn't it funny how people respond to a different accent? Mine is different because I still have the remnants of my Rhodesian background, and although I never spoke Afrikaans, I have the undertones of a South African accent. My experience of the reaction to this, was that I was either hard of hearing or stupid, and people spoke to me in loud voices, enunciating their words ever so slowly, ending with a slight cock of their head and 'do you understand'? To top it all I would respond with 'Ja', (pronounced Yah) which is 'yes' in Afrikaans, and that really upset their whole interpretation of me, because I didn't know that it signified a yuppie, middle class person. In addition, my education included precise pronunciation and equally precise use of the English language which only added to their confusion. Fortunately I was able to see the funny side of this remarkably patronizing conclusion that a different accent can invoke, I still experience this reaction now, and I still can't drop my 't's'. It seems that once a foreigner, always a foreigner, and the identification of one, largely comes down to your accent. Regardless of how hard I tried to blend in with these new people, I knew then, as I know now, that I would never be completely accepted as one of them, which is funny really because my ancestry is almost entirely based on English heritage, and a lot of my ancestors were recognized military officers, physicians, and high ranking members of the church. One was a personal friend of Queen Victoria. My children however quickly picked up the local accent, and nobody would identify them as anything other than British born and bred. I suppose it's how you react to this that decides your success in making a new and happy life within a new country. I learnt to use it to my advantage, and gave up trying to fit in completely, and I accepted that although I had adopted England as my new home, if it wasn't completely reciprocated, so be it. I have friends who have become very successful financially, and their greatest desire is to be accepted by the upper class they socialize with, perhaps they feel if they are rid of their accents, and other traces of their pas, they will be more acceptable. Sadly, with all this however, you can never change your country of birth, and why try so hard to eliminate your history; it's essentially part of who you are. Where you've come from shouldn't be shameful, it should be indicative of how you've managed the enormous changes of leaving a familiar past for new challenges. In other words it requires courage and vision, and surely if you have that, you have a strong foundation to build on.

I didn't need an ice breaker in any situation, I was one. People gravitated towards me because I sounded different, so I must therefore have a story to tell, and this enabled me to meet people and make friends. People relaxed with me easier than they do with their own, they could let their guard down to a foreigner in the safety and security of their long established and secure roots. The standard niceties could be relaxed because the assumption was that I wasn't aware of those standards therefore, they didn't have to be rigidly maintained. I found and still find this refreshing, and it still fascinates me that most people react to openness and discussions of a more personal nature than the weather quite easily if they don't feel threatened. I don't have the typical British reserve, and people seem to respond to that with relief a lot of the time.

I am digressing again.

We soon discovered what a 'local' was, and established one of our own. The pub culture here is probably extremely damaging to a semi committed recovering alcoholic, and Bruce loved the variety of beer, the accessibility and the social aspect of it. 'It's exactly how we can meet people and make friends', he said.

I enjoyed the atmosphere and novelty of the pubs too, and Bruce was soon back into regular and routine drinking. He was still reasonable in his behaviour though, and I believe this was because of us being in a strange place with strangers, and until we established our roots he felt quite insecure. I was all he had at the moment, and we were still finding our feet in this new life.

The children settled in remarkably quickly, and they soon had a wide circle of friends. This was also the advantage of being from a strange country, and Africa in particular was fascinating. They were asked if we'd lived in a mud hut and whether they had had pet lions and rode elephants. They didn't try hard to dispel these notions, and initially made themselves out to be some sort of Tarzan and Jane who'd survived the ever so frightening jungle. Eventually however they had to admit, that it wasn't quite as primitive as that, and they had seen a TV before, and even knew how to use a telephone, not just tom tom drums. We spent many evenings laughing about this, and they used it to their advantage. It was wonderful for them; they could invent a completely different past for themselves, including Jack being a surfing champion? Their street credit was at the top of the scale. They loved this new life, and we were closer as a family then than we had ever been. There were a lot of adjustments we had to make, and these were made as a unit. We had to walk everywhere, to work and school, and only on the very odd occasion, for instance pay day, did we take a cab home after doing the shopping. Mostly the kids would meet me after work, and we would haul bags of food and drink home, and it was a good few miles. The absolute wonder and realization of their new opportunities came home to them, when they were told they going on a field trip to France. They were going to another country as part of school work, this was amazing for them and for me, it was just what I had dreamed of for them. The world was now on their doorstep. Bruce and I worked hard and volunteered for any overtime, we needed every penny we could earn, and eventually we were in a position to buy our own home. This was a first for both of us, and we were thrilled. There was a stipulation however. My parents had visited us, and they were considering leaving South Africa to come and live in the UK. My brother and his family had moved to Redhill now, and it made sense for them to live here. Emma, who had been devastated when her beloved grandparents returned after their holiday, was ecstatic. My dad apparently was reluctant, but my mum had made up her mind, so that was that. My brother and I did feel it would be best for them too however, as they were struggling financially in South Africa, and the general situation around safety and being able to afford healthcare was worsening. I think my brother felt that although he'd settled the other side of the world; he was now being invaded by the very people he'd chosen to keep a distance from. He loved his parents, but he preferred to enjoy a selective lifestyle in as much as the amount and frequency of his time spent with them. I was excited about them coming to live here; I still loved my mum, and had that continuing hope that one day I would achieve enough to gain her approval and love.

Therefore, the house we bought would have to be large enough to accommodate them too, and that way, they would help with the deposit, and in return they would have a financially secure retirement, rent free. I was so excited about buying our own home, and of course absence makes the heart grow fonder, that I really believed it could work. If only I'd known that this would be the root of my complete personal downfall.

My temping job had become permanent, and Bruce had been in permanent employment too, and we met all the criteria necessary to buy a property. The four of us spent week's house hunting, and I couldn't believe that we were looking for a home of our own, I suppose I had a dream of how it would look, and I was particularly cautious about finding the right one. I'd just about given up; when in November he persuaded me to go and look and one of the properties we'd hesitated in viewing. It was absolutely ideal, and we fell in love with it. The children loved it too. It was huge, with three bedrooms upstairs, an enormous living room, and even larger kitchen. It also had a toilet downstairs, a study, and very large extra bedroom. The garden was manageable and it overlooked a large public pond with all sorts of wild birds. We put an offer in immediately and entered the confusing and frustrating world of buying a property. It progressed slowly and with the normal frustrations anyone experiences buying a house, and we had also included most of the furniture that the previous owners were selling in our purchase. We didn't have any furniture of our own, and all I'd collected over the last eighteen months was linen, cooking utensils and the such like. Bruce's nephew had come over from South Africa, and was staying with us, and we all moved in. I absolutely loved this house, apart from it being ours, and owning a property for the very first time ever, I just loved everything about it. It needed a lot of redecorating, and that was so exciting, to personalize your own home, what could be better.

40

S oon after we'd moved in, I got a call from Bruce at work, to meet
him in town later. He sounded strange, and when I pressed him
about it, he said he'd just been made redundant. I was shocked
and frightened, how were we going to cope now, were we going to lose
everything we had just achieved. We went to the pub, this was our
home from home now, and Bruce was relaxed about the future. He
said he'd made enough contacts to enable him to start up on his own.

I was really scared and didn't share his confidence and enthusiasm,
but we talked and drank for hours, and it's amazing the assurance you
find in alcohol.

As it turned out, it went as well as Bruce had predicted, and we
had to go to London to 'buy' a company. We chose the company name,
employed recommended accountants, and were both Directors. How
cool is that, we had our own company, and I was co-director, oh and
secretary for the company. Bruce worked hard, and made a lot of
money in a short time, and in the meantime we were preparing for my
parents to come and live with us.

During all this relationships had changed. My relationship with
Bruce had begun to regress to how it had been in our first marriage. It
was as though we both slid slowly into familiar roles, he the abuser, me
the victim. When we'd decided to come to the UK, and for a while afterwards, I had been the strength, emotionally and mentally supporting the family through this transition. I had felt needed and useful for

perhaps the first time in my life. As they all settled in though, my role lessened and eventually reverted to what it had always been, mum and wife, and as their strength increased, mine diminished. I became the needy and reliant one. Bruce was the main breadwinner, and although I was working I believed that I couldn't possibly survive without his contribution. I wouldn't have been able to buy a property or anything, and would have had to rely on benefits of one kind or another. I didn't want to do that, I wanted to earn my money. My relationship with Emma had deteriorated slowly, but increasingly. She was a typical teenager, and had reached that argumentative, know it all age. She wouldn't contribute to the housework, or even keep her own room tidy, unless we had a huge argument about it, and I was the one who continued to try and maintain some sort of discipline. Bruce didn't want the unpleasantness of it all, but he became involved when Emma told him I was being too hard on her. Then he would have a total go at me. She was extremely moody, as teenage girls are, and swung from a cheerful fun person to swearing and hateful in moments, she was totally unpredictable and that wasn't unusual for her age. One minute she was in love, the next she wasn't, her best friends changed regularly as they also experienced the extreme highs and lows of hormonal change. She had now however learnt and become adept at manipulating us, which is a normal teenage trait, if they are given the opportunity to use it. She constantly played her father against me, and enjoyed the power it gave her. She would watch on, as he would scream and shout about what an evil mother I was to her, and I often caught her smile out of the corner of my eye, during these arguments. Bruce smoked in the garden, and Emma would join him, normally straight after I'd told her to do her homework, or get off the phone, or tidy her room, and I would see her look at her father as though her life was so terrible because of me, and he'd comfort her. When they came in, she would smile at me, and he would shout at me. Once he got going, it became reminiscent of my fathers vicious lectures about me literally being the spawn of the devil. I had gone full circle with Bruce, I was back now, where I'd been all those years ago, and I didn't know how to change it. Emma often lied to see me get a tongue lashing from Bruce, and one of these incidents was so deliberate and unkind, it scared me. We had a large table in the kitchen, and I had come home from work to find her washing all over it. I asked her to take it upstairs to her room and put it away, as we needed to use the table later. She ignored me. Sometimes I would have just done it myself, but lately I'd decided to dig my heels in, otherwise no lesson was learnt if I kept doing it for her anyway. I went into the lounge and settled down with my glass of wine, and every so often called to her to take her washing upstairs. This was always met with 'I'll do it later'. A couple of hours later, Bruce came in, and of course the first thing he saw was the pile of washing on the table. He asked me what it was doing there, and I told him I'd asked Emma to take it to her room, as it was hers. He called her down, and asked why she hadn't cleared her washing away. A look of shock crossed her face, and she said 'I did Dad; I don't know why it's back on the table'. I couldn't believe what I was hearing, and then she looked at me and shouted, 'it was you, I took my washing up, and you've brought it down again, to get me into trouble'. Dear God, I must have imagined she said that. 'What are you talking about?', I said, I've been here watching TV. 'You're a liar' she screamed, 'you're always doing things like this to get me into trouble with Daddy, you are pathetic', and with that she pretend sobbed as she ran up to her room. In that moment, I thought I had lost my mind, I couldn't believe what I'd just heard, and I started to tell Bruce, that she had just blatantly lied, in a horribly nasty way. He didn't give me the chance, and he called me every name he could think of, including his latest personal favourite, that I made my daughter so unhappy, that if anything ever happened to her, it would be my fault. Lately, because she'd been dramatic about everything in her life, Emma would often say things like, 'if Nigel breaks up with me, I'll commit suicide, I couldn't live without him'. This extended to her hair not looking nice, a skirt too long, or not having the latest designer trainers. Everything warranted 'suicide'. Well clearly Bruce had taken these dramatics seriously indeed, and was now telling me, I would be responsible. My child hated me, my heart broke.

I looked forward to when my parents would be living with us, they would see what was going on, and I would have a support network, and then maybe, we could sort things out. I knew I was drinking more than was good for me, but I must have been totally deluded to imagine that happening. There were a couple of other incidents that worried me; one in particular frightened me enormously. The first involved my Jack Russell puppy. I have always loved dogs, and at last I had a puppy, I adored him. During one of Emma's and my increasingly frequent arguments, she was standing at the top of the stairs yelling and I was at the bottom yelling back. It was about her going out, and I had said no. The puppy was at the top of the stairs one moment, and tumbling down the stairs the next. Jack had been standing with Emma, and screamed at her 'why did you kick Podgy down the stairs', he was distraught. She denied it at the top of her voice, but the lie was obvious in her behaviour, it was a 'he who protested too loudly' scenario. The second incident however was much worse, and could have been potentially ruined lives. We were in the process of redecorating the house, and I had invited my brother and his family over. They had two little boys now, and Emma hated both of them with a disturbing passion. The reason for this was that they were her granny's grandchildren too, and granny wasn't allowed to love them, because that took her love away from Emma. Emma and Jack were in her bedroom, painting, and we were in the garden preparing a barbeque. Joe and Alex were sitting on the edge of the porch directly under Emma's window, and in those horrifying seconds, I saw Emma at the window, just before an unused, heavy tray of paint fell out of the window. It was flat, it hadn't been tipped out, it had been dropped out, and if it landed on the children, it could break their necks. I screamed and ran towards the two little boys, knowing I would never reach them in time. Everyone had turned, and saw that tray falling through the air, there was nothing we could do. The tray of paint landed inches away from them, and it burst open with the force, spraying them with paint. They got a fright, and started to cry, and I turned and ran towards Emma's room. By the time I got there Jack was outside the room, and Emma had locked the door. Bruce was behind me, and I screamed at her to open the door. What had she done, what in God's name had my child tried to do. I was angrier than I had ever been, and Bruce was shouting at her to open the door.

She wouldn't and Bruce broke it down. For the first time ever, I saw him angry with her, and in the face of this she was hysterical. She hadn't had enough time to concoct a reasonable story, and the first one thing she'd knocked it out of the window accidentally. When I challenged this, by the way it had fallen out of the window, it didn't spin or twist, it just came out flat, she said was that the wind had blown it out. The tray was still sealed and very heavy, and it was absolutely impossible for the wind to blow into the room, and then blow a piece of paper out, let alone this kind of weight. I was livid, as we all knew she had deliberately dropped it out, and she could have killed, or very seriously injured my brother's children, because she was literally insanely jealous of her granny's affection for them. I slapped her across her face for the first time and the last time ever, and I walked out of the room.

My brother and his wife were clearly much shaken, and they just said they wanted to leave, go home and get their boys cleaned up and calmed down. Jane, my sister in law was white as a sheet. What could I say to them, we'd all seen the tray fall, and it was as clear to them as it was to me, that it had been a deliberate act?

This scared me to my core regarding Emma's mental state. I knew she idolized her granny, but this was serious, this was beyond the norm. Bruce stayed talking to her for some time, and when he came down, I said we had to do something about what had happened, and suggested arranging therapy for Emma, so that she could perhaps learn to control this terrible jealousy. Bruce said he believed Emma, that it was just an accident, and this was so typical of the way I treated her. I was making it much worse than it was, just to discredit her in any way I could, and then he contradicted himself by saying that if she had actually dropped it out of the window, it was probably because of me anyway, and the way I treated her. If anyone needed therapy in this house it was me, he concluded, and it was time I had a good long hard look at myself and my behaviour. I really did think I was starting to go mad, I was being held accountable for her action. I despaired, didn't he understand that the more he allowed her to get away with unrepentant and rebellious, the less she would learn that out in the big wide world one day, it wouldn't be quite so reasonable nor forgiving. He was giving her free reign to believe that she could get away with anything and everything, and this made me afraid for her future. Emma came down a while later, and behaved as though nothing had happened, I suggested she phone her uncle and aunt and apologise, and she said 'what for, the boys weren't hurt were they'. I called them to find out how they were, and all Jane said to me was that they would never leave Emma alone with their boys again, they never have. I felt that my saving grace would be my dad; he was a doctor after all and had studied enough psychology to understand where I was coming from. They would be here soon.

41

Bruce berated me on a daily basis regarding my relationship with Emma, which I considered reasonably normal when I compared notes with other mums with teenage daughters. They experienced friction, rivalry, and constant bickering and nagging too. I knew that mine was different in respect of Bruce not working with me regarding the children, and clearly against everything I suggested Emma should be doing, but I began to seriously doubt myself, and started believing that perhaps I was the mother from hell that he insisted I was.

My parents were due to arrive within days, and I realized they would need a lot of emotional support, as once again they had moved country. I knew their main motivation was living close to Emma, as well as the rest of their family, but that didn't detract from the fact that they were older now, and it was quite traumatic for them at this time in their life. I had decorated their room, with my sister in laws help, although she wouldn't bring the boys, and bought new beds and other bits of furniture, in the effort they would be comfortable and feel at home.

The day before I was really excited, and I also really believed that I would find allies in them, and they could help me understand Bruce's bizarre behaviour with regards to my relationship with Emma. I knew he was drinking heavily, and the abuse had taken another turn, but the impact that this was having on Emma was my primary concern. However, to have considered their support might rest with me was a flight of the imagination.

The night before they arrived, Emma had asked to go out to a party with her current boyfriend. It was a friend from school and it was her sixteenth birthday. I was reluctant because we had to be at the airport at seven the following morning, and as she had been longing for this day to come, I thought she might be tired after a late night out. The normal screaming and shouting ensued, that I hated her, and I never wanted her to have any fun, and I always spoilt things for her, and on and on, and then true to form her father stepped in, and said of course she could go.

Her current boyfriend Greg and other friends of theirs came to fetch Emma. They were walking to the hall where the party was being held, and Daniels dad was going to give Emma a lift home. I did the usual embarrassing thing warning about the dangers of 'ecstasy' which was the much talked about drug, alcohol, and don't be late, but have fun anyway. Emma gave me a look that should have sent me to an early grave, and her father matched it with one of his own. I was anxious about her going out that evening, there had been a tragic case of a young girl in the news recently, who had 'just tried one ecstasy pill', and had gone into a coma. I'd always talked openly and honestly to both children about the dangers of drugs, and we often allowed them to have a glass of wine with a roast dinner or on a special occasion with us. My attitude was that if it wasn't forbidden fruit, so to speak, it would decrease the allure, I couldn't however adopt this attitude with drugs, as I had always been terrified of them and had never even tried cannabis.

They had been gone for only about an hour, when the phone rang. When I answered it, and heard the background music of a party and a strange voice on the other end, asking if they were speaking to Emma's mum, my blood ran cold. 'It is', I said. 'This is Sophie, a friend of Emma's', the young voice said. 'Is something wrong with Emma', I was shouting now. 'You'd better come straight away, she's collapsed on the dance floor and we can't wake her up'. Dear God, what had happened to my child, had she taken drugs, what had happened in such a short time? 'What happened Sophie?' I was screaming now. 'We don't know, she was dancing and then she just collapsed'. Sophie replied. 'Call an ambulance, Sophie, can you do that, and give the address and directions quickly', I was crying now with fear, 'I'll be there as fast as

I can, just call the ambulance'. Bruce had heard my hysteria, and I just said to him that I would explain the call in the car, but we had to go now. Jack was crying with concern, and I told him he had to stay at home, I would let him know what was happening as soon as I could, and we ran for the car. I drove like a complete maniac to the hall, and was literally out of the car whilst it was still moving. I ran into the hall, and my daughter was slumped in a chair, vomit all over the front of her top, and her eyes were closed. I shook her and called to her to wake up, open your eyes, please open your eyes. She reeked of alcohol, and she didn't seem to be breathing, and it was then we heard the sirens of the ambulance. The paramedics rushed in, and I was hysterical and incoherent, because I didn't know what had happened and I shouted for Greg, surely he would know what had happened. I was also screaming at the paramedic to wake her up, was she alive, was she breathing, until he eventually told me to calm down. I couldn't, where was Greg and Mathew the other friend who had come to fetch her. Nigel eventually appeared and I thought thank God, he might be able to tell us something. Nigel was totally drunk, and didn't even know his own name. What had happened, they'd only been gone for about an hour. I started asking if anyone had seen Emma drinking, and then someone said she and the others had arrived at the party drunk. The ambulance was rushing her to hospital, and I had to go with her. If she woke up in the ambulance she would be frightened. I swallowed my panic about being in an ambulance and going to a hospital in a way that was my absolute worst nightmare. My child needed me, and that was all there was to it. Bruce followed in the car. In A&E, they were concerned about her condition, and there were medical staff all around her. They knew she'd had an enormous amount of alcohol, but she'd taken something else, and they needed to find out in a hurry in order to treat her appropriately. I had to go back to the party, and find out, my child's life could be at stake. I decided to take the calm approach this time, I had probably terrified the kids with my panic, and although I drove like a demon, I walked in calmly, and asked if anyone could please find Greg, or someone who could tell me what Emma had taken. It didn't matter who told me or what it was or whom she got it from, the hospital needed to know in order to help her, and there would be absolutely no repercussions, I would just be forever grateful for their help. It worked and one of the teenagers told me Emma

309

and her group had arrived very drunk, and she had complained of a headache. Someone had given her a card of over the counter painkillers, and someone else had seen her take about ten, laughing drunkenly, that she would make sure her headache went. I wanted to scream at them, 'if you saw her taking them one after the other, why didn't you stop her', instead I said 'thanks for your help', and I got back in my car, and drove like a mad thing back to the hospital. They now knew not to pump her stomach, and she basically just had to sleep it all off. She was taken to a ward, and cleaned, and Bruce and I sat with her. He looked at me and said I was lucky she hadn't died, otherwise I would have had to live with it on my conscience, as he believed she'd tried to commit suicide because she had a mother like me.

There was nothing more to do for Emma, she was deeply asleep, so I went home, and I sat with Jack to calm him and console him, he was distraught that his sister was in hospital, and wanted her to come home. Bruce had gone to bed, and I sat up for the few hours that remained before we had to go to the airport to fetch my parents. I didn't feel excited anymore, I felt numb, I wanted to see my daughter and I wanted my child home, I was tired, and I'd had the biggest fright of my life. I made excuses for what Bruce had said, he was in shock and distraught after all. I wanted to see my mum, have a hug, and have her tell me it would all be alright. They arrived, and after the artificial smiles of greeting, I had to explain why Emma wasn't there. I'd seen the disappointment when they hadn't seen her with us. I told them what had happened as briefly and simply as possible, and whilst I was telling them, my mum looked at me with stern disapproval. 'How had I allowed this to happen to her beloved granddaughter, I clearly hadn't been looking after properly, well that would all change now that they were here?'

We dropped them at home, and had to get to the hospital to meet with a psychologist before Emma could be released. Because she had technically taken an overdose, she, and we had to undergo an assessment before they were confident to release her. When I walked into the ward, she was sitting up in bed, and she smiled at me and said 'Hiya, like your top, you alright, why are you looking at me like that, I didn't do anything wrong'. My mouth dropped open, and she went on 'I just had a drink and took a couple of pills, why do you always have to exaggerate everything; you just want me to get into trouble, don't you'. I went to her, and told her I was thrilled to see her looking so much better, and how desperately worried I'd been last night. 'How are granny and granddad?' she said, 'I hope they aren't too worried about me, I'll say sorry to them when I get home, that I wasn't at the airport.' I felt as though I'd been thumped in the stomach, her father walked in, and her face crumpled, and she held her arms out to him. He hugged her and she said 'I'm sorry Dad for worrying you, I'm so sorry'. I walked out of the ward.

The psychological assessment showed that there had been no deliberate intent to self -harm, she'd been very drunk, and hadn't realized how many pills she was taking. Apparently they had organized for an older sibling to buy the booze, and they'd hidden it in the bushes at the top of our road, and they had all drunk as much as they could in as little time as possible. It was some years later that I discovered that her father had known all about this plan, and had thought it was typical teenage fun.

We arrived home, and Emma was treated like a heroine coming home from a victorious battle. Understandably everyone, including me was happy that she was unscathed by her experience, and she was home, but there was no remorse, she didn't believe she had done anything wrong, and this was endorsed by her grandparents. They hadn't been with us for twenty four hours and I already felt like an outsider. What was it about me that I seemed to see things so differently to the others? I knew it was a group of teenagers experimenting, and it had all gone horribly wrong, but shouldn't a lesson be learnt from this. Surely some boundaries should be put in place; something to indicate that what happened was unacceptable and shouldn't happen again. It was also about example setting, and if Emma was treated like this, as though nothing had happened, and it was ok to do what they'd done, what about Jack. What would he learn from this, that he could one day do the same and know he wouldn't be reprimanded? I tried to communicate this to Bruce, and got the same old lecture about my shocking treatment of Emma, and that I got off on punishing her. He also said I was probably disappointed she'd survived, if she hadn't that would have made me happy. Jesus, there was that stabbing pain again, the one that sucked the breath from my lungs, the one that seared my heart and mind. Why did he constantly tell me I didn't love my child, I did want to mete punishment, I wanted to ground her, I wanted her to know that what they did was wrong, I was terrified it could happen again if it was considered acceptable behaviour, I wanted to protect her. I couldn't, and as my parents were of the same opinion as Bruce, I realized I had no support network now in any way, manner or form. I was frustrated and angry, it felt as though once again, my daughter had been taken away from me, and although she was there physically, the emotional chasm between us appeared to be impossible to cross. It takes two to come together, and it was clear in how she looked at me, that she had no desire whatsoever to leave the stronghold she was in to even consider crossing that void. What hurt even more, was when she walked into the house with her grandparents and father, and she looked over her shoulder at me following behind, her eyes locked with mine, and in that look I knew she wanted more than anything to shut the front door in my face, leaving me outside. My daughter hated me, I was a thorn in her side, that look said it all. 'I wish you weren't here, I wish I could just be with my dad, granny and granddad, I wish you'd get out of our lives'.

42

I felt isolated, and if I was to put a time to it, I think it was about then, that I started to shut down to life, and it was deliberate and intentional. I believe it was that day, that I wondered how I would survive this emotional desolation. The reason to try, was my son, I think I knew my daughter was lost to me, but he wasn't and I would not let him go. I knew with an absolute certainty that he loved me, but how could I depend on him to sustain me, I couldn't rely on my child to realize my desperate need for love and acceptance, what an awful burden to give someone so young, and someone you love. It wasn't a conscious decision, it just seemed to happen, but I didn't fight it hard enough, and then not at all, I welcomed the oblivion it provided, I was comforted that it dulled the pain. When I knew I was losing control, and it was controlling me, I let it happen, I didn't want to fight it, I didn't want reality, I wanted to be in this lonely, dark, angry, sad, unreal world I created. In it, I didn't feel, I didn't care, it didn't hurt anymore, you see, I drank, every day, most of the day, and every night, as much as I needed to make me sleep, or pass out, I spent the next year locked in my self inflicted alcoholic world.

This didn't happen overnight; it crept up on me slowly. I'd been drinking socially ever since we came to the UK, and by that I mean, joining Bruce at the pub some evenings after work for a few drinks, and those evenings that we went straight home, we both had our drinks anyway. My drink of choice at the time was white wine, Bruce's was beer, and red wine. Initially, it would be one or two glasses, and then as I began to revert into my victim mode, it extended to a bottle of wine a night. I believed that was reasonable, and so did most people. It helped me relax after a busy day at work, and it softened the sharp edges of the tense and unpleasant atmosphere at home. Friends from work regularly went to the pub at lunchtime, and we all had a glass or two of wine, and I became accustomed to this.

Perhaps, if I'd continued with my life as it was then, things might have been different, then again, I don't think anything would have changed, I believe I had already started on the path to self destruction, and I might have travelled it less quickly, but ultimately I would have reached the same destination.

My parents settled in quickly and easily, and my life as I'd known it prior to their arrival changed irrevocably. It was sudden and I reacted by increasing my alcohol intake accordingly. It was fight or flight, and I didn't have the emotional resources to fight, so I took flight in the bottle. Emma now spent all her time with my parents in their room. She regarded them as exclusively hers, and even Jack was made to feel like an intruder when he went to sit with them. They weren't confined to their room, but I think they chose to spend most of their time there as opposed to joining us in the front room, especially after I'd been stupid enough to try to talk to my dad about my concerns regarding Emma, in particular, the incident with the 'falling' paint tray. He was a doctor after all, and I hoped he could advise me on how best to deal with her obsessive jealousy and rage. You would think I'd leave things well alone, and let them get on with it regarding her upbringing. I just couldn't let go, and I was scared for her.

I was on leave for a couple of days, and the children had gone to school. My parents and I were in the kitchen, and I said there was something I wanted to talk to them about and hopefully my dad could give me a professional opinion. I told them what happened that day, and the time Podgy was kicked downstairs. I was hoping to keep it professional, and get advice and direction from someone in the know, it didn't happen. Emotions ran high, and I was told there was absolutely nothing wrong with Emma, it was an accident, and I should look to myself, perhaps if I sorted myself out, and stopped being so negative about her and stopped making mountains out of molehills, things might change. I felt like a little girl again, it was all so familiar, my dad got on his soap box, and he laid into me verbally. Amongst everything he had to say which covered my early childhood onwards, he also told me he hadn't wanted to come and live in the UK, but my mother had persuaded him to so they could help me sort out my life. Where the hell did that one come from, I was slow on the uptake, but understood, as he ranted, that this was as old as I was. Nothing had changed over the years, clearly I was still the scapegoat, and responsible for anything and everything he found unpleasant or challenging in his life. I was gutted, and went and opened a bottle of wine, poured a glass, downed it in front of them, poured another, felt the pain dissolve, felt the 'fuck you' attitude take over with the third, and although his mouth continued to move, and his voice grew louder, I didn't hear what he said, I shut down, and eventually with a look of utter contempt my mother took his arm and led him from the kitchen. That was the last time I tried to talk to them about anything to do with Emma, or anything much at all really, apart from the weather and other superficial subjects.

My relationship with Bruce changed too. Some nights we would meet at the pub after work, and these evenings felt conspiratorial, especially when my mum phoned to tell us to come home for dinner. This angered Bruce, and I took pleasure in this anger, it felt like I had an ally against the enemy. He would rant about the fact that no-one would tell him when to come home, and I was pleased this wasn't directed at me. I would play his annoyance, feed it, make it grow, try to get him on my side, and it would feel it was working. He would say my mum was too controlling, 'what have I always tried to tell you', I would respond eagerly. He soon started to consider that they should think about getting a place of their own, but he lacked the courage to talk to them openly and honestly about it, so it was just talk really. That was enough for me though; I believed it indicated he wanted us to be a family again, without external interference. I would hug myself mentally with delight, I was winning wasn't I, soon my parents would move out, and we could get back to normal. Sadly, there was no 'normal' to get back to, nothing was normal in our family anymore, but that didn't bear thinking about, so when these thoughts crept in, another drink quickly swept them away. During these evenings, I would pander to Bruce's every whim, agree with everything he said and did, I thought it would bring us closer, I felt as though he loved me, and when he was insistent and said 'drink up, you're falling behind', I believed he was enjoying being with me. I didn't see that his tolerance for alcohol was much higher than mine, he drank faster and I worked hard at keeping up, and by the time I was too drunk to realize, I didn't know that I always got home much more under the weather than he was, and that he made certain he pointed this out, I would laugh when he said to the family, 'look at her, can't take her anywhere once, its always got to be twice, the second time to apologise for the first'. We were drinking buddies weren't we? He was my husband, my mate, and the alcohol led me to believe he was my friend. I'd forgotten how angry he'd been at my mum, and when he kissed her hello, gave her a hug, and said he'd had to bring me home because I'd had too much, I would giggle and think he was joking, he'd had more, he was teasing me, it meant we were growing closer, it meant it was getting better, it meant he liked being with me. When he walked into the kitchen and poured me another glass of wine, it was thoughtful and generous, and it meant he wanted our evening together to continue, oh this was fun, this was how it should be, this was, and then of course there was nothing much more, I'd passed out on the couch. I didn't see or hear what went on after I'd 'dropped off', that was a blessing. Then there were the evenings that we didn't meet at the pub.

As soon as Bruce and I got home from work we got stuck into our respective drinks, again with much refilling of my glass by Bruce. These were perhaps better evenings to begin with, as I chatted to the children, well that's not quite true really, I chatted with Jack whilst cooking dinner, and soon after, I would quickly fall asleep on the couch, desperately trying to stay awake and pretend I was alert on the one hand, whilst willing sleep to take over on the other. Bruce was also spending more and more time on the computer, and I'd discovered it wasn't work, but porn web sites that became more sordid as time went on. I considered myself to be broadminded, I'd watched 'blue' movies, and seen porn before, but this was different, there was nothing artistic about it, and he wasn't looking at woman's bodies as a thing of beauty. The sites he chose, displayed women and men with strange fetishes, multiple piercing, and then he went onto sites where men and women shared really perverted fantasies and sex. To begin with, he would call me to go and see something on the computer and then show me some of these sites. When I expressed disinterest and displeasure, he told me I was frigid, undesirable, and ugly and he had to find his satisfaction elsewhere like the websites he spent hours looking at. It got to the stage where he only came to bed in the early hours of the morning, if at all, and what he did whilst closeted in the study; I really didn't want to know about. I resolved my feelings of inadequacy as a wife, whose husband preferred the internet to her, with a few more glasses of wine. Sadly it didn't anger me, I felt insulted and decided that I had not only failed as a daughter, I was failing as a mother, now as a wife yet again, basically I was a total failure. I drank more, to quiet these familiar feelings of inadequacy, and to reduce the fears that as my life went on, I continued to disappoint anyone and everyone who was important to me. I just could not achieve my ultimate goal, and that simply was to feel loved and valued, I was so tired of just being tolerated.

This may sound like I am justifying my drinking, that's not my intention, I am simply explaining where I was at, at that time in my life. Choosing to drink reality away, ultimately destroyed any chances at all that I ever had to feel loved, it wasn't possible, even if someone had felt that way about me, I was so consumed with self loathing, nothing would have been able to find it's way in. The first few drinks gave me Dutch courage, the next few, blunted and blurred the insults and, and after a few more, I became verbally assertive to aggressive. All the things I had wanted to say over the years dribbled out in not so veiled criticism, condemnation and deprecation. This was directed mainly at Bruce, but at times included my daughter and parents, and this only served to send me spiralling downwards, because there is always a morning after the night before. Most of these mornings I would wake up morbidly remorseful, and the crushing guilt virtually suffocated me. It took a while for the fog to clear and for me to remember what I'd said and to whom. I didn't have too much to worry about regarding my actions, because I was never drunk in public, and the worst of it would be that I would simply pass out quietly on the sofa. I did wobble about and slur my words as I approached that stage, but the booze loosened my tongue, and it was vicious, malicious and unforgiving. I felt a bit like a volcano as each evening progressed, the early part, I was like the magma rising to the surface, and then inevitably the eruption. The force of this depended on the intensity of the attack I was under, and who the enemy was. At this stage only the lava erupted, and I spewed it out hoping it hurt, wanting it to

317

burn and scar whoever was in its destructive path. Bruce was ruthless in taunting me, and belittling me, watching whilst I responded by having another drink. I would think, I can control this, I will not take the bait, I will not react, then again I knew that the more I drank the less control I had, and he would smile knowingly, sensing the imminent eruption, and when it happened, he would laugh, which incensed me further, until I was bordering on hysteria, spewing insults and hatred, tears streaming, alcohol and fury taking control, what a mess I looked, what a state I was in. Knowing another 'show' was on my parents would come in and look at me with absolute disgust and contempt, Emma laughed in repugnance, and Jack watched on, helpless and hopeless, pity and a deep sadness and fear etched on his face. Night after night this went on, it became routine, and then there were always the mornings after the night before. Bruce enjoyed this part of the day, and he was quick to tell me how dreadful my behaviour had been the night before. He would describe in detail things I had said, and sometimes I couldn't remember saying some of what he told me I had. I panicked and believed I was having blackouts. I could remember, somewhat vaguely all that happened before I passed out, but now it seemed that I was blacking out more and more. This confused and frightened me, as what Bruce told me I'd said, I couldn't recall at all. I grovelled and apologised, and in an attempt to make up for the awful things I had said, I made Bruce's sandwiches, I made sure the children had everything they needed before school, I hugged Jack, and told him 'it was alright, things would get better, this was just a very bad time for me', and 'I would try not to have too much wine tonight', knowing it would all happen again. My parents would ignore me, and I always left for work early, to get out, to take my aching overwhelming guilt, sadness and weakness away, trying to separate my worlds. Nobody at work knew what a total complete and utter useless and worthless human being I was, and I had eight hours in the company of people who treated me normally. 'If only they knew', I would think, 'they wouldn't want anything to do with me', this terrified me, it was also so wearing though, because I would sit at my desk, laugh and joke with my colleagues, respond to their standard 'have a nice evening', with a fantasy, and try to remember what I'd told them about the evening before. Every evening and weekend had to have a slightly different story to be authentic, and as far as they knew, I lived a normal life, I might drink a little too much, my tell tale breath, but then again everyone at work enjoyed their drinks and socialized passionately. Everything about my day was artificial, an act for their benefit and mine, but it was very tiring, very wearing, and there was always the constant fear of the night ahead, and the never-ending internal battle and the personal commitments and promises that I made to myself. I would retain control, I would have a drink, but I would not allow myself to be antagonized, and for an instant I would believe I could do it, and then a cruel voice would whisper to my mind 'who are you fooling, you know you won't, you know you can't', and I knew that voice was right. And then there were my lunch time sessions at the local, which I clock watched for.

As the morning wore on, and the effects of the alcohol wore off, my feelings of paranoia nearly overwhelmed me, but knew it wasn't too long until the next glass of wine, and I clung to this as though my life depended on it. Woes betide anyone who delayed me, when the clock struck the hour I was out and rushing to the pub, and eventually I would quietly put my phone on voice mail, and go to the ladies about five minutes before to prevent any sort of delay. I told anyone who was going that day that I'd get in the queue for them, hence my rush. I liked to think they believed this. Deep down however, I knew they knew there was a problem, especially when I had that first glass of wine in front of me, and I couldn't pick it up with one hand. I was shaking too much you see, I was clever enough to disguise this with 'the glass is too full, I'll just sip it a little first', whilst the glass remained steady on the table. Or I would lift it with both hands, in an invented toast. I always gulped the first one down, and commented on how thirsty I was, and of course I always bought two large white wines, 'to save wasting time in a queue, in the limited time we had'. I inevitably managed to squeeze a third in during this time however, and would sometimes drink it at the bar, so the others at the table didn't see me. I would then return to the table empty handed saying I hadn't had time, and decided to leave it. The attitude towards drinking was very relaxed within the office, as most of the employees were young sales people who frequently came in with debilitating hangovers, and more often than not, they too rushed to the pub, to top up their levels, or reduce the effects of their hangovers, so I comforted myself with this, and once those drinks hit home, the paranoia disappeared, the anxiety converted to tranquillity, and the feeling of all, I didn't really give a shit. Although I had to put more effort in, I managed my job as before, I never gave anyone reason to pull me up over my work. Through the haze of alcohol I was very conscious of maintaining my standards, not only to disguise how much I was drinking, but also because somewhere tucked away in my fog, I desperately wanted to have a clear work record.

43

Out of the blue, Bruce came to my rescue, or so I believed. One weekend, he suggested I give up work. He was making very good money with his business, and as he said, his earnings alone would provide more than adequately for us. He said he felt it was time I had a break, I'd worked for some years now, ever since our divorce, and as we fine financially, I could spend time redecorating the house, and perhaps more time with my parents would build bridges. I asked him why he was suddenly suggesting this, as we hadn't discussed it previously and I had never inferred I wanted to give up work. He told me he'd been thinking about it for some time, and waited until he was certain we could easily afford it, and now he knew we could, he'd decided to mention it. I was delighted initially, who wouldn't be really, being given the opportunity to live the life of 'ladies what lunch'. Mind you I didn't really have anyone to lunch with come to think of it. I had relatively few friends, they took up time and energy, none of which I had left to give. Anyway, I decided it would be best after all, as this constant secrecy regarding my drinking was taking its toll, and it would also mean that I could leave whilst still respected by my colleagues. I knew that at some point it would all fall apart, it couldn't continue the way it was for much longer, and it was becoming hugely mentally and physically demanding keeping up this façade of normality. There was a tiny little voice however that reminded me I would lose whatever shreds of independence I had, because it would mean

I would then depend entirely on Bruce for everything. The stronger voice, the gullible self serving, victim said 'it will be wonderful, no more sneaking about, living on your wits and nerves, afraid people will know exactly how far you've fallen, you will be able to keep your dirty little secret just that, a secret'. I willingly conceded.

I handed in my notice the next day, and it was met with the standard regrets, 'we will be sorry to see you go', and yet was that also a sense of relief I glimpsed. It couldn't be I reasoned, nobody knew, did they. My last month at work went quickly and before I knew it, it was my last day, and there were all the presents and normal farewells, the standard evening at the pub, and I felt elated and relaxed, looking forward to the days ahead where I'd nothing more to worry about than the housework, not even about when I could have my next drink, it would be on tap, no worries.

Over the next months, any restrictions I had imposed on my drinking slowly fell away. I tried to stick to having my first drink at noon, but that soon became an hour earlier until I was having it as soon as I woke up, in a coffee mug of course. I tried to hide it from my parents and resented their constant presence, and my lack of freedom. I knew I could openly sit and drink all day, but there was still some dignity left, and I would sneak a quick glass in when they weren't watching. I was now drinking whisky, and my change in drink came about in a very strange way. In one of the rare reasonable conversations my parents had with me, they, and I, acknowledged how much I was drinking, and my dad suggested I shift from wine to a more pure alcohol, as if I was going to continue to drink, it would be better for me. I took his advice, and fast tracked it to hell. Now that I no longer worked, Bruce had me right where he had wanted me. I had stopped driving completely, as I knew I was a risk on the roads, so I walked everywhere, it also meant that the children and I had to rely on him for lifts, and I lost probably my final use to anyone in the family. He knew I was now completely powerless financially, emotionally and mentally to leave him and this fuelled his abuse. He was vindictive and malicious, and enjoyed watching my pain and distress. He reminded me of a child who deliberately tortures animals slowly and intently, getting real pleasure as they pull legs or wings from insects one by one, observing their suffering, thrilling over their desperate struggle for survival, the growing panic and desperation, the eventual knowledge that it is over, their time is done, and then the blessed relief from the pain as they are deliberately crushed to death or just die anyway. That was the difference, I didn't have that release. I thought about it of course, many times, but I couldn't do it, not even attempt it. I had got as far as holding the pills in one hand, and the whisky in the other, and I knew I would go to sleep forever. In the deepest recesses of my soul a message always came through. It was that 'life could be more than this, it wasn't time for me to leave it now, there was a purpose, there were choices, and "they" were with me.' So much of life being; that changes occur when 'everything is at the right time and in the right place'. I felt that my 'right time and place' never seemed to come, and I'd like to say, that I was motivated, comforted even uplifted by this, but I had to listen to that message many times before I actually heard it.

Both children had lost all respect for me, and used my drunkenness to their advantage. They would often tell me I hadn't given them their pocket money, and even if I did remember I had, it was a vague unsubstantiated memory, so I gave them more. They would be going out on a Friday night and say 'see you Sunday'. 'Where are you going?' I'd ask. To stay the weekend with one or other of their friends they would tell me. 'You didn't ask me?' I'd say. Of course we did, and then with derision, you just don't remember anything anymore mum do you, and they'd go. I didn't argue, how could I, what right did I have, I'd taken this action, I was responsible for the reactions.

Bruce felt more powerful by the day now, and one night he was snoring louder than ever. He snored every night because of his excessive drinking. I shook him gently a number of times, and it continued, so I shook him awake. He went berserk, to the point where I was frightened enough to run from the bedroom, he chased me down the stairs and into the lounge. 'What's wrong with you', I said, 'you were snoring'. 'Don't you ever fucking wake me up again, I work unlike someone, meaning me, and I need my sleep'. 'You're crazy', I replied, and went to walk away. He hit me hard across my face, and I fell onto the coffee table. I'd screamed in fear and pain when he hit me, and my parents rushed in from their bedroom. 'What on earth is going on? My mum shrieked. I was still sprawled on the coffee table holding my face, and I said 'Bruce just hit me because I woke him up, he was snoring'. My parents looked at us, and my mum said 'you both better get back to bed, we all need our rest', and they went back to their bedroom. Bruce looked at me smugly, and then turned to go upstairs; I stayed and slept on the couch. That was that then, it was clearly acceptable for him to hit me as far as my parents were concerned, they didn't even voice disapproval, this from the man that always told my brother 'a man should never hit a woman, not under any circumstances', these 'circumstances' or being woken for snoring was obviously the exception.

Bruce used his most powerful and terrifying abuse tool ever one day. We were sitting in the lounge, and he suddenly said that he was considering having me sectioned. 'What does that mean', I asked. 'Getting you locked away in a mental institute' he said. Oh dear God, my stomach knotted so hard so suddenly I thought I was going to throw up. 'Why?' I whimpered, tears starting. 'Because you are an alcoholic and a nutter, and you make me sick', he said, and went on, 'then I will have everything, the children, the house, and I won't allow them to let you out, you can rot in there for the rest of your life' he said. 'Where has this come from?' I asked, crying. 'I've been thinking of it for a long time, and I'm just waiting for the right opportunity', he replied. 'I'm also thinking of calling Social Services in, so they can see you're an unfit mother, and that will add to my case' he continued. I couldn't breathe, the anxiety was terrible, I felt like I was choking with fear. I was terrified of hospitals, and a mental home was my worst nightmare, because you couldn't get out, I would be trapped in there, I would be drugged, I would never see my children again, I would die in there'. In my state, my phobias were exaggerated and there was no sense of reason, I believed what he said, and I firmly believed he would do it. I wept and begged and pleaded with him not to call Social Services in, not to have me sectioned, I would do anything and everything he asked, don't take me away from my children. I would try and get better, I would try and be the wife he wanted, I would do anything, and for a long while I did. I gave in to any and all sexual perversions he wanted to try out, I was his whore, I cooked whatever he asked for no matter how ridiculous or complicated it was, I ironed his shirts over and over until he was happy with them. I poured his drinks, I ran his bath, I agreed with everything he said, regardless of what he called me. I massaged his body and his ego day and night, until eventually he must have got bored with it all, tired of his slave, time to take action.

One night I was lying on the couch, as normal, and passed out, as normal, and woke what seemed seconds later to slaps on my face, and my mother screaming at me hysterically to wake up. What's happened I slurred, what's wrong? 'You've had a fit', my mum screamed. 'What, I just passed out', I said, there was no pretence anymore, say it how it is. The children, my dad and Bruce were all looking at me as if I'd died and come back, why I hadn't stayed for Gods sake, it would have made it all so much easier. Well I hadn't done anything like that; I'd just gone to sleep. My parents and Bruce were whispering and I heard the word Ambulance. That was enough to send me hysterical. 'I don't need an ambulance, I'm fine', I shouted, 'I'm going up to bed now'. I was beside myself with fear, this is just what he wanted, to get me into any sort of institution, and then he would make sure I stayed there. I screamed at them not to call an ambulance, and said whoever did; I would never speak to them again. 'Lie here a while, so that we can watch you', Bruce said and then huddled in a threesome with my parents talking in hushed tones. I turned to talk to the children. They'd had a fright, and Jack was crying. I told him I was fine, of course I hadn't had a fit, everything was fine. Nobody apart from Bruce had been in the lounge when I supposedly fitted, so they didn't know what to believe. Jack told me I looked ok, and I said I was.

Bruce and my parents came and sat around me, and said I should just give it a little while before I went to bed, so they would be sure I was alright, and I agreed. I'm not sure how long it was before there was a loud knock on the front door, it couldn't have been more than about ten minutes, and when I heard it, I knew. Two paramedics walked in with a stretcher, and I knew that Bruce had his opportunity to get me into a hospital. Clearly if I went to hospital they would know about my drinking, and they would put me away to sort me out. This was his chance, and he'd obviously been planning it. I gave him the opportunity tonight by being alone with him. I knew with remarkable clarity that I would not go with the paramedics. They asked exactly what had happened, and I made an enormous effort not to behave hysterically. Bruce started to tell them, he'd been sitting watching tv with me when I suddenly threw a fit, and described something from a horror movie. I waited for him to finish, and then told the paramedics that I'd had too much to drink tonight and had simply passed out. I felt fine now, embarrassed and very sorry that we had wasted their time, but I hadn't known they'd been called. They did the routine checks, blood pressure, pulse, and eyes, and all the while I sat calmly explaining that I was anxious as I suffered from 'white coat syndrome', and them even being there would send my blood pressure up and my pulse soaring. They seemed surprised that they had been called at all, and as they couldn't find any indication of anything being wrong, but suggested I could go in for further tests if I chose to, I refused politely but emphatically. I suggested instead that I would make an appointment with my GP the following day and let him check me over. They left, and the saddest thing of all was the utter fury on Bruce's face, and the disappointment on his, my parents and Emma's faces. They had thought their problem, me, was going to be taken of, but it was still sitting there. I think if we'd been alone, Bruce would have hit me. The following morning, he told me that my mum had called the ambulance, and when I asked her, she said it had been Bruce. I chose not to speak to my mum, I believed she had called them at his insistence, whichever way it had happened they had all betrayed me.

It would be nice to say this incident encouraged me to change my way, and I gave up drinking, sadly that only really happens in the movies, it did change things for me, I spiralled down even further, if that was possible into my hell hole.

44

My body was now probably more dependent on the alcohol than my mind was, and when I woke up in the mornings, as soon as I got out of bed, I shook physically. My vision was blurred and my head swam, and there were mornings that the only way I could down the stairs to the kitchen was on my bum. I shook so hard as I poured that first drink, that most of it spilled, and I drank it as though it would save my life. It did feel that way though, I was helpless without it. No sooner had that first one hit my stomach, than I would be stumbling to the toilet as it rocketed up my throat and spewed out of my mouth. Sometimes I didn't make it to the toilet. The second one, stayed down, and by the third, the shaking stopped, my focus cleared, and my head stopped swimming, and I could function again. I hardly ate now, I couldn't, food nauseated me, and my biggest fear in life was that I would run out of booze. I managed the basics in my appearance and attire, and had no desire or energy to do more than keep clean and dressed. I hardly ever left the house, unless I was grocery shopping, and that was always after I'd been drinking. I either got a cab home, or Bruce would take me, he'd sit in the pub across the road whilst I did the shopping, I was grateful for the lift. The days blurred together, and I existed, nothing more.

At night when I went to bed, my foggy mind swirled and whirled in a torturous turmoil. Love, hate, calm, anger, peace disquiet, who am I, what am I, why am I, useless worthless, turmoil, round and round the merry –go –round, my mind was a carnival of pain. This enormous deep surge would come from my belly, up into my throat, then my head, and the sobs racked my body, my throat ached, and the tears would spill incessantly. What was I crying about, nothing , everything, this was what I had become, I couldn't get out, I was trapped, my self fulfilling prophecy, I was useless, and worthless to everyone, even to me. I was pathetic, I was a total waste of space, I was nothing. In a self pitying defiance, I would think, 'well you've all got what you wanted now; I am what you always said I was'. 'Look at me', I shouted in my mind to 'them', 'look at what I've become, look what you've done to me'. Smug satisfaction, this was what they had done, and then, that other voice, the one I didn't want to hear would always speak, softly, quietly, but with the force of a well honed razor sharp sword, it would cut through these mawkish thoughts, and say 'Oh no Cheryl, look at what you've let yourself become, look at what you have done to yourself'. 'Stop it, Stop it, you don't know how it is, you don't know how it's always been, you have no idea of the pain, I hate you, leave me alone', I screamed mentally in reply. The same voice answered, 'I can't leave you alone, I do know the pain, you see, I am you, I am that part of you that will fight this'. 'I can't fight it, I don't want to fight it anymore, I'm tired of it now, I give up', I would reply, and I would beckon and will sleep in, that blessed relief of unconsciousness, relief from the battlefield that was my mind.

One night, sleep was slow in coming, and another of those messages came through. This one for some reason I took seriously, somehow it bypassed the blur and fog, it cut through to my core, it spoke to my soul, and I listened, and I heard it, 'you are dying', it said, 'You now need to choose to live or to die'. I knew the time had come that was inevitable, my body couldn't take much more, I knew by the way I felt and looked, that if I continued as I was, I would die soon. I also knew with absolute mind numbing fear that exploded through my senses, that I would have to give up drinking to live, I would have to face reality, all that pain again. After a long while, when the fear eased, I understood that my life as it was, was like the tide, it ebbed and flowed, the pain, was my sea it hadn't gone, it had just changed, and now there was fear and guilt, and the only time my sea ebbed was when I was asleep, it flowed, breakers of pain, guilt, shame and despairs, even when I was drunk. I was truly in hell, and I couldn't get out on my own, but for the first time in a very long while, I understood I wasn't alone, I'd just assumed I was, I'd been deaf to the messages.

That night I spoke to my angels, sure they'd forgotten and forsaken me a long time ago, they hadn't, they were the voice of reason I'd fought, they had told me to choose now, they were giving me a chance. It was a life changing moment, I didn't deliberate for days or nights, my soul wouldn't allow procrastination, and that in itself was my miracle. That night when I spoke to my angels, this is what I said; '*If you can give me the strength and courage to survive, to face life again sober, if you can walk with me and stay with me whilst I stumble along this path, if you can help me leave this hell, this very dark place I am in, and guide me towards the light, I will never come back to this place*'. '*If you can still love me, if you can forgive me, that gives me hope, something I never thought I would feel again, and if you can do all this, my promise to you is that I will spend the rest of my life in giving back and paying forward*'. I slept.

I woke up very early the next morning in a state of total panic, I remembered the commitment I'd made the night before, and I was terrified. I crawled out of bed, and along the hall, and then bumped down the stairs on my bum, I couldn't walk, my whole body was shaking with anxiety and with the dt's. I managed to pour whisky into a mug, spilling it all over the kitchen counter, and then using both hands put the mug to my mouth and drank deeply. Of course it all came straight up, and this time I only got as far as the kitchen sink. I tried to muffle the sound with my hands, and the burning liquid spilt through my fingers. The second drink stayed down, and I took the next one into the lounge with me. I sat, drank deeply and the shaking slowed to trembling. I knew I'd given my word to stop drinking, but in the cold light of day that seemed impossible and improbable. Perhaps I could negotiate a new time frame, it wouldn't make any difference really, and I hadn't made any broad statements to anyone about this, so no-one could sneer at yet another empty promise. There was that voice again, 'why then have you made such a desperate and impassioned plea for support, what is different in the morning that wasn't true last night?' Well for one thing, I feel better this morning, I thought, and I knew that was only because I had poured alcohol into my body, to quiet the awful symptoms of withdrawal. That scared me even more, was that how it would be, that I would have to go through days of wishing I could die rather than feel like I did first thing every morning before I got to the booze. The whisky had calmed me, it warmed me and comforted me, and it was poison, killing me, physically, mentally, emotionally, withering my soul. I sat, hunched over on the sofa, my head down, my hands clasping the mug between my knees, and my body rocked, back and forth, back and forth, whilst my tormented mind tried to contemplate the torture my body would endure, and then, a life without alcohol, with pain, and the petrifying return to a reality that was alien and unreal, I didn't know what was real anymore. The strangers that were my family, nothing could nor would ever be the same again, at least this hell was familiar, my pit was my refuge. Head bowed, hands clasped around a fresh drink, rocking, back and forth, back and forth.

The voice of my mind said, 'You will die then as you now live, alone, angry, and out of control, is this the legacy you choose to leave your children. I knew Emma was loved, and would be cared for, as well as I knew Jack had been segregated to 'my camp', and would be treated accordingly. How could I leave my son alone to fight and de-fend me, even in death, his only weapons would be love and loyalty. These would be defended and defiled, how he could possibly emerge safe, stable, let alone victorious. What of his future, my choice would impact on his expectations and opportunities, the wrong choice would destroy trust, and hope, create pain and anger, the sins of the mother visited upon the child, would he turn to an artificial solace, would his heart and mind ever heal. He was my only glimmer of light in this very dark place, and I could snuff that out, or sustain it, he was my light, and I was his. If mine died, I was the keeper of his flame, and surely nurturing this light was my responsibility now, as giving him life had been. My love for him had never wavered, it never would, 'love conquers all?' in my war though, death was a fierce soldier, fight-ing for everlasting peace.

Regrets, everyone has some, some have many, not all have the op-portunity to put right the wrong, sometimes it is impossible, out of their control. This is your choice, make it and either choose to live, reclaim your life, or die knowing you could have lived.

I saw myself, a pathetic figure, thirty-seven years old, hunched and rocking in a place that didn't feel like home, nowhere did, who was she, she was still a victim, only this time, a victim of her own abuse. Where was the survivor, was there a shred of courage left, if I could snatch that shred, grasp it, hold it, I knew courage came hand in hand with hope. Later, when no-one else was about, with trembling hands, brimming eyes, and a heart filled with fear and shame, I called and made an urgent appointment to see my doctor.

EPILOGUE

Thus began a new path, an entirely new journey, and one I will share with you soon, in my next book. I will ask you to walk with me again through all the terror, the pain, the hope, the joy, the failures and the victories that lay ahead, the twists and turns that life continues to throw at me. It has taken me some years to decide to write this book, and it has perhaps been my greatest challenge ever. You see as you have walked in my shoes through all these pages, shared my most intimate feelings, thoughts and experiences, shared my joy, my laughter and my tears, so I have relived these moments. Whatever reading this has meant to you, for anyone out there who has shared one or more of my experiences, whatever your beliefs, and no matter how bad it's got, there is always a way out, and once you reach rock bottom there is only one way left to go, and that is up.

I believe, I am on an endless journey through eternity, and however extraordinary it may seem, all my experiences are meant to be. Those I choose to learn from and grow with in this lifetime; I won't have to endure in the next. I also believe that ultimately we all have our place and purpose, and in sharing my life with you, I believe I have found mine.

ISBN 142512952-8

9 781425 129521